PATHS OF CHANGE

Strategic Choices for Organizations and Society

Revised Edition

Will McWhinney

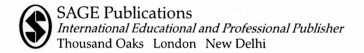
SAGE Publications
International Educational and Professional Publisher
Thousand Oaks London New Delhi

For information address:

SAGE Publications, Inc.
2455 Teller Road
Thousand Oaks, California 91320
E-mail: order@sagepub.com

SAGE Publications Ltd.
6 Bonhill Street
London EC2A 4PU
United Kingdom

SAGE Publications India Pvt. Ltd.
M-32 Market
Greater Kailash I
New Delhi 110 048 India

Printed in the United States of America

Library of Congress Cataloging-in-Publication Data

McWhinney, Will.
     Paths of change: strategic choices for organizations and society
/ author, Will McWhinney.—Rev. ed.
        p.   cm.
     Includes bibliographical references (p.   ) and index.
     ISBN 0-7619-1017-4 (pbk.: acid-free paper).
     1. Organizational change.   I. Title.
     HD58.8.M38   1997
     658.4′063—dc21   97-4628

97 98 99 00 01 02 03 10 9 8 7 6 5 4 3 2 1

Production Editor: Sherrise Purdum

Contents

The processes we have for resolving complex issues in organization and society are not adequate to the complexity of our times. I tell some tales of my personal route to that conclusion.

The current methods of resolution are unable to "decide" on critical issues requiring new translogical operations. We need to call on a third order of change to resolve the issues during this era of rapid transition.

I propose a science of practice, a meta-praxis, to identify and organize methods that transcend the limitations of our existing methods. I base this science on the assumption that human beings use diverse and incompatible concepts of reality.

The deepest sources of guidance for working undecidable issues appear in story and myth, particularly the myths of creation and heroes' tales. The meta-praxis recognizes these sources and presents paths of resolution that employ narrative, historical, and "rational" approaches to complex issues.

Consciousness and the use of language leads to the formation of divergent concepts of reality. Each of these "realities" is available to everyone. Due to varying backgrounds, however—natural or nurtured—each individual is biased in the use of the different realities.

The biases, and particularly the dominance, among realities greatly influence one's behavior in stable and predictable ways.

I present a model articulating a universe of four alternative realities. The properties of the pure realities are striking and lead to new insights about a number of areas of behavior, including leadership and follower relations, creativity, and, most centrally, the need for translogical modes of making choices in complex situations.

The logical discontinuity of the realities indicates that there is no way to logically "move" between the realities. Disturbance of any relationship among the realities leads to conflicts because they do not share logics, values, criteria of acceptability—they differ *ontologically.* Any attempt to make changes engenders conflict.

Conflict is primary. Only through the establishment of cultural norms is conflict managed and through the use of narratives are issues resolved.

I explore the strategies we must employ to effect changes, recognizing that any change will require work involving two or more realities.

The concepts of change and resolution developed here strongly suggest a parallel to what Gregory Bateson calls Learning III. Thus I identify this meta-praxis as being founded in an acceptance of third-order change processes.

The third-order processes transcend the logical tools that Western cultures have been using since Aristotle's time, and thus their development calls for entirely new translogical operations.

Change is accomplished by acts that we traditionally recognize as design and "problem solving." The basic mechanisms of problem solving create changes in a given reality according to the rules of a second reality.

Problem-solving tools can be classified according to what realities they involve as given and as controlling and how they must be used accordingly in different paths of resolution.

I identify six classes of familiar tools organized via the model of alternative realities. They are presented to indicate their appropriate relation to the qualities of the users and the strategies of change.

Significant changes, like those required to deal with the complex issues of contemporary society, are resolved along *paths of resolution* underlying the "stories" that guide our engagements with the issues.

There are two grand archetypal paths that pass through (involve) all the realities in opposite sequences:

The *renaissance* path matches closely the path of return-for-a-better-start known from biblical times on.

The *revitalization* path matches closely the patrilogical planning model that is commonly used in Western cultures.

Both paths have parallels with historical and ancient spiritual traditions of transformation.

I also recognize the particular importance of two extreme paths—the *creative* and the *dialectic*—both of which have major roles in resolution.

All remaining paths of social change—political revolution, urban redesign, organization development, sociotechnical analysis, liberation theology, and so on—can be viewed as paths of problem solving passing through a subset of the realities.

The choice of paths of change depends greatly on the availability of the appropriate types of leaders and populations, perhaps as much as any other factors, such as culture and economic conditions. The qualities of both the leaders and their populations are significantly determined by (or correlated with) the dominant worldviews.

In this chapter, I describe

a topology of *styles of leadership* that is related to the map of realities and in turn to the paths of resolution.

a first look at a theory of *followership* that examines the forms of subordinate relations we see in Western societies, and

the *forming of cultures*, which calls for differences in the ways we resolve issues. I suggest two processes of culture formation that have been important elements of the Western heritage for three millennia and indicate how two additional culturing processes develop from this basic pair.

I explore the role of *courage* in the selection and development of paths of change and show the relation of courage to the three orders of change.

In a brief section, I look at the interplay of courage, belief, and logic, organizing the thoughts of a number of people around the notion that "we live by those propositions whose validity is a function of our belief in them."

The formal conclusion of my study of meta-praxis is that conflict is avoided by making changes in accordance with the path of the myths and stories that guide our lives. Change is most effectively accomplished when we have uncovered the core stories of the relevant cultures and use our skills and courage to advance along the paths that are natural to our person, organizations, and culture.

I conclude with an appreciation of the difficulty of the task of moving beyond the issues that now plague our societies, using two metaphors, one characterizing the culture in which we live, the other pointing toward that which may develop.

List of Diagrams

Chapter 1. Alternative Realities

Chapter 2. The Dialectics of Change

Chapter 3. Modes of Change

Chapter 4. Paths of Resolution

Chapter 5. Leaders, Followers, and Culture

Chapter 6. Courage for the Journey

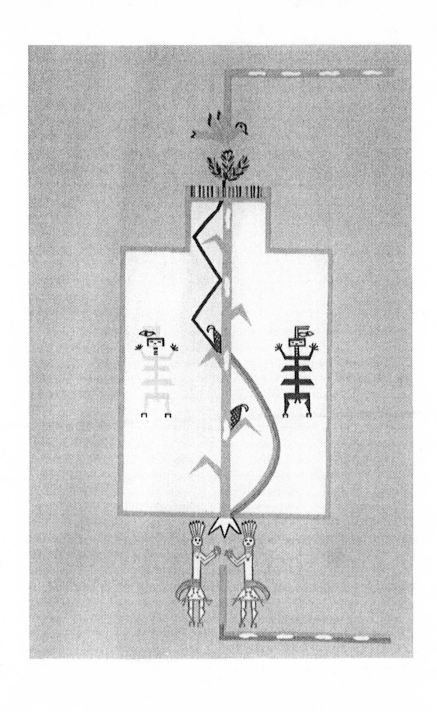

Preface

I was pleased when Sage asked me to revise *Paths of Change* on the occasion of publishing the new edition of the companion "field book." I first looked to see how well the original writing stood up against societal changes that have occurred in the past 5 years. I find the match is still good. My concern with the increasingly unmanageable *complexity* that initiated this study 25 years ago has become even more significant over the past 5 years. This is partially because a new language has evolved for understanding complexity and chaos and there are new tools for dealing with them, such as those presented in this work. The need to tune one's paths of change to the environment and the available but scarce resources is increasingly relevant as human societies edge closer to chaos.

I revised the text to reflect an increased attention to managing conflict. The end of the cold war mentality helped us recognize that simplistic attempts to frame all conflicts—crime, drugs, disease, and terrorism—as "wars" is ineffective if not counterproductive. We now recognize the need to better discriminate among sources of conflict and those responses that are effective. In a recently completed work, Tamara Bliss (1996) used my theory to understand the diverse ways in which activists affect corporate behavior on issues of environmental and public policies. She recognized how social advocacy groups and their corporate targets use competitive and cooperative strategies in the "games" they play. This reflects back on the basic theory, producing the major revision included in this edition, Interlude III. Bliss's study led me to see more clearly how the change model contributes to conflict resolution. It provides a systematic way to describe the great conflicts in Western societies between the analytic and expressive, the sacred and the secular, and the artistic and moralistic lifestyles (McWhinney, 1995) and to place these and lesser conflicts on a map of strategic alternatives using the work of Helen Weingarter (1993).

There have been changes in the past 5 to 10 years in American corporate practice that we did not anticipate. Commercial and industrial firms have been adopting open system management at a higher rate over the past few years—flatter organizations, more use of teams, more concern with customers. We did not anticipate that these adoptions would be driven by the opening of international labor markets. Instead, we anticipated benefits from increased productivity, both in the meaningfulness of the work for employees and for an improved economy. We did not anticipate the negative effect on employment that has torn apart the fabric of American society. Again, we must learn the lesson that we seldom have the power to solve a problem that does not cause additional problems in its wake. Such failures give support to my belief set forth beginning on page 9 that we need a general approach to managing change, what I call a *meta-praxis*. The purpose of the book stands to support our ability to manage complexity and to do so by managing change in a changing world. It does so by presenting a theory of change and, with its companion volume, the tools of social practice.

CONTINUING DEVELOPMENT OF PRACTICE

As support to the application of the theory, we created a "field guide" for the practitioner, *Creating Paths of Change* (1993). This work contains both core strategies for effecting change and instructions on using specific tools for change efforts in organizations and communities. It has been a useful field guide and textbook. Sage Publications is now printing it in a second edition (McWhinney, Webber, Novokowsky, & Smith, 1997) as a companion volume. The new edition supports the trend in practice to use various forms of *narratives* in both understanding organizations and communities and in effecting change. It is gratifying to see the powerful results of using the expressive tools to help organizations find new ways of operating and new meaning in their work.

Over the years since the publication of these two volumes, managers, consultants, students, and I have used the theory and the field guide to discriminate among different worldviews, leadership styles, conflict resolution, and paths of change in *Fortune 500* companies, schools, health systems, and grassroots programs. In some cases, OD professionals find a tool in the handbook that makes a management meeting more productive. In others, a leader suddenly awakes to the effects of his style on his team. In still others, a whole stream of changes in the production process is coordinated. The most significant changes occur when leaders become clear in choosing between the conformative paths that *revitalize* an operation and the adventuresome paths that lead to *renaissance* and the birth of new initiatives.

REFERENCES

Bliss, T. J. (1996). *Leveling the playing field: How citizen advocacy groups influence corporate behavior.* Unpublished doctoral dissertation, Fielding Institute.

McWhinney, W. (1995). "The matter of Einstein square dancing the Magritte." *Cybernetics and Human Knowing, 3*(3), 3-24.

McWhinney, W., Webber, J., Novokowsky, B., & Smith, D. (1997). *Creating paths of change* (2nd ed.). Thousand Oaks, CA: Sage.

Weingarten, H. R. (1993). International conflict and the individual. In W. Z. & H. K. Jacobson (Eds.), *Behavior, culture and conflict in world politics* (pp. 177-196). Ann Arbor: University of Michigan.

Acknowledgments

This book has been long in its development. Its origins are in my undergraduate studies with the philosopher Philip Stanley at Union College, who first lead me to find philosophical understanding in events in everyday life and, with his wife, welcomed me into their own everyday life. The specific work began in discussions with Bob Andrews (UCLA) and was supported by colleagues and the many people with whom I joined in organizational and community projects. All along I have had encouraging and insightful conversations with Ian Mitroff and Tom Greening. I particularly acknowledge Burkard Sievers (Wupertal, Germany) for sharing with me his appreciations of myth and showing me the etchings of A. Paul Weber. My work has been greatly aided by the questions and clarifications that came from the "reflective practitioners" who study with me at the Fielding Institute. But all would have been for naught without the sustaining trust and insightful examples with which my wife Bonnie McWhinney supported my work.

I used a lot of editorial help in the writing. My first coworker was Stephanie. . . . Six months into our working relation, she was murdered in her home by a man who had just been released from prison. He had been incarcerated for the same crime 10 years early and was released without ever having psychiatric evaluation or therapy—the issues about which I write are not abstract. Valerie Murphy's appreciative readings were always encouraging and her reconstructions always caught my spirit as well as intent. John Kroll and John Bergez taught me a great deal about communicating while critiquing the prose.

* * *

I have quoted material and used ideas from Roy Wagner's *The Invention of Culture* (University of Chicago Press, © 1975, 1981 by Roy Wagner), by permission.

The *Pollen Twins* (sand painting), photograph by Herb Lotz, is provided courtesy of the Wheelwright Museum of the American Indian, No. P1#4.

Introduction   Journey to Resolution

The impetus for asking the questions that led to this book carries the quality of paradox that continues to characterize its contents. In the early 1970s, most us in the West saw that Western cultures had reached a discontinuity, a sudden break in the rate of development that foreshadowed the end of the Industrial Age. The 1960s—really the dozen years from 1962, the year of the Cuban missile crisis and the publishing of Rachel Carson's *Silent Spring*, to 1974, the year of the debacle of Cambodia— were the turning point. That decade both opened opportunities and led to a societal confusion that we now recognize as signaling the end of the era, the end of millennia, the birth of earth consciousness, and perhaps the end of international war and sovereign states. The changes were massive. They affected individuals: Vietnam veterans were not hailed as the patriots they expected to be, and Black Americans found opportunities they had long deserved. They affected the meaning of power: We came to know that no one wins a war. They affected our values: Western youths no longer had clear paths as they entered adulthood and the world of work. Western culture is no longer assured that it is dominant in the world or even permanent.

In trying to understand all this, we came to realize that we do not have a theory of change, of intentional action, by which to explain what has happened in the recent decades or predict the events of coming decades. What explanations we have are conventions of our society that account for our actions. These were sufficient for us as long as our culture was stable and coherent and as long as we did not need to make significant cross-cultural interventions. But neither condition is holding. The evidence is in the continuing surfacing of anomalies as we go on trying to resolve issues. The evidence is the resilience of major social issues such as homelessness and the drug wars and in the persistence of anomalies such as the assignment of the healing of social ills to the judicial system or the supra-anomaly that our rationalistic society does not allow for anomalies.

The heart of the problem may not be that our times are becoming more complex but that our ability to resolve conflicts fails with a loss of cultural vigor and upon confrontation with different cultures. Complexity is a sign that our methods are no longer adequate to the task. It is a sign that the modes of thinking that originated to solve the issues of ancient Greece and industrializing Europe are not sufficient for the third millennium. The purpose of this work is to lay the groundwork for a theory of change that will give us the power to organize and deal with the issues of our times.

The appearance of complexity calls forth a variety of responses in people, ranging from depression to a frenetic search for solutions. For many of us in America, the first response on awakening in the 1960s to the deteriorating conditions of Western society was to attempt to do better what we had been doing, working harder and smarter to solve the issues. My upbringing and profession supported this approach. I was on the faculty of the School of Management at UCLA during these years. My immediate professional focus was on reconceiving what a student of management should be learning to be effective the 1970s. But this focus was repeatedly broken by the intrusion of events into the cloister of Industrial America—the Kennedy assassinations, the Watts Riots in which Blacks burned their own ghetto, the wars in South East Asia. It was clearly not enough simply to refine past learning. Rather, we needed, at least, to reconstruct organized industrial work to bring it in line with a world perspective and to develop communities out of an expanded personal consciousness.

The complexity of the changes facing industry and its employees had rendered much of management education obsolete. Computers, "T-groups," international business, and affirmative action weren't even recognized five years earlier. The simple models of profit maximizing, climbing a career ladder, and retiring a respected millionaire now seem to be a self-parody accepted by both students and faculty. Our first collective response to the rapid rate of change was to subject all the students to a yearlong confrontation with the ambiguity of values in the corporation and community, international issues of ecology, markets, and power, and the losses of personal meaning that came with the Vietnam war. The level of novelty in the early 1970s was so great that we could spend the entire year exposing students to new issues without ever recognizing that all we had provided the students was an open door to chaos. We could not say where our society should be going; we lacked a satisfactory image of the world they should be trained to master; and we had no adequate strategies with which to encounter the complexity. The grand models of rationality that had been provided by economists, operations researchers, and political and social scientists of both left and right persuasions were increasingly recognized to be devoid of empirical content. Much as we tried to ignore the evidence, the usefulness of our rationality seldom extended much beyond the schoolbook problems. *Suboptimization* became the euphemism that obscured the fact that, when our governments and corporations used new management tools to solve problems, they invariably produced greater messes than they resolved.

The Cuban missile crisis, in which Kennedy took his stand against Khrushchev in 1962, was a critical turning point not only in the cold war but in the survival of the planet. Appropriately, it became the subject of an extended study into the rationality that led to this momentous resolution. Graham Allison's landmark study, originally published in 1969, attempted to identify the logic by which the sequence of events leading up to the crucial withdrawal of Soviet missiles could be explained. He presented three diverse models, based, respectively, in the theories of the "rational actor," organizational behavior, and bureaucracy, to explain what had happened. Each explained some aspects of the crisis well, but no single model presented a sufficient argument. For example, the rational actor model assumes that, once a policy is accepted by the decision makers, it will be implemented. Rather, as Allison (1971, p. 267) points out, implementation normally follows in only about 10% of the cases. Each model was of some use, but it appears that Allison would need an indefinitely large number of distinct models to account for the outcome. Like the ancient astronomer Ptolemy, he needs more and more "epicycles of explanation" to deal with each new aspect of an issue. He has no rule for knowing if he would ever have enough rationality to predict outcomes or direct decision making in any crisis that mattered.

As the excitement of the 1960s settled down in the mid-1970s, our faculty group awoke to the same fact—we didn't have a sufficient basis for teaching the management student how to handle complexity. We had neither theory nor practical heuristics by which to guide an approach to the major issues facing a person, organization, or society. We lacked a general science of practice—that is, a *praxis*—that we could use to formulate and attack issues. We had learned how to scan the world for information and categorize what we found according to concerns of the different stakeholders to an issue, and we had built models of endogenous and exogenous variables and learned to be futurists—but with very little sense of what we would like the future to be. It became apparent to us and many in the West that we didn't know what to teach future managers and CEOs. We had not learned sufficient means by which to

- formulate issues
- set boundaries on issues that we would deal with
- set objectives for our organizations or ourselves
- select the tools to be used in dealing with the issues
- make space for alternatives, especially in the face of overt conflict

All we had were some good narratives about how these questions were being handled, such as Allison's story of the missile crisis, Norman Cousins's description of the end of the *Saturday Review,* popular accounts of how Robert McNamara's "whiz kids" ran the Pentagon, and a lot of old wisdom about military strategies and resolution of personal issues that we had little skill in translating into a modern context.

Further, each instructor in the required MBA course approached complexity from his own discipline—economics, operations research, political science, behavioral science. We lacked rules by which to combine the logics of the diverse disciplines. Allison's analyses proved themselves inadequate. As we reviewed other studies, we found that there simply was no rational model for dealing with issues. We regretfully concluded that major social, political, economic, and personal decisions could not be made from a strategic and rational view.[1] Our tools appeared to be nothing but well-established conventions.

The conditions that led to complexity also gave birth to opportunities. While we were encountering our lack of skills for teaching others to resolve complex issues, I, along with other consultants and social designers, was working to create new modes of organizing work that would transcend issues of the Industrial Age. Our aim was to enhance the quality of working life, of the community, and of economic productivity. This effort, which now appears to have been grandiose, aimed to produce more effective workplaces based on open systems concepts, existential psychology, and community development. We believed that, by using tools arising from these new fields of inquiry, we could achieve a general and sustainable improvement in the quality of community and working life, providing personal, social, and economic good. Our optimism was supported by our success in creating microcosmic prototypes—new factories, parts of organizations and communities—efforts we imagined would propagate throughout the multinational organizations of Western industrial society and revitalize the inner cities.

By 1970, there were a number of such prototype developments. Most widely publicized were various sociotechnically designed plants, such as Volvo's in Sweden and Pet Food's in Kansas, and various major community developments such as cooperative labor-management engagement in Jamestown, New York, or an artist-driven project that rebuilt Watts (in Los Angeles) after the race riots in 1965. Some of the work at industrial sites was so successful that owners, such as Procter & Gamble, kept their green field, open-system, high-performing production factories under tight wraps to prevent competitors' breaking their advantage. These successes and a few urban projects appeared to produce exemplary organizations and communities that were harbingers of a postindustrial society.

Along with many others who had experienced such successes, I "got high" on the possibilities. "Doing what we had been doing, better," might work. These *open-system organizations*, variously configured, provided for participation in decision making, for work designed in response to individuals' psychic and physiological needs for social interplay, and for power sharing. They were sensitive to their environments and they produced goods with significant reduction of cost. The systems were, it seemed then, the foundation of efficient social democracies in the workplace and community. Indeed, some of the plants continue to operate, more than 20 years later, at high efficiency and with outstanding humanity, and the communities are healthy and thriving.

But utopia is still far off. Few of such leading organizations as General Electric, Procter & Gamble, Alcoa, or General Foods have supported replication of these models within their own boundaries. A few organizations have adopted and sustained open-system organizations re-dressed as "Japanese management" but even fewer have provided worker control through employee stock option plans (ESOPs) or similar modes of participation in ownership. At the site of the prototype of all these organizations, the famous Ahmedabad weaving shed experiment, which has persisted for more than two decades, no attempt to replicate it has been successful (Miller, 1975). There has been almost no spread to other sectors of society, government, education, or health. We can see some resilient successes in urban redevelopments, such as in Newark, New Jersey, but it be would a stretch to name more than a dozen enduring examples.

There were indications of difficulty even in the first international Quality-of-Working-Life (QWL) conference held in 1972. Even then it was clear that we could not expect the new model to be acceptable in all forms of work or institutions. Not all employees and rather few managers would participate in humanistic approaches to designing their environments, and in only a few companies and communities would workers or residents come to control significant resources and opportunities. Limitations became apparent, and skeptical queries or outright opposition came from all sides—from students of the labor movement, religious communities, teachers, technologists, economists, and managers. As we fell into the disillusionments of the 1970s—the losses in Vietnam and the energy crises—it became even more evident that we lacked models for self-sustaining large-scale improvement in "quality of life" in the workplace and the community. It was obviously easier to start prototypes than to propagate them. Regressions have been more common than sustained changes.

The proliferation of New Age organizations has not been what many advocates had hoped, but I would be unduly pessimistic to deny that there has been change during the past two decades. There have been shifts in the way most U.S. organizations operate that have made an impressive contribution to quality of life. The most important changes are in the social setting, in opening opportunities for women, in greater attention to health and stress, and in a growing appreciation of consciousness. Some industrial organizations and community projects that have approached social change through concepts of network formation (for examples, see Trist, 1985) and organizational transformation (Levy & Merry, 1986) have shown vitality and reproducibility. Yet the slowly increasing rate of success is not sufficient to establish that a "paradigm change" has taken place.

By 1978, the weaknesses of our understanding of strategies for dealing with complex issues was so obvious, both in the world at large and in the small world of management education, that a faculty group at UCLA formed to identify teachable strategies that would give the student some power to cope with the complexity we had failed to corral. As we worked with various methods arising from all manner of disciplines and cultures, it became clear that in the microcosm of our committee we were encountering the very phenomena we were studying. To build a theory of change would require us to confront our immediate conflicts. The diversity that was our burden turned out to be its merit; we had variously been trained in the ideologies of science, Marxism, Western legal practice, sociology, humanistic psychology, and diverse religious traditions. We did not need an external issue to provide conflict; every discussion of the various methods of resolution produced conflict, sometimes handled in a scholarly fashion but often with the anger and contempt that arise from fear. The best the committee could do was to categorize our collection of methods into four distinct types that had varying degrees of acceptance in Western management work. This was useful, but we lacked both an overall rationale for the collection and an ability to specify the conditions under which any method should be used.

This failure became the committee's most significant contribution. From examination of the unending conflicts that arose in the group's discussion, I sensed that the source of conflict was in the *premises and decision operations* used by an individual or group and *only secondarily in the content of the issue itself.* This idea is the seed from which developed the central thesis of this book.

BASIC PROCESSES OF RESOLUTION

The conflicts that arose in our committee's discussion were never resolved. Our differences in style persisted into the classroom, and the course developed at UCLA ultimately failed just as our work had failed to disclose the basic processes of resolution. The recognition that the conflict lay within our operational methods, however, provided a fundamental approach to resolving issues. We had been overlooking that which lay at our feet, as I now think our entire society has been doing. What we missed is that *human conflict arises from the means of resolving conflict.* Conflict is self-generating and self-feeding. We cannot look forward to resolving conflict by eliminating scarcity, by ensuring democracy, or by any other *substantial means.* We need to look at the ways in which we organize the reality within which conscious, choice-making human beings operate. The conflicts that are most difficult to resolve are those that arise through the ways we organize our thoughts, not, as in the natural world of plants and animals, from shortages of or lack of access to resources.

As I became acutely aware that the method itself is the fundamental issue, a book titled *Alternative Realities* by Lawrence LeShan (1976) caught my attention. LeShan proposed that we could account for a lot of social behavior if we assumed that people came from different understandings of reality. He held that there were four general types of beliefs about reality in Western cultures. His four classes are suggestively parallel to the categories of methods of resolution our committee had identified, thus supporting the hypothesis that differences in methods of resolution produced conflict in society at large, based in the different concepts of reality maintained by people of different disciplines and persuasions.

This insight provided the base for creating a fundamental model of the processes of conflict resolution. It led me to the argument that

change is differently understood within each of the concepts of reality
that are held by significant portions of our (Western) populations. It is
for this reason that, in any attempt to change a situation, we engender
conflict. From this I come to the basic premise that *conflict arises out of
attempts to make changes*. The resolution of conflict and the resolution
of complex issues share the same framework: Both depend on dealing
with differences in the image of reality maintained by the various parties to the issue or conflict. Clearly, such differences are not the only
source of conflict, but I propose that, when the problems arising from
the scarcity of resources are factored out, the remaining issues can be
best understood through this proposal.

I spent the next few years developing this concept, further organizing
the methods of resolution, and exploring the qualities of the realities held
by different parts of the population. The differences in views of reality
held by individuals appear to be deep and stable,[2] so the model of conflict resolution will have pervasive applications. The fundamental premise highlighted above applies to all manner of conflicts among workers,
neighbors, spouses, community members, and political leaders. It applies
particularly to societies in which those of similar beliefs join into cliques,
professions, and political parties. The premise also concurs with various
other worldview schema such as those of Pepper (1942) and Burrell and
Morgan (1979). Through experience in a variety of settings, I have elaborated on these worldviews, coming increasingly to realize that I needed
not only a context of realities to understand and promote change processes but also a way of choosing our paths through territories of multiple realities. This has led to the use of *stories* and myths as central
elements in achieving resolutions. I am exploring these uses of story, ex-
perimenting in practice, and finding ways to articulate the underlying
theory for resolving conflicts and complex issues.

This work now forms a *meta-praxis*; that is, it is a theory of ways and
occasions on which various modes of resolution should be employed.
It is a means of moving out of one's own construction of reality and
entering into a dialogue with multiple realities to reframe one's own
and others' experience in alternative frameworks.[3] It does not call on
new methods for problem solving—all the methods I refer to are
known and in practice. (Chapter 3 illustrates these correspondences at
the level of daily practice.) Rather, I present a mapping of alternatives
that makes clear the relation among methods and allows us to understand the impact of our approaches on resolving conflicts and issues.
The strategy and methods are general; they apply to any situation, to
issues involving individuals, groups, communities, and nations. Of
course, we would not consciously call on such a strategic approach
where simple problem solving is adequate. But, with the increasing

complexity of our lives, less frequently can we successfully treat a situation as though it were a simple problem. The boundaries are seldom sufficiently defined, the intentions are contradictory, and the opportunities are not specified. We must step back to pursue a course, a path, through a "mind field" of competing realities. Understanding the alternative realities provides the requisite structure, but I propose that the choice of path should arise out of our histories, new and ancient, conscious and unconscious, personal and cultural.

Use of a meta-praxis is, first, appreciative; it helps us comprehend a situation. Second, it guides us to the methods of resolution that are most likely to be effective. And, third, it can be used to anticipate problems and organize efforts to minimize the impact of different views of change in situations where change must occur. A meta-praxis is an instrument of strategy by which we select the skills and tools needed to achieve resolutions. Its construction also points to the weakness in our current modes of conflict resolution, by establishing that these modes are almost entirely dependent on the conventions of the cultures in which they are used. As such, they are likely to fail us most significantly in times of greatest need. In this approach to meta-praxis, I both provide some direction for creating methods that transcend the limitations of local cultures and suggest that we must move to a new level of engagement, a *third-order change,* to find the direction to resolve complex issues. This meta-praxis is a first proposal, going beyond the rationalities that us served well over past centuries but are no longer adequate in themselves to deal with the human agenda.

THE READER'S JOURNEY

Meta-praxis, and thus this book, is about strategies for resolving complex issues and bringing about change. The arguments here are about our use of alternative realities as the undergirding of the processes of resolution we use in our daily lives. This analysis precedes the decisions we make in the flesh and blood world of enterprise, military campaigns, social issues, and family quarrels. Thus I am not providing a cookbook for the practitioner—but that is in preparation. Rather, I am laying the groundwork for how people resolve these grand and messy circumstances of everyday life. The particular issues discussed as applications of the meta-theory are introduced here to exemplify, to connect ideas with the reader's experience, and to provide a playing field on which to test our understanding of such issues as the plight of the homeless, the conflicts in the Middle East, marketing strategy, or ways of rebuilding a community. It does not replace the textbooks of method for any of those arenas, yet it should make their use more fruitful and the outcomes more enduring.

To explore what lies beneath the surface of issues, I first lay out a map of worldviews, of realities (in Chapter 1). Like a road map, it has four corners. These represent the four pure views of reality on which I base this work. Each pure reality is the logical (ontological) underpinning of a worldview. Each manifests a variety of typical behaviors that we associate with belief in that world. Inward from the corners of this map are places identified with combinations of beliefs, "places" representing beliefs that use a combination of the pure worldviews. The map is a first crude representation of this meta-space of realities. In subsequent chapters, this territory is further characterized in a succession of dimensions dealing with problem solving, paths of change, leadership, followership, and cultures. With each elaboration, the territory will become more tangible and familiar. Also, it may become clear that the geographic metaphor will eventually get in the way of further development of the theory and practice. I sense that, in my next presentation of theory, I will replace it with some combination of storytelling and a new *vector logic* of which I currently have only a dim image. I anticipate that in this development we will find a new companionship between analytic and symbolic modes of change.

Next, I present an elementary theory of change (in Chapter 2). The theory is based on the notion that the concept and meaning of change differ with underlying beliefs about reality. That is, the meaning of change depends on the concept of reality one holds. Beliefs about reality support different processes of change that in turn lead to inconsistency, paradox, dilemma, and contradiction. I build on a variety of examples of our inability to produce satisfactory rationales for resolving issues. This is particularly obvious when the parties to a decision are from different cultures—the "two cultures" of C. P. Snow's novel of conflict between scientists and humanists—or when the parties are of different religions, class backgrounds, or national traditions. I maintain that the ground for conflict is always present among those of different cultures or even different beliefs in reality. On most occasions, the members of such a mixed group let their fundamental disagreements go unrecognized and unresolved. Most people, most of the time, construct blinders, fictions, obscurations that allow them to overlook their diversity. But, if the content or degree of the contemplated changes is deemed significant, the change efforts themselves produce conflicts that are unresolvable by any method that is framed in the same worldview as is the problem. The larger the movement, the greater is the likelihood that the change itself will call out open conflict regardless of the content of the issue.

In complex, novel, and threatening environments, conflicts emerge as persistent issues. The attempt to resolve homelessness in contemporary America perfectly illustrates the degree to which local efforts accumulate into large issues. Economists, social workers, and innovators call on incompatible arguments to support their solutions. It is unlikely that any of their proposed solutions would satisfy them all. In short, we need nothing more than the call for major change to produce deep societal conflicts that will become self-fueling.

The various methods of change appropriate to the different realities are described in Chapter 3. They are labeled according to familiar terms such as *analytic, participative,* and *innovative.* Each is based in a different combination of reality assumptions, and each serves different purposes and requires different resources. And, naturally, each requires a different kind of person for its effective execution. These modes form the building blocks of the paths of resolution. And this is as far as the rationalistic approach can take us toward resolution. Issues can be framed in these languages, but our approach to resolution must be located beyond these logics within expressive modes.

I open the discussion of the paths as expressive forms in Interlude IV with a tale of two industrial leaders telling each other stories on a mountaintop.[4] In the following chapter, I illustrate a way in which their archetypal tales form the basis for two grand paths of resolution and suggest that most of the paths of resolution used in the Western world are variations on the plot that underlies these two tales. These grand paths of resolution I label *revitalization* and *renaissance.* I show there is an essential and surprising relation of these paths to familiar concepts of conflict resolution, social and political change, and organizational design and development.

With the introduction of the paths as the archetypal forms of the stories that guide resolution, I have the two main components of the meta-praxis in place—the strange territory of multiple realities and the paths that transverse it in the resolution of conflicts. So, in Chapter 5, I form the context in which to consider the processes; that is, the leading, the following, and the generating of cultures.

The final chapter is about taking action—who and where. First, it is about the courage to act; then, it is about the care that must be taken in not setting into motion the counteraction that will negate any resolution that is attempted. In many circumstances, we may resolve a conflict without any apparent change, allowing those of each reality to see the outcome in their own terms. Second, it is about the choice of a path in the stories that enables us to transit through territories that are otherwise alien and uncooperative. This meta-praxis is about creating journeys that lead to resolution.

   Presenting this new theory is not easy. There is much here that will
not be comfortable for the reader to accept at first look. While the subject underlies the familiar grounds of personal social and political life,
many of the concepts I introduce are unfamiliar; the questions have
seldom been confronted; and, by its very nature, the material will be
seen variously as bizarre, irrelevant, overly complicated, or even blas-
phemous by readers coming from other quarters of the map of reality
than my own. But, as is appropriate to this topic, if the work were not
so difficult, I would know I had concocted something insufficient to
the task. The disagreements you have with this work initially may be
a sign of its pertinence. Later, when the paths have become familiar,
its explanation can be rendered elegantly simple.

I

High-Definition TV, 1981

In the intensity of great conflicts and deep social issues, there is so much at stake and so much trauma that it is difficult to understand later what actually took place and just how the resolution came about. This is certainly true of the Cuban missile crisis that Graham Allison studied so extensively; yet the possible explanations of that crisis continue to expand. In less life-threatening situations, in conflicts less compressed in time, the process of resolution and the inherent difficulties in achieving resolution are more visible. The example that follows shows that the conflicts underlying a relatively benign issue can be seen more clearly.

In fall 1981, I sat in on a conversation among the executives of an East Coast media company that both transmitted programs and produced TV sets. They had met to discuss how their company should respond to the news that a Japanese company had made a breakthrough in creating a high-definition television (HDTV) system for closed circuit distribution.

There were five men central to the discussion: the CEO and the vice-presidents of production, marketing, human resources, and finance. Each had been in charge of the same functions for years. They knew each other well. I recall a few of their phrases verbatim but have reconstructed most of the conversation.

Paul, the CEO, opened with the announcement of the Japanese breakthrough, then asked how they should respond.

STEVE: I knew it was coming! Now we know it's a "go," Research and Marketing can figure out the impact on the industry. Can't do much till we know, but it won't take long—they've been waiting for this!

MIKE: Oh come on, Steve, why waste time collecting data? What can it tell us about a fantastic opportunity like this? I've already been on the phone with some closed circuit people about a Super-Satellite Circuit.

13

The Japanese say we can start putting together the components. We could have an operating system by next fall.

SUMNER: What about the backlash from the cinema and TV production people? They're invested in the present and this is going to have a big impact—we'd better look at the consequences before we move. You know the new technology will produce an even greater disadvantage than the VCR for the millions who are limited to what's on the networks. Can you see what is going to happen when high-definition takes over all the new movies and live sports?

ALEX: You guys are way off. This is going take years. There is just no way to do this quickly. If they *did* pull it off quickly, it would knock the industry for a loop. We have got to get the lawyers to block the introduction until we are sure of access. Then we can pace the development to get our capital out of our regular production. We don't want this disruption now.

PAUL: Here we go again. It's hard to believe you are looking at the same world. I hear some good arguments. Mike, you are right about this being a great opportunity; the announcement does change our world. But would it really have much impact on society, Sumner? And what will be the long-run cost of disruption [to our current production]?

MIKE: Alex, time moves on but you stand still. It moves on, ya' know. That is all sunk cost. If RCA or Zenith hops on to this, our markets are gone no matter how carefully we shift our capital.

ALEX: That's why we need to bottle this up in regulations.

STEVE: And we'll sit here blocking and arguing while somebody else is getting their development program under way.

ALEX: It's impossible to do it in 18 months.

SUMNER: Somebody at SONY said that about the "Walkman."

The conversation continued for some time, the five men arguing among themselves about what effect it would have on the company and their divisions but getting nowhere—a reflection of their different worldviews. The CEO let the discussion go on, listening for any one point that would dominate all the others. He was also questioning his own leadership on this kind of an issue. At one point, focusing on the comments of Steve and Mike, he said:

PAUL: The direction you two suggest often looks the same. You both act with great assurance. You, Steve, because you know your facts, and you [Mike] because you don't. Neither of you trusts anyone else. One needs evidence and the other just needs runners to carry out his fantasies. Your styles present me with opposite risks. Mike, you maximize the risks; you've produced the greatest successes and the greatest losses. Steve, you minimize the risk by studiously tracking down all the unknowns, but you take so long that you miss the big ones—expensive insurance! Your arguments are impeccable. You tell me something can't be done, then Mike pulls it off. When I most need clarity from you, I get confusion.

STEVE: Just let me get the data. . . .

SUMNER: That's what you don't get, Steve. Mike isn't interested in your data and I doubt it's the kind of information that I—or Alex—can use. We need to do a lot more consideration of what we want to happen here.

PAUL: So much for a consensus. I need a summary of the issues from each of you this afternoon. I'll look them over tonight and we'll discuss it again in the morning.

The next morning brought no definitive answer; nor was one ever forthcoming. The company eventually gave up all efforts to develop HDTV.

In the nine years after this conversation, no single company or regulatory body has taken a positive position, though millions were spent exploring the possibilities.

In 1985, I repeated this conversation to the researchers at RCA's Sarnoff Laboratory. They laughed a bit at themselves but were dismayed because this same conversation was currently going on at their laboratories with the same lack of closure. In 1988, I used the conversation in a workshop at the Bell Laboratories. The response was one of even more discouragement, an intensified version of the reaction at RCA. It seemed to the scientists that there was no process to transcend the irresolution and conflict that consumed their management.

What has always struck me in this conversation was that the CEO and the four VPs never at any time recognized that the guiding criteria for each person came from completely different worldviews. There was no way they could agree. In brief, their views were as follows:

Steve: "We can do it this way"—a statement of potential, of opportunity

Mike: "I have the solution"—a statement of imposition, of one person's will

Sumner: "We should be careful of others' opinions"—a statement of social concern

Alex: "We have to play correctly"—a statement of rightness

With such divergence, there could be a shared action program only in an absolutely monolithic culture, and even then Mike would have had to have thought the program was his. The CEO sensed the incompatibility but never overtly attempted to push for closure. After the initial discussion, he worked one on one with his staff in the way least offensive to the person to whom he was talking. Often, he found no workable compromise. Some budget was approved for research, and there were a lot of conversations with media business people and with Washington lawyers, but nothing happened with HDTV. Gradually, even the production of TV sets was phased out.

I have held onto this example because the four VPs perfectly match the worldviews I have found in studying complex issues. They were not an odd collection of difficult men but a representative selection from a Western population. Their performance taught me once again that we cannot look to "rationality" to resolve complex issues. The more assiduously we pursue "rational" approaches, the more deeply we will become mired in the anomalies obscured by our cultures. We have to look elsewhere for understanding and somewhere else for leadership.

On December 17, 1990, AT&T, together with Zenith, announced they had a feasible all-digital HDTV broadcasting system to present to the FCC in 1991.

In April 1996, the *LA Times* reported that "a group of American and European companies demonstrated a new HDTV format in Las Vegas that is expected to be approved for all broadcasters by the Federal Communications Commission later this year." November 14th, the *LA Times* continued this tale of diverse worldviews:

> A digital television standard first proposed three years ago by an alliance of broadcasters, television manufacturers, consumer electronic firms, and a handful of computer companies has been languishing for months at the FCC, following lobbying this summer by . . .

1 Alternative Realities

At birth, each of us is given a particular Beginning Place within the Four Great Directions of the Medicine Wheel . . . giving us our first ways of perceiving things, which will then be our easiest and most natural way throughout our lives.

—Storm (1976)

Over human history, every society has created methods to systematically achieve change. In some, its members have consciously chosen to turn the responsibility for change over to their gods and emperors. People in most societies, however, recognize that most changes, small and large, do not result from things "just happening" to them. Rather, they result from actions taken by purposeful, sentient human beings. For the most part, and certainly in the West, societies operate through technical, political, and social methods to decide issues of state, commerce, and personal life.

Since the end of World War II, intended or "planned change" (Bennis et al., 1964) has become a professional practice at the personal, organizational, and societal levels, through individual therapies, organization development, and various forms of social reform from Gandhi's nonviolence to Paulo Freire's "pedagogy of the oppressed." Having explicitly developed a great variety of *modes of creating change*, we can now see that most changes are outcomes of directed efforts, some chosen more consciously than others. We attribute less to accidents of our own lives or to the vagaries of monarchies, technological imperatives, and natural events. Corporate life is not left to its markets, nor are communities allowed to sprawl haphazardly except by our wishes. Greater threats call for greater responses—we no longer live passively in the shadow of nuclear war and ecological catastrophe. Thus we need to become students and practitioners of *intentional action*.

It is becoming apparent that we create an arguably large part of our problems and issues in the very act of trying to resolve them. We create the messes we are in, sometimes by blatantly destructive acts but often unwittingly in the course of dealing with other problems. With the increasing power of mankind to affect the natural environment, we are increasingly creating havoc through acts of hubris—choosing our actions as though we could foresee the outcomes. The clearest examples are in the ways we have manipulated the natural environment, as we have seen in the impact of the "green revolution" and the cutting of the rain forests in the tropics.

Given our realization that our efforts yield unintended results, it is all the more amazing to me that we have not created a science of change. I know of no comprehensive monograph or text covering the major issues in the practice of intended change, though, in just the last three years, there have been a number of works responding to this need. There have been some excellent partial efforts or arguments set in particular institutions, for example, Piven and Cloward's (1979) discussion of poor people's movements, John Friedmann's (1973) work on urban redevelopment, and Noel Tichy's (1983) study of technical, political, and cultural dynamics in corporate organizations.

Our theorizing has been limited, but we have a respectable historical justification for these limits. Until recently, the approaches to change in particular settings served us adequately for the level of interdependence the change theorists and practitioners recognized. The omissions and errors that follow from problem solving did not accumulate fast enough to demand attention. They fell beyond the borders of our concern. As we approach the twenty-first century, however, the vast increase in the human population and the expanding technological impact of civilization have eliminated our border areas; now we have no borders beyond which we can throw our social and technological trash. The discarded by-products of problem solving are thrown back into our societies to congeal into the issues that threaten human existence. Our civilizations cannot survive without resolving the complex issues that face the planet. We need to have an overall map, a descriptive theory, of how to deal with our critical human issues—if for no other reason than to have a place to map our failures and move beyond them.

Resolving a complex issue produces a macro change in a society, an organization, or even in the life of an individual. Resolutions do not solve issues but transform situations radically so as to *dissolve* problems or render them solvable (Ackoff & Emery, 1972). For example, creating a positive work environment dissolves problems such as absenteeism, slow response to customer and client demands, and negative attitudes toward the employer, no one of which may have been addressed directly in the resolution effort. Resolving the larger issue makes it easier to deal with the residual problems. For example, if workers come to trust the integrity of a corporation's ownership, then it is easy for the management to get changes in work rules.

The success of a resolution is the degree to which

- it frees the organization, society, or individuals from one or another of the horns of the dilemma that had frustrated prior attempts when the issue was treated as though it consisted of separable problems, and
- it does not create new problems in its (immediate) wake.

The limitation in the second criterion simply recognizes that it is unlikely that any resolution will fix forever the major issues in a society. All that this criterion calls for is freedom from problems arising from the change effort itself.

In practice, the criteria for a resolution differ in accordance with the worldviews of those involved. The differences in worldviews arise from diverse concepts of cause, meaning, and satisfaction that lie beneath the way that those who hold those views define the problem. Issues, as defined here, do not have preestablished, unambiguous structures. They are usually laden with a complex of beliefs, values, and emotions. As a result, the route to their resolution is similarly ill-structured and depends on the espoused realities of the participants. What is *at issue* is seldom visible at the inception of the efforts that aim to resolve "it," if for no other reason than that not all the parties to the resolution have identified themselves.

For example, the *problem* of disposing of the waste from atomic reactors did not become an *issue* for decades after the first reactors began generating electricity. The waste issue was seen in the 1950s as complex but of local interest only. Its national and global implications did not become apparent until much later. Conversely, we can see what happens when we treat a pervasive issue as though it were but a problem. An example is the failure of an American Black child to achieve in school. Typically, the situation has been treated as problematic, something that could be solved by a simple if massive effort, such as offering better schools or offering courses in self-assertiveness. Such efforts had a noticeable lack of impact on the issue that spawned them. No list of identified causes or responses to them would by itself resolve an issue.

The very origins of the two words *problem* and *issue* indicate the differences between them. *Problem* is derived from the Latin, to "throw something at." *Issue* is a word for "outflow." So I will use the words here as follows: *Problems* are solved by throwing resources at them; *issues* are flows—usually the turbulent intermingling of various streams—that must be comanaged.

Typically, we deal with "problems" as contained within the levels of social intercourse such as that of the family, the neighborhood, or even the nation-state by sequentially using the methods of psychology, politics, technology, history, ethics, and economics. The result is that each effort to solve a problem creates new problems. We must treat each such complex as an issue, as that which flows from fundamental inconsistencies in the social fabric.

The typical analytic approach to resolution specifies that we need to identify and characterize the tools (modes) we have available with which to work on issues. With an understanding of the tools and their impacts on the whole situation, we should be able to use those tools in response to problematic situations. Before I followed that logic, I began an inquiry that led into the sources of conflict themselves and hence to a key discovery—namely, that conflict can effectively be understood as a product of the differing *means of implementing* change that are employed by people who hold differing beliefs about reality.

The attempt to solve a problem involving people who hold to different realities provides a classic case of the vicious circle. The attempt itself produces problems, because of the differing beliefs the actors hold about the meaning of change. Once a population starts on the path of problem solving, the society becomes a *self-generator of problems*. Because there will always be conditions that call for change, and thus a constant initiation of problems, our search must be for strategies that *manage a stream of problems* at least as much as for means designed specifically to solve problems. This is the function of a meta-praxis—to present strategies or, more accurately, paths—for determining the particular modes of change that can best be used for resolution of an issue.

Anyone who has been involved in an effort to change a system—family, corporate, or community—knows that a simple discussion of the change can generate a surprising amount of heat, even among people who seem to share common goals. I believe the underlying cause of that conflict is the different worldviews of the people involved in forming a solution, and the approach for resolving issues and conflicts I am proposing in this book is based on that premise. When the change under discussion is minor, the conflict is easily suppressed, either because of our habits of conceding to general opinion or because our worldviews are sufficiently overlapping. That is the case most of the time.

The five executives discussing the development of HDTV, for example, shared a corporate goal but held distinct worldviews. Their differences were displayed not only in the positions they took but in their personal styles, in the ways they made choices that reflect those differing worldviews. I propose that those differences are the source of the conflict—the issue under discussion is but the current "trigger." This paradoxical implication, and the unpleasant implications that conflict is inevitable, suggested to me that we need to inquire at a deeper level for the underlying and pervasive source of conflict that enters into every issue.

The differences in operating styles that appear in the characteristic behavior of individuals form distinct patterns, arising from the way those individuals define the "things" that make up the world, from their sources of knowledge, from their sources of agency and moral responsibility, and, surprisingly, from their modes of leadership. Those patterns are popularly given such labels as "the bureaucratic personality," "the scientific mind-set," "the do-gooder," and "the creative type." The persistence of such tags assured me that these patterns of behavior are stable and definable. Thus encouraged, I began a search for a model that would explain how these differences in style might produce conflict and account for the varying responses to change that occur among any given population.

We seldom argue with one another over "what is," or even "what I say is so," as long as we do not imply that our words are intended to change anything. I may state that the moon is made of green cheese and I am the King of Hearts without getting into any kind of conflict—unless I want to make something happen on the moon or in the Kingdom of Hearts. Conflict is intimately related to change, and change engenders conflict. But why? Why should change lead to conflict? There are certainly many ways to explain this, but I find that many of the phenomena of conflict can be understood by looking at how it can arise from differences in *the ways in which each of us constructs reality.*

Differences in belief about reality produce (or accompany) differences in our sources of meaning and knowledge, value processes (morality and ethics), and attitudes toward authority and freedom. The most conflict-inducing aspect of differing realities, however, comes in response to the simple assertion, "I did this *because* . . ." or the companion question, "*Why* did you do that?" That is, the greatest single source of differences in the way people think arises from the assignment of *cause*. For example, there are those for whom the world is determined by prior circumstances,

who totally believe in First Cause or destiny—either cosmic or circum-
stantial. For these people, any activity designed to create change is at best
foolish and at worst evil. For others, it is unthinkable—immoral and in-
human—not to make every effort to redirect the course of events. For another group, meaning arises from an interpretation of law, god-given or
scientifically established. For still others, such as Lewis Carroll's Humpty
Dumpty, meaning is created on the spot, by one's say-so!

We ask questions of "why" and "what for" out of our own values
and to determine those of others, to see the intentions and criteria behind their choices. In one concept of reality, values are the foundations of belief, while, in another reality, a consideration of value or
social responsibility is meaningless. For the scientist and engineer,
"why" is a quest for knowledge. For others, "why" seeks intention,
guilt, or bias. These differences are decisive. They arise from differing
realities and they fuel conflict whenever a group of people get together to make something happen.

We do not have to go beyond differing beliefs about cause to find
the sources of unavoidable conflict. We don't have to assume that either party is evil or even that they have opposing goals. Conflicts arise
from constructions of their minds, from the beliefs and styles by
which an individual or group makes a choice; only incidentally are
they in the content of the issue. It is therefore in terms of the source
that the conflict must be resolved.

Differences in the construction of reality provide not only the conditions of interpersonal, social, and international conflict but also the
patterns through which we organize society. Those of similar mind
tend to group together in communities, professions, fraternities, and
nations. Thus the differences among people are reinforced and their
conflicts are exaggerated. The maintenance of one's reality may require accommodation, ritual purge, angry confrontations, and out-
breaks of violence. Reality is a precious good, not to be released
simply to save a life or an empire.

Any social change, even a threat of or a plan for change, becomes
the occasion for the separation of a community into subgroups of common sensibilities. The pressure leads to the segmentation of a population along political lines, or by academic and artistic discipline, or
cultural heritages, or in other groupings based on like beliefs about reality. Boundaries are established to reify the differences between
groups in territories and laws. Even societies tend to emphasize and
support particular worldviews, denying the expression of other
worldviews. When segmentation is induced by the prospect of
change, the stability of a social system is reduced. Minor differences
escalate into threats against the identity of the subgroups.

Any attempt to systematically resolve conflict therefore needs to recognize the dynamics of interaction among different views of reality, that is, different worldviews. Thus it seems appropriate to explore the "geography"—the diversity of worldviews—and to develop strategies of dealing with the conflicts that arise from the differences. This is the subject of *meta-praxis*—designing strategies of resolution out of a recognition that human beings do not share a common ontology. The first step is to define a map of realities on which variously appropriate approaches to resolution conflicts can be played out.

A Map of Realities

The basic operating assumption of this meta-praxis is that changes take place when boundaries between the logics of alternative realities are transgressed. To make this notion graphic, I introduce the metaphor of a *map of the territories of the various realities*. This map covers a range of alternatives that appear to include all the concepts of reality of the current Western cultures.[1] At the four corners of the map, Diagram 1.1, are the pure archetypes: unitary, sensory, mythic, and social realities; in the spaces between are located various mixes of the pure beliefs and behaviors such as we ordinarily find in the people we encounter.

This map is similar to other constructions that organize perceptions of differences among individuals, cultures, and societies. They define categories such as the paradigms of which Kuhn (1972) wrote, Pepper's (1942) four worldviews derived from his root metaphor theory, Burrell and Morgan's (1979) sociological paradigms, Gebser's

Diagram 1.1 Four Realities

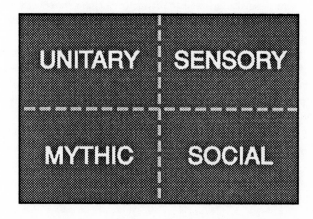

(1985) historically based levels of conscious development, the variety of models based on information processing styles—for instance, see Quinn and McGrath (1985)—Bolman and Deal's (1991) managerial types, and many more.[2] Some of these characterizations were created by observing clusters of behaviors; some, representing stages, arose from a theory of development; and others, like the reality system I am presenting, arose from deductions about characteristics along two or more dimensions. The four-quadrant model I present here characterizes realities according to the qualities derived from an exploration of my two-dimensional map. Its inspiration was the evocative characterization of biographies reported by Lawrence LeShan (1976)—images he derived from historical and psychobiographic research on leaders, scientists, artists, and entrepreneurs in Western societies. He proposed that these striking individuals participated in one or another of four alternative behavior systems, so different that he could not imagine that these individuals had similar views of reality. I took LeShan's work a step further, seeing in his characterization an intimation of underlying beliefs about reality from which I could generate his archetypes. Deductions from this structure match closely the qualities of LeShan's extraordinary people, and mixtures of the types provided descriptions of the worldviews of ordinary, everyday people.

The alternative realities are systems of belief and behavior that characterize a person. They can be seen in worldviews, artwork, styles of leadership, legal theory, modes of argument and of creativity—everywhere that human beings express their understanding of the world. Each describes the way a person explicitly or implicitly understands what is real and thus how these beliefs about reality lead to characteristic behaviors. These are characteristics that are relatively stable, perhaps set from birth or early childhood as has been claimed by many traditional peoples such as Hyemeyohsts Storm in *Seven Arrows* (1972).

Note that, in describing these realities, I make *no statements* about what *truly* exists or what *really* causes what to happen. I take reality to be essentially unknowable; any image we have of reality is, at best, a belief. However unreal these beliefs are, they are persistent. I find that these patterns of belief are characteristic of people over all of Western history, being variously developed and maintained in different cultures and times. In part, my evidence is the similarity of the various constructions mentioned above. Of course, in acknowledging that people use diverse concepts of reality, it would be foolish to say any one of these schemes is *true* or that its reality could be tested empirically. Rather, the intent is to show that, by creating clear images, we can discriminate more richly and make choices more strategically. The spirit of this inquiry is *not the discovery but the creation of images* that help people make choices in practice.

Plurality and Agency

The map of realities has been grossly simplified so that it can be seen as a familiar "flat" map, a space defined by two dimensions. In the usual map, these are measures of width and depth. In this map, the two dimensions are the *degree of differentiation among the elements of reality* and the *source* of movement, that is, of change. A location in this territory is given by the answers to two questions:

1. *Does the change move things toward being more alike or more different?* The changes toward alikeness are *monistic*; the changes toward difference are *pluralistic*.
2. *Is the cause of the change an external, natural condition or are there intentional acts of change?* The external change assumes *determinism* while that produced by the free agent is *volitional*.

The answers to these two questions locate a reality on a map of two independent axes (dimensions). These axes are measures of plurality and of agency (see Diagram 1.2).

The first axis runs from the extreme of monism to pluralism. It distinguishes the idealists from the realists and the theorists from the empiricists. It distinguishes between those who hold the universe to be essentially a unity and those who hold it to be a *multiplicity*. Believers in the monistic assert that all things are one and that our perception of separate things is only a convenience, a habit. The reality has no spatial or time differences; all separations are simply nominal. One form of the belief holds that the universe and everything in it are simply expressions of the Oneness of God. In recent decades, the unity position has garnered new respect in physics with the status of relativity and Unified Field Theory and in philosophy and psychology with attention to various forms of gestalt thinking.

Those at the other end of this axis hold that our perceptions are of separate things that as true entities *in fact* exist separately. My pencil is something different than my automobile; yesterday occurred before tomorrow; and you are not me. There has been a long-standing faith in the existence of basic, undividable elements in the universe, beginning with the Greek atomists and continuing until now in positivistic science.

The paradoxical quality of each of these diverse positions is obvious when we think about communicating from either position: The need to communicate at all denies the unity, but the ability to communicate suggests that the separate parts share in an encompassing wholeness.

In a pure logic, there would be only the extremes, *the one* and *the many*. I find, however, that monists accept *some differentiation*, treating differences as articulations of *the true reality*, and pluralists accept, as a convenience, the concept of wholes.[3] We can experience the impact of the paradox of these opposites by comparing the worldviews of a religious dogmatist and an empirical scientist or those of an artist or entrepreneur and a clinical psychologist or nurse. The concepts of reality held by these very different types of people clearly lead to paradoxical assertions and, in action, to conflicts. One cannot act consistently in both worlds simultaneously; it is not only that they describe incompatible premises but they also lead to different ethical approaches, different explanations of phenomena and causality, different rules of evidence, and so on. The arguments can carry into a science, say, in arguments as to whether mathematics is created law or discovered fact or into politics in the debates between those who hold doctrines of "right" and those who argue for "fairness."

An important intermediate position along this axis is *dualism*, a concept fundamental to many philosophical positions. It divides the world into two opposite forces, such as light and dark, good and evil, mind and body, or yin and yang. Another intermediate position is represented by quantum theory, which sees the world in terms of distinct units in a continuous field.

While this monistic-pluralistic debate has always been part of Western thinking, it has become more problematic during recent decades as the dogmas supporting the extremes have become less maintainable by their true believers. The dogma of Newtonian science (multiplistic) is losing its hold; so is that of traditional Western religions (monistic). More people are recognizing the paradox of the extremes and experiencing incoherence, which manifests itself as mental and spiritual discomfort. The paradox becomes particularly visible as the old paradigms fail and are succeeded by the rise of new mystical—and authoritarian—regimes. Recognition of differences on this dimension are particularly important because differences between unity and multiplicity have historically given rise to the most powerful social conflicts—such as religious wars and persecutions—and the tensions are most aggravated by rapid social change, for example, the failure of economies and cultural norms.

The second axis—agency—extends between those who hold to a *deterministic worldview* and those who believe they have the free will to create their own worlds (*volitional*). This dimension was expressed in Greek mythology as the difference between Apollo and Dionysus and the life-styles they represented. We recognize them in the difference between the rational and the romantic or between the conservative and the liberal.[4] Extreme determinism accepts the universe as given, as destined to follow a path that conforms to a cosmic logic, ordained by God in a religious viewpoint or arising from nature in a scientific one. Some call the determined the *rational*, but I don't use this term because of its implication of correctness or validity. Those who believe in a determined world do not accept that change can occur through human volition: The world follows its own path and we are merely spectators, passive participants in our own fate.

Extreme volition, on the other hand, asserts that the individual is the source of all that happens. In the extreme case, solipsists find no limitation on their behavior because they do not believe in the existence of any other person or thing. Short of this extreme are beliefs that support the ability of the person to choose and to make a difference thereby but that recognize limitations, some arising from the nonhuman "natural" world and others from a recognition of the choices of other persons. The paradoxical qualities in this dimension are apparent, for as May (1975, p. 84) indicates, "Freedom and determinism give birth to each other. Every advance in freedom gives birth to a new determinism, and every advance in determinism gives birth to a new freedom." This paradox appears most clearly at the extremes. As one comes to believe that one has created everything, there is nothing by which one can discriminate between what happens and what is chosen. Conversely, to be totally in tune with the universe creates a feeling of freedom, of having everything happen that one would wish to have happen. I develop the consequences of this paradox further in the section in the next chapter on *counterinvention*.

Whether one can believe in the joint occurrence of free will and determinism or that some domains are determined and others free is not clear from arguments in the literature.[5] Take prayer, for example. Does the act of praying imply both acceptance of the omnipotence of the deity and our ability to affect the outcome? I suspect most of us mix our beliefs, according to the recipes of our worldviews.

The space defined by these two independent axes forms a map on which we can plot different concepts of reality. There are four extreme archetypes: monistic-deterministic, which I call the *unitary*; pluralistic-deterministic, the *sensory*; monistic-volitional, the *mythic*; and pluralistic-volitional, the *social*. These extremes give character to their quadrants, although all individuals hold worldviews that are combinations of the four pure realities. A person's dominant quadrant simply expresses the worldview from which he or she will be choosing actions on significant matters.[6]

For example, a pure pluralistic-deterministic (sensory) worldview supposes that there is lawful interaction among the multiplicity of things that make up the universe. This position is associated with the

Diagram 1.2 Dimensions of Reality

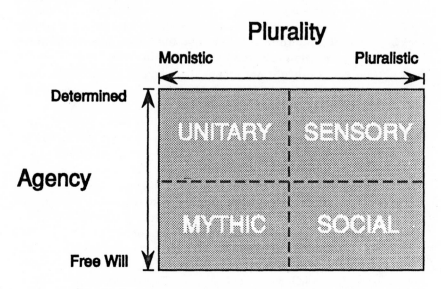

rational, scientific worldview that has been idealized during the Rational/Industrial era. In the opposite quadrant, the monistic-voluntaristic worldview supposes an anarchic world, chaotic, free of the abstract categories of space and time—a view that I and LeShan label the *mythic* reality. Its occupants are solipsistic and asocial. A less extreme view in this quadrant would characterize the creative minds of artists and entrepreneurs.

In Diagram 1.2, I present these four realities with the dimensional labels—the dimension of agency is along the vertical, the dimension of plurality is along the horizontal. Any point on the map not in the extreme corners represents a belief system that allows a mixture of the archetypal realities. This map is only a visual aid. The analogy to a territory should not be carried further.

The alternative realities, as presented here, constitute a basis for categorizing all manner of beliefs, attitudes, and behaviors; that is, all worldviews within at least the Western World.[7] A worldview is derived from the properties of reality and includes other characteristic behaviors and roles that a person believing in such a reality is likely to demonstrate. I use the term *worldview* as a more encompassing characterization than the term *reality*. For example, I may speak of a unitary reality as providing premises for making strategic decisions; I may also speak of people with a unitary belief system who will tend to adopt certain ways of behaving according to the reality they espouse. An authoritarian worldview, for example, is a complex of beliefs and behaviors that tend to arise in a person dominated by a unitary concept of reality.

This map of realities is a strange map; it changes form according to the place from which one views it. A navigator using a terrestrial map assumes that the map is the same regardless of where he or she is. In this model, however, the reality itself changes with the location of its reader. The changes are like the ones Alice experienced as she moved through the looking glass. The rules change; what one cares about changes; and one's abilities to change the scene varies from "place" to "place." In the extreme, a person may only see a single form of reality, thus limiting the view to a given set of rules, values, and opportunities. In a more typical view, a person sees a "real map" that includes a region around his or her location (beliefs) and a fuzzy region that he or she accepts for the sake of social graces. One of my purposes in publishing this work is to provide a platform from which to see the map without the need to traverse this entire countryside. This work provides a view of the myriad idiosyncratic realities without a need for denial or acceptance of the total range of realities.

No person or group operates entirely out of a single view of reality, as defined here. Nothing happens "where one is"; there is no action within a single reality for one's actions come from the interface of one view of reality with another. Any attempt to operate solely within one or another reality signals a pathology—fantasy behavior, uncompromising commitment to a principle, indecisive questioning of one's perceptions of others' feelings, and so on. Conversely, an articulate, elective balance seems to be the mark of a healthy and mature person, culture, or society. As we look at the ways in which the realities are used in combination, however, it will become evident that, by any logical rules we can construct, any action—that is, any change—is necessarily *arational* or, more hopefully, transcends rationality. Every human action, every attempt to change what is, involves us in logical contradictions because the logics of the realities are not compatible; the logic of one is outside of the logic of another. Thus the paths of change are *alogical* or paradoxical. The reason for the alogicality will become more obvious as the totally different bases on which the four realities are built are described in the following chapters.

This set of alternative realities provides the basis for understanding the modes of resolution of issues. In the following sections, I describe each of the four alternative realities, giving the defining characteristics of the pure realities. I have summarized these in Diagram 1.3 and added a few other characteristics that lead to other arenas that are ultimately of interest but that cannot be described in more detail here

Diagram 1.3 Characteristics of the Pure Realities

Quality	Sensory	Social	Unitary	Mythic
The Source	Nature	The Other (in relation to me)	Logos—The Truth	The Self
What is it (Onta)	Objects—things	Feelings, expressed interpersonally	Ideas and principles, articulation of laws	Symbols
Cause of it	Efficient	Intentionality	Formal	Exercise of *will*
Relations	Things act on each Other	Connect via processes of valuing	None—no separation	None
Test of Reality	Observability—direct or indirect	Feelings/values	Consistency with the truth	None
Source of Information	Senses	Self engaged with others	Direct experience of oneness, deduction from rules	Oneself
Moral Judgment	None, no values	Concern for values held by others	None, no alternatives acceptable	Total responsibility, others are not recognized
Changes by	"Going with" the environmental imperative	Social Interaction, no inherent stability	Interpreting ideas in accordance with principles	No change, just creation
Operates in	Necessity	Openness	Certainty	Identity
Seen in	Creature comforts, science	Social exchange, organizing	Mathematics, law, devotion	Play, creating, leading
Comes from	Environment	Society	Culture	Person

without too great a diversion from the search for modes of resolution. Attempting to make these descriptions points to that absurdity we live with—but valiantly attempt to overcome—that one can seldom speak for the other with assurance. More explicitly, one cannot describe a pure reality from within its logic. So the descriptions I provide are *about* the realities. I will say things about a reality that would not be said by someone operating from within it. Conversely, if I talk about my reality, it will appear absurd to you if you do not have access to that same reality in yourself. In writing this book, I am counting on your having such access that you will know out of your own experience what is meant, even if it sounds very exotic from a "normal" position.[8]

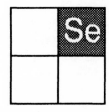

SENSORY REALITY

This world is, after all, a certain way.
—a contemporary historian[9]

The sensory reality is based in the belief in a pluralistic-deterministic reality in which that which we touch, smell, see—that which is sensed—is what is real. It presumes the existence of *prima materia*, substances detectable directly or indirectly by our senses that are related to each other and to humans as part of the natural environment that represent the "certain ways" of the world. This is the reality of the practical person, of science and commerce. It is the espoused belief system of the educated American, certainly of natural scientists and, oddly, also of social scientists and psychologists. It is so pervasive that the majority of Americans have grown up to assert its *reality*, no matter how uncomfortable it may be or how ill-suited to one's personal and ethical views.

I grew up within the educated American establishment, so it is easy for me to accept that the foundation of our being is *the physical reality*. In this world, we move about, find sustenance, and engage with other living beings. The sensory reality is the world of our habits, the environment of our evolution, wherein the forces of nature (whatever those are) produce our sensory awareness, our scales of time and place, tactile pressures, and motion, of taste and odor, our visual impressions of color, shape, movement. We, that is, the great majority of us, so accept the sensory impacts in every moment of our lives that it is hard for us to articulate what are its qualities. Our immersion approaches that of the proverbial fish that do not sense their watery world. It is hard to accept that our worldview is *constructed* by our needs to feed, protect ourselves, and procreate. Particularly with the emergence of scientific methodologies during the past few centuries, the world of things has come to be "reality," so much so that, in the contemporary Western world, any other assumption is treated by most people as a superstitious or religious belief.

The sensory reality is a world of raw sensation, wholly lacking in structure. We come closest to knowing it in the direct awareness of sensorially received data, without the intervention of preconceptions. Of course, we never perceive the raw existence. There are habits built over thousands of years that mediate our perceptions through concepts we have developed of shape, form, hardness, color, texture, and so on. In practice, the sensory reality is created by the ways we have come to know; some ways are buried deep in our nervous systems, such as the rules by which we decide how far away is something that we see; others are learned rather naturally, such as the ways we learn how tastes are produced by the way we combine foods; and still others are learned intellectually, such as the ways we measure electric currents and the age of the universe. Thus the sensory reality is the world of aconscious animals, sensualists, and "hard" scientists. In considering ideas of sensory reality, I don't argue whether I can ever engage with the *prima materia* itself; rather, I argue how reliably I follow the rules of observation.

The sensory reality is centrally related to mortality—to birth and death—created by a drive for growth and a fear of want. It might be called "the evolved reality" for it is what we have come to sense through the joint evolution of our environments and our physiologies.

Belief in the sensory reality is conservative and economical; the world is simply made up of that which is or, as far as we know, of *signs that stand for* what is. This belief assumes there is something out there that can be detected, so that the more we understand, the less we will be surprised by what we find and by what happens. Our sciences are developed to reduce the chance that anything that comes along will surprise us. (Is it not wonderful how *unsuccessful* they have been?) The sensory reality is, after all, about what is.

The characterizing qualities of the sensory reality are laid out systematically in the following subsection, as are those of the other three realities in succeeding subsections. These qualities are the ontological characteristics that deal with what is real (the *onta*) and how the elements relate (the causes of "things") and, as deduced from these basics, the sources of knowledge and meaning, the modes of change, values, and moral judgment, and the criteria for action.

Major Characteristics of Sensory Reality

1. *Space, time, and material objects are "real," existing independent of the observer.* Through observation, we can gain an increasingly accurate view (knowledge) of physical reality.

2. *The onta of this reality are objects of the senses that can be detected more or less directly with sensory instruments, either natural or artificial.* I use the Greek root *onta* for "things" to avoid being trapped within the current connotations, because the "real things" in other realities have quite different properties.

3. *The relations among onta are determined by the continuity of nature; nothing is created that does not arise from something that happened before.* The bald belief is that everything is determined by prior circumstances.[10] There is no room for willful determination of events by human beings or other creatures.

4. *All events flow from a first cause (from the "big bang," the point at which our current scientific theory says it all began).* The relation among onta and the forces that relate them is *efficient cause*—that is, everything that occurs follows from some set of prior or concurrent conditions.

5. *Concepts of change.* The extreme form of the sensory reality denies any possibility of making changes. All is predetermined. It denies any meaning to an intentionality that a person, organization, or society would choose to redirect a course. When the term *change* is used, it denotes simply reification, making what must be made by the "laws of nature." Humanly directed action is paradoxical; it serves to cause that which will happen anyway. The (strange) role of the scientist is to see that nothing happens in the future that is not predicted (or predictable) from the past. In this sense, "to attempt to change" shows a failure of understanding that change cannot be achieved. Thus the drive for change, sometimes characterized as the pursuit of the technological imperative, amounts to following the natural course of history. To do anything else would be inefficient and ineffective and would deny the fundamental lawfulness of the universe.

6. *Criterion for action.* Does it work? Will it work? This too is paradoxical, for there is no choice about what action one takes. But the validity of this criterion is supported by the sense that "working" is an indication of achieving harmony, ignoring the contradiction implied in recognizing any source of action that is not "natural." The only form of cause is *efficient*. Thus the question of criteria exposes an anomaly. On strict consideration, such a question is acceptable only as a convention, without substance.

7. *Lacking free will, there is no moral responsibility.* The sensory reality involves no recognition of values, thus no recognition of moral or ethical

questions. In every belief system, however, the accepted system is valued as the only acceptable one. Thus the acceptance of determinism
denies that any set of rules for determining what is (real) could have a
place. Any expression of heresy regarding methods of establishing
that which is valid represents an attack on the fundamental value of
the sensory reality.

Every society lives with a very large dose of sensory reality. One
cannot get through a day without operating as though one were a part
of a material reality. This is the reality that has its foundations in our
physical being. For people who hold strongly to this reality, the sensory is all that it is necessary to know. As humans gained the capacity
to form concepts, however, other images of the way in which the
world works have emerged; we form symbols, we make moral choices,
and form images of God. So, while the human mind continues to use
the sensory apparatus that it gained in its earlier animal forms, it has
access to other ways of engaging with the world. We have constructed
additional views of reality with which to create, explore, and guide
our actions. The idea that we do construct our worldview is itself the
basis for the *social reality*, described next.

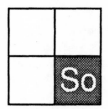

SOCIAL REALITY

Social reality is a humanistic view of mankind, an acceptance of different viewpoints, histories, and moral codes as well as of the conflicts
that such acceptances engender. The beliefs of social reality are centrally concerned with the feelings and values of human beings; these
beliefs hold that feelings and the values derived from them are the
only basis for assigning reality to something. In the extreme, a person
who holds fully to this worldview would say, "If it does not matter to
someone, it does not exist." The key is "mattering," for the social reality is a feeling/value phenomenon, not a question of physical energy
and form. This is not a denial of the sensory reality, it simply holds
that mattering is a question of human concern. We can see the play of

this reality in the arguments about the allocation of tax monies to grand science projects such as moon voyages. Those of a social reality sense that it makes no difference whether the moon is made of green cheese or not. Such allocations can only be justified if they contribute to the felt quality of life on earth.

The objective world of the social reality is the shared consensus among the perceptions and feelings of a population. It arises in the individual awareness and is *constructed* through the interaction among individuals. What comes to be treated as real is what one cares about and values, for these valued constructs become the onta of the social world. In the extreme, the only things that exist are those that a society values enough to maintain as entities. Ideally, individual preferences would converge onto a shared "objective reality," so that sensory and social realities would approximate each other. But, with diverse histories, the appearance of new ideas, and unshared feelings, those of social belief will continually sense an ambiguity about what "reality" is. This ambiguity, and the failure of the pluralistic source to converge on a single reality, are central qualities of the social reality. Maurice Friedman (1989, p. 10) epitomizes the relations among those with a social reality:

> The mystery of word and answer that moves between beings is not one of union, harmony, or even complementarity, but of tension; for two persons never mean the same thing by the words they use and no answer is ever fully satisfactory. The result is that at each point of the dialogue, understanding and misunderstanding are interwoven. From this tension of understanding and misunderstanding comes the interplay of openness and closedness, expression and reserve, that mark every genuine dialogue between person and person.

This tension in the social reality is exemplified in the character of Hamlet, who is hesitant, self-observing, driven to distraction by the impossibility of knowing whether his reality is "correct." The attempt to make relations and to share feelings and constructions creates the "social reality." For those who hold the social worldview, the universe is defined, if not created, by the private and public dialogues of valuing minds.

While the concept of the social reality has gained respectability only in the last few decades, the worldview is well recognized and its adherents are many. Of the four, it is the reality most associated in this society with the "feminine" viewpoint and with those of a service mentality. So we find that almost everyone in the counseling and social welfare professions, in organizational development, and to a slightly lesser degree in family medicine, nursing, and school teaching predominantly holds a social worldview.

The social reality is emerging as a new view, characteristic of Americans, though its origins are ancient. Its principles were clearly postulated by Immanuel Kant in the eighteenth century and are concurrently incorporated in the theistic movements (for example, the Society of Friends) out of which grew the personal and the communal modes of worship that flourished along with the prosperity of the colonies and the U.S. frontier. This view of reality became more widely acceptable in the Romantic movement of the nineteenth century. By the twentieth century, it came into general acceptance as reflected in such creations as social welfare as a governmental function rather than a charity, with the emergence of psychological practice, and in the concepts of the rights of all to public education. Fifty years later, in the era of the "flower child," social reality as a life-style gained the impetus that now deeply affects not only the personal view but also the conduct of business and the organization of community life. It gained intellectual respectability in the work of Alfred Schutz (1945/1967), as popularized by Berger and Luckmann (1967). Paul Watzlawick titled his 1984 work on constructionism *The Invented Reality: How Do We Know What We Believe We Know?* During the past two decades or so, social scientists have increasingly recognized the social reality as fundamental even while espousing the traditional methodologies and validity of the sensory worldview. Further support comes from the historian Evelyn Underhill (1961), who noted two similar paths of development in ancient Greek society in her work on mysticism.

Major Characteristics of Social Reality

1. Objects, space, and time are arbitrary constructs of a physical reality inaccessible to the human mind. The worldview is *constructed* collectively by the willful activity of sentient beings.[11] In this reality, the images one has of the world are created intentionally, by choice; the social reality is teleological.[12] "Objective" knowledge is developed by the agreement among observers as to what they will assert is the culture's worldview.

2. Feelings are the onta. In his *Rules of Sociological Method,* Durkheim says, "The first and most fundamental rule is: Consider social facts as things." Feelings are social facts. They are objects, but they are not defined in terms of energy or physical dimension or limited by the physical laws of conservation. The values derived from feelings cannot be objectively compared as there is no calculus of values within the social reality or "law of conservation" of values.

3. Relations among the onta and their values depend on social process. Lacking an independent source of values, and a "real" world directly accessible to the sentient being, there is no standard for comparing feelings (utilities) or even what we identify as sensations in an objective manner that has not passed through the minds of one or more human beings. "Constructivism necessarily begins with the (intuitively confirmed) assumption that all cognitive activity takes place within the experiential world of a goal-directed consciousness" (von Glasersfeld, 1984, p. 32).

4. *Causality is final.* That is, events are produced by intention, acting in a world created by the diverse humans who exist therein. We make things happen purposefully. (Without purpose, the world goes on according to its habits.)

5. *Concepts of change.* "Change" is a constant companion to the construction of reality. Within the social worldview, all communications disturb the balance of values. Change is thus the normal condition, a part of the natural course of interpersonal relations, of life and death, of social movements, and of the shared understanding of the phenomenological world. Life is interaction and awareness of difference.

6. *Criteria for action.* Does the change produce outcomes that are *fair* to all those involved? Does it support interdependence? Does it allow openness to alternative views? While the notion of fairness may seem narrow, it is the general form of the concern that one's values, thus reality, are taken into consideration. To not have one's feelings considered is to be literally "wiped out."

7. *Responsibility.* The joint condition of free will and pluralism creates a recognition of a multitude of individuals with volitions of their own, each able to affect the world according to his or her power. Thus each is responsible for the other. Ethics arises in the recognition of the other as a valuing/valued creature. Ethics, as the science and practice of social valuing, is the particular province of the social reality. I differentiate ethical behavior from "right" and "truth," which is prescribed in unitary thinking. The social is the only belief system of these four (and thus the only one in Western thinking) that recognizes moral and ethical questions. This follows because, without intention and free will, there are can be no responsibility, and, without pluralism, there can be no concern for another person.

As all the above suggests, the formation of the "social" reality is paradoxical. In the denial of an accessible objective universal structure, the social reality is essentially a collective private reality. This paradox enters our daily world in the operation of democracy, for its truths lie not with the individual's value but must be established by the "will of the majority." So, at its heart, the humanistic reality provides an arena for conflict. The tension that accompanies such irresolution frequently leads people of a social reality to wish that there were a single truth that confirmed their values and, in that wanting, leads them to end up espousing the exactly opposite reality that I label "unitary."

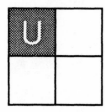

UNITARY

For most of recorded history, the unitary belief system, monistic and deterministic, has dominated human societies. This is not to say that the unitary reality is the most used in the daily business of survival but that it is the reality that underlies the processes by which humankind regulates itself. It is the reality of the spirit and ritual, religion and law, mathematics and the theoretical sciences. In the pure extreme, we find the blissful world of romantic idylls in which one experiences the self-transcendence of all dualities, the sublime unity of the Hindu samadhi and holy ecstasy, world without time. Yet, with only a suspicion that others deny this one worldview, the unitary belief leads to a world of autos-da-fé and holocausts called down by Inquisitors to enforce the unique "truth" of religious and political movements. The unitary is the world of *true believers* (Hoffer, 1951), of ritual, sacred art and architecture, and the machinations of bureaucratic regulations. "Only magic [the unitary] knows fanaticism" (Gebser, 1985, p. 354). Equally it is the reality of the profoundest simplicity that encompasses the cosmos. Albert Einstein so deeply believed in the principled universe as to say:

> Our experience justifies us in believing that nature is the realization of the simplest mathematical ideas. . . . With them (natural laws) it ought to be possible to arrive at the description, that is to say, the theory, of every natural process, including life, by means of pure deduction. (Einstein, 1934, p. 3)

The unitary reality is familiar in daily life as the belief system through which we establish roles, form organizations and political states, authorize and forbid actions, and interpret the dogma of the eternal universe. It is the world of form that is manifest in mathematics, law, custom, ritual, and many fine arts. Its characteristics are order, consistency, and conservation. There is a freedom from making choice. Moral decisions are decided by authorized interpretation of the writ. For there to be an ethic, there needs to be choice that is lacking within the unitary reality. It is a world of interpretation and elaboration inasmuch as the purpose and ends have been preformed.

Across the range of appearances that arise in a unitary reality, there are important commonalities that lead to using the same strategic approaches to change. For common usage, however, I initially identify two strategies: those generated in response to an assumption of unity and those generated when the unity is threatened, that is, when the person or society sees around itself a shadow of something foreign, a "dark side." I label these strategies, respectively, the holistic and the dialectic. The holistic is dominated by the expected unfolding of the ordained story. Evangelistic sects exemplify this worldview. The dialectical worldview comes from a perceived need to replace the established, but inaccurate, truth and from the struggles that come with the replacement. Such a worldview is common among revolutionaries, artists, scientists, and critics whoseperceptions come from seeing from "the outside." The holistic aims at amelioration, at cleansing the present of imperfection. The dialectic aims at revolution, at an often fiery spiral of thesis and antithesis on the path to the realization in a new synthesis, a new statement of truth. Thus, among those whose primary belief is unitary, we find ecstatic spiritualists, mathematicians, authoritarians, and doctrinaire revolutionaries, as well as a variety of cynics.

Of the four realities, the theoretic structure of the unitary has been most exhaustively studied. In addition to its relation to the nominalistic tradition in philosophy, the great majority of religious (both spiritual and theological), legal, political, and dialectical discourses are set within the unitary assumptions of reality. It is the reality we associate with authoritarianism and with disciples.

As indicated at the beginning of this chapter, one cannot discuss the pure position from within that position. In this case, the pure believer is captured in a wholeness that allows no articulation, thus no description. The true believer operates in an ecstatic oneness that renders it impossible for comparative or analytic descriptions to have any meaning. So, what we are characterizing is this worldview from outside, using words that would be alien to the person within it.

Major Characteristics of Unitary Reality

1. What truly exists is the Oneness, the totality. Space, time, and any other distinctions are *nominal*; they are but appearances, conveniences of expression. The sensed world is a manifestation of that totality, an expression of god or of the honored ancestors of one's culture. Its pure form is without form or delineation. Einstein said, "For those of us who are concerned physicists, the distinction between past, present and future is an illusion, however persistent" (Prigogine, 1980, p. 203).

2. *The sole existence, that is, the onta of the unitary work, is the logos, the Word, the authority.* There is no thingness separate from it. In the various manifestations posited by the philosophies and religions, more and less complex hierarchies of ideas (concepts, laws, classifications) are articulated as an interpretation of the One as needed for a particular occasion. These articulations render the unitary worldview comprehendible—particularly to the pluralistically minded—by postulating nominal "things" as parts of structures with which to manage daily life. The formal structure or organization is the epitome of the unitary world, whether of the City of Heaven, the U.S. government, the ABC Manufacturing Company, or the family of John Jones. Individual people gain reality by defining roles for themselves in organizations and communities, by becoming articulations of the whole.

3. *Relationships are the product of the articulation of the whole into parts and thus by definition are hierarchical.* Relationships are posited and formulated in structures of "laws" that need no "earthly" foundations; they are not grounded in sensory reality. The law, in its various forms, is the manifestation of the process of structuring; it is the regulatory mechanism of a particular organization of the oneness.

4. *Cause is formal.* What happens, happens *because* it is deduced from the Word according to the current interpretative procedures. In some cases, it is based in a sacred writ; in others, in a tradition of social regulation. There is no sense of effect—without acceptance of time or space as dimensions of reality, there can be no sense to an efficient cause.[13]

5. *Concepts of change.* Change cannot be formulated in the unitary reality. There are two radically different modes of resolution of an issue that arise in the unitary reality: the holistic and the dialectic. The holistic mode calls for a reinterpretation of the law that might entail a change of the roles of those interpreting the law. That which others might call *change* is considered but clarification, harmonization, or the return to the utopia that is inherent in the universe. The dialectic assumes that the current form either is in error or is an approach short of the final truth. It assumes the current dogma is a violation of the ultimate utopian condition and calls for a fundamental reinterpretation in the service of the inevitable. Neither mode involves change. Both utopian movements and the Marxist revolutions of this century are better understood as *retrogressions* to a better world that had been

"known"—though not experienced—rather than as progressions toward a new world. We can also recognize that science considered as a deductive mode of understanding is similarly a study of the past done to assure that the future is not unexpected.

6. *Criterion for action.* Without justification for action, there is no meaning for a criterion of action within the pure unitary worldview. For the unitary worldview, action is *staying in tune with the flow of events*; it is avoiding choice by never getting out of line with the truth system. Or, in the dialectical view, it is to move swiftly to end the plurality of views, crushing the strongholds of error. Change does not bring the unitary any expectation of joy or relief. On the contrary, one who holds to unitary reality believes it is better to remain in an unhappy (depressed) state than to experience the trauma of taking on even the possibility of new truths. In the practical daily world, if a person holding to a unitary belief recognizes even the possibility of another truth, change becomes a question of membership, of switching from one truth to another. That is, membership and truth are complementary. Consideration of another truth is heresy—note that *heresy* is from the Greek *hairein*, to choose.

7. *Responsibility.* To remain "at one" and to support others in so doing is the basic responsibility to the unitary. One cannot be wrong except in the heretical act that violates the unity, and guilt due to a violation of the unity is resolved by the process of *at-one-ment*. Choice is heresy, is evil. It is the only evil in the unitary belief. It forces one to see doubt, an idea that would open questions of "the truth" that are unresolvable. What passes for an ethic is the system of rules. So, strangely, the unitary reality that is the base for religion and law has no room for morality or ethics. As we have seen, they are solely the province of the social reality.

To an even greater degree than the pluralistic realities, the unitary reality is everywhere confounded by paradox. The unitary assumption denies reality to any particular structure and thus to any specific lawfulness. The logic denies any particular organization of the universe. So this reality that is most associated with strict law and reliance on a code of behavior lacks an essential justification for any law or order. It is understandable then that whatever is adopted must be held to fiercely for there can be no support for a particular belief external to the belief system itself. As William James (1963, p. 71) saw it, "The slightest suspicion of pluralism, the minutest wiggle of independence of any one of its parts from the control of the totality would ruin it." With no foundation on which to rest, great structures must be built that can sustain themselves from accidents of the moment. In such a world, the inhabitants must be self-binding, that is, a *religio* (from the word from which *religion* comes.) Paradoxically, a religion is that which is created in the absence of anything in which to believe. The one suprahuman structure that has been available and used by various cultures is that of mathematics, particularly numbers and geometry. Sacred geometry has been the basis of sacred architecture and rites for all of human history. Belief structures built by the Pythagoreans on rudimentary number theory have been carried into most mystical traditions in the West.

A second paradox arises in the expression of unitary thinking. Clearly, languages based in the pluralistic foundation of nouns and verbs—as are all the European languages—cannot adequately express the unitary concepts. Thus a language such as English can only be a coding *pointing to* unitary ideas. The sacred geometries and the Jewish Cabala have tried to solve this dilemma in one way; mystical traditions have tried others. References to the process languages, for example, of the Hopi Indians, suggest there are ways out of the errors, as viewed from the unitary reality, made by inappropriate linguistic modes of distinction.

A third paradox is even more problematic for the resolution of conflict. This is the paradoxical condition of having two totally opposing behavior—that is, attitude—sets—the holistic and the dialectic—derived from the same view of reality. It should not be surprising that behavior in the most conflict inducing of the realities is also the most obviously separable into a holistic, conflict-free worldview and the source of violent, obliterating fury. The unitary is the reality of *power* because it depends on maintaining absolute boundaries around the acceptable beliefs and knowledge. Paradoxically, it also requires total surrender of one's ego. Within the unitary worldview are found primitives who have not yet developed independent egos as well as those who are working to transcend the ego (Wilber, 1981). Those who are most concerned with retaining power ultimately must totally surrender it to fully accept their belief.

The fourth reality, the mythic, is also a domain of power but one based on the ability to *create* the world one intends.

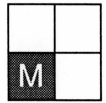

MYTHIC REALITY

> His mind bloomed in the most far-fetched and beautiful
> fantasies, and he believed to be fact what was merely
> beautiful. He believed it with such a lively faith, with the
> faith which engenders works, that he decided to put into
> practice what his folly suggested, and by sheer belief in it he
> made it true.
>
> —Unamuno (*Don Quixote*)

The mythic reality—of all the realities—provides the most fascinating insights into the resolution of issues. It is the least understood and the most mystifying. The behaviors of a person with a mythic worldview seems the most unreal, yet, if we are to understand the creation and evolution of systems and the behavior of great leaders in almost every field of human endeavor, we need to understand the impact of a reality of monistic free will. The "mythic" is the creator of symbols, of ideas, unhindered by the limits of what already is present for persons of the other reality beliefs.

The mythic reality combines belief in free will with a monistic concept of the universe. In the extreme, the worldview is wholly solipsistic. If I were to speak from the mythic view, I would say (to myself): "All the world is my creation; you, my readers are my creation; I people the world, I create its phenomena, and I assign it in time and locate it in space—which themselves are given meaning by my thought." Quoting from Bradley (1966, p. 218), "I cannot transcend experience and experience is *my* experience. From this it follows that nothing beyond myself exists; for what is experienced is the [self's] state." Experience and my creation are indistinguishable, so that which exists does so because I gave it meaning by volition. LeShan (1976, p. 90) describes this world as one in which:

> Nothing is arbitrary; nothing occurs by chance. Everything has meaning and is charged with implications and power. Things, however, may look arbitrary because it can be hard to trace the connections between the various parts of a unity as these connections, from the sensory viewpoint, range over objective and subjective, past and future, things and symbols,

until they come to that one arbitrary act of will underlying the whole thing that neither needs explaining nor is explainable.

The moment we think of people who act as though each sees him- or herself as the only existing being, we sense the presence of greatness and/or madness. Certainly, the great leaders of the world—the charismatics, the painters and architects, the impresarios, the movie moguls, and the megalomaniacs—hold strongly to the mythic worldview. Unamuno (1967, p. 142), describing this way of being, said:

> That's the way, My Lord Don Quixote, that is the way of naked courage, insisting aloud and in the sight of all, defending one's claims with one's life; that is the way of creating any and all truth. The more one believes in a thing, the truer it is believed, and it is not intelligence, but will, which imposes the truth.

And so it was that

> Churchill idealized [his people] with such intensity that in the end they approached his ideal and began to see themselves as he saw them. . . . So hypnotic was the force of his word, so strong his faith, that by the sheer intensity of his eloquence he bound his spell on them until it seemed to them that he was indeed speaking what was in their hearts and minds. . . . [T]hey conceived a new idea of themselves which their own process and the admiration of the world has since established as a heroic image. . . . They went forth into battle transformed by his words. The spirit which they found within them he had created within himself from his inner resources. (Berlin, 1980, p. 14)

All mythics are not so grand in their impact nor so elevated in their worldview. At a primitive level, the mythic reality is an unrestrained world that has not yet accepted a "reality principle." Mythic persons manufacture their environments. For instance, the devotees of voodoo believe they can control other people or things by affecting an "aspect" that symbolizes the whole, and other mythics create symbols that give meaning to society through the arts or technologies. The extreme exemplar of a mythic as solipsist is described by Ernst Becker (1973, p. 76) as a "full blown schizophrenic [who] floats out of his body, dwells in an eternal now . . . not subject to death or destruction."

In the most elevated manifestation, the mythics come to represent the whole, leading society through knowledge and experience, as Churchill did, or through the compassionate insight that great spiritual leaders have demonstrated. The worldview of their followers becomes indistinguishable from that which the mythic persons symbolize; followers of the Buddha become Buddhists; of Christ, Christians. Ultimately, we cannot say whether the mythics create their worlds or personify them. To lead and to be led are indistinguishable in the highest attainment of mythic unity.

Out of pathologies of the mythic belief, however, arise deformed and incomplete worlds. The pure mythic as sole creator, and thus the sole site for feelings and desire, is unable to conceive of ethics questions, to consider what would be good for other people or understand what they offer or lack. Only as a person also participates in a social or unitary reality can questions of ethics or rightness be entertained.

If I were of a pure mythic reality, I would not be writing to you or even to myself. I would be writing out of the joy and pathos of creating the audience, the stage, the script, the score, the characters of the play I live. The writing and all it describes are one with me; I allow their plurality only to ornament my world and articulate it with my desires. Paul Valéry spoke as a mythic in saying, "I am in a world which is in me." Whereas a unitary reality is a world of abstract law, mythic reality is a world of *story*. The world is my story, created and to be created: "Whole civilizations rise from stories—and can rise from nothing else. . . . Myths, told for their own sake, are not stories that have meanings, but stories that give meanings" (Carse, 1986, p. 168).[14] Carse indicates the mythic person to be the generator of stories and "myths," and, while this connection will be developed in later chapters, the reader should not identify the mythic reality simply with story as fictions.

Describing the mythic from the viewpoint of other realities is, of course, a denial of the mythic reality. So the readers of this book, who I know will not be pure mythics, must know that all thinking, talking, writing, and even the discussion of mythic behavior itself is, from the mythic's viewpoint, an absurd exercise that I (the mythic) engage in to illuminate the ingenuity with which my creations explain *their* existence. (You cannot discuss the mythic, or any other reality, with a pure mythic person.) With this forewarning of contradictions, I describe the properties of *the* world.

Major Characteristics of Mythic Reality

1. The only reality is that which I have created. Its apparent parts are articulations of that which I have elaborated. It is not meaningful to say that there are or there are not real things separate in time, space, and energy. That which is is what I have created.[15]

2. The onta are symbols. Reality is the meaning given to experience by symbolization. The power of a symbol is the degree to which it orders that experience for me. (One view of the mythic world—admittedly contradictory—supposes there to be a god of which I am the agent. That god presents me with the unformed experience that I symbolize and, in a sensory realization, materialize.)

3. *Relation*. "Nothing is arbitrary in the mythic mode; nothing occurs by chance. Everything has meaning and is charged with implications and power" (LeShan, 1976). In being given meaning, "things" are created. No laws determine what is possible; what is created is. As in every aspect of describing the mythic reality, we see paradox, not because it is more paradoxical than other realities but because we so unfamiliar with its properties that we see it freshly. What consistency there is comes with the creation of stories, that is, through fabrics of meaning. "Story" sets the form of meaning, and the accidents of the moment clothe it.

4. *Causality is will and intentionality*. I could equally well use the term *final*, as used to describe the social form of causality, but, without any sense of another, *willfulness* conveys a clearer sense of both the strength and the fragility of this cause of the world's manifestations. Will as cause is foreign to the Western sensory mind but not to others. The voodoo belief makes no essential separation of part and whole, thus nothing is illogical in the part controlling the whole. It is simply a matter of focusing will or intentionality. The voodoo magician conjures a symbol related to some object or person and, through an act of will, affects aspects of the whole. Powerful symbolization, "arbitrary acts of willing" initiate new stories, which, like genes, are autopoietic and self-maintaining. The Christian story is one such *willing*, perhaps all of modern science is another.

5. *Concepts of change*. Paradoxically, a believer in the pure mythic world *does not experience change*, for it is always the created world that is. A mythic creates in the moment the total existence—present, past, and future. For the solipsist, that is it; there is no change. To the sensory or social observer, the mythic person may be inducing unending, unpredictable, and chaotic change while the mythic just sees what is as the exposition of the story. Of course, when the mythics recognize and enter the pluralistic world, they may "make things happen." If they are not in tune with the environment, the effect is chaotic and self-destructive; if they are deeply attuned, as were Beethoven and Shakespeare, Churchill and Mao Tse-tung, Buddha and Christ, they have immense power to change everyone's world yet remain themselves always in the unchanging eternal.[16]

6. *Criteria for action*. The pure mythic reality provides *no criterion for action*, there being no restraint on one's choice. One chooses a daydream. But if a mythic person were to make a choice, he might ask, "Does it work?" From outside of the mythic reality, we would rephrase it to

ask: Does my world work? Or, Does his world work? Paradoxically, the criteria for the near mythic and the near sensory extremes are expressible in the same phrase—*does it work?*—within the limits of my boundaries or understanding. A second criterion, which may not logically depend on the mythic assumptions but seems to accompany the mythic act, is *elegance,* which is attained by creating order by simplifying where there was complexity.[17]

7. *Responsibility.* The mythics are totally responsible for the world they have created and exist within. There are no laws other than those created, no actions except those willed, and no other being to accept fault for any manifestation. This view of responsibility can be expressed this way: "I cannot even say that it did not happen the way I wanted it to; if it happened, I wanted it to." Of all the realities, none is so harsh, so demanding, as the mythic's. The mythic person carries the burden of the world *and* lacks a sense of morality—lacks any need to take care of another, any reason to "do good." How can one be moral if there are no others who have feelings, values, and intentionality different than what I have given them? *The mythic is amoral and unconstrained by any ethics issue.* Looked at from outside, mythics are uninvolved in what is around. That is not what is felt by others, however; powerful mythics may have an immense impact on their communities, leading to one of the most confounding paradoxes of the mythic reality.

The mythic's belief that he or she has created all leads us to believe that we are, in our own reality, created by his or her belief (in us). Most of us have had the experience of feeling larger, more important, more alive in the presence and the afterglow of a powerful charismatic leader, a great artist, or a saintly person. We come away from a masterful performance of a work of genius feeling touched and made grand simply by having been there. We are enlivened by following in the footsteps of Gandhi, of Mao, and unfortunately of Hitler and other Pied Pipers. For those caught in his spell, a mythic may appear to be the god who is creating them; conversely, for the mythic, we are the evidence of (his) self-creating essence. In this entanglement, the mythics, unintentionally and illogically, become responsible for their offspring. It is easy to see why a mythic, overcome by such responsibility, might retreat into solipsism—thus leaders, such as Napoleon or Nixon, as they fail, come to deny reality, and their lieutenants build asylums that isolate them from the world of their followers.

The mythic reality leads to a variety of behaviors that at first seem bizarre. With further consideration, it provides a straightforward explanation that allows us to recognize much that is commonplace—in particular, artist's work, leadership, and followership. Individuals strongly dominated by the mythic world may be labeled "narcissistic" and, at the extreme, schizoid. (I find that such labeling locks us into the causal analyses appropriate to deterministic worldviews and denies us access to the powerful worldview of the mythic.)

As in the case of every other worldview, no one can operate from the extreme position; operating even close to the extreme appears pathological. In the mythic reality, the feasible extreme is solipsism, a state others view as insanity (schizophrenia).[18] In typical mixtures with other reality beliefs, a person who combines the mythic with the sensory may be an entrepreneurial producer—Thomas A. Edison and John Sculley are examples; with the social, a facilitator of creativity and change—IBM's Watsons, father and son; with the unitary, a prophet, leading others into his or her mythic belief system—Mary Baker Eddy, the founder of Christian Science.

It is not likely that any human society has been dominantly mythic. It would be hard to build a culture dominated by a population of so-lipsistic people. Among modern Western cultures, we might think of the Hollywood studios of the 1930s, but Spain, with its echoes of medieval dreams, has the most pervasive component of mythic think-ing in its arts and at the fringes of its everyday life. The epitome, and the parody, of the mythic person is Don Quixote, and the mythic image, "the castle in Spain."

Comment

While the mythic reality provides greater freedom and opportunity than sober and rational people expect from life, that very freedom to create images is the source of its greatest danger, which the nonmythic person calls narcissism, schizophrenia, or egotism. The *double* of the personality can take over, putting sensory reality aside to create the il-lusion of asylum within which the mythic person cannot distinguish his or her reality from the universe itself. Even when mythics are in touch with other realities, they live with intimations of omnipotence and immortality. The tragedy in their lives is captured in the title of Ernst Becker's *The Denial of Death* (1973). The burden is expressed in this telling sentence: "To renounce the world and oneself, to lay the meaning of it to the power of creation, is the hardest thing for man to achieve—and so it is fitting that this task should fall to the strongest personality type, the one with the largest ego" (Becker, 1973, p. 173). So the ultimate difficulty for mythics is denial of their egos. Humankind has found the mythic both the most difficult to live with and the source of the greatest and most distinctively human contributions. The mythic reality, in which everyone participates to some degree, is the space of the created. And, according to Jean Gebser (1985, p. 545), "Only those will succeed for whom the present becomes a time-free origin, a perpetual plenitude and source of life and spirit from which all decisive constellations and formations are completed."

COMBINATIONS OF REALITIES

It is clear from the examination of the pure realities that it is both dangerous and unlikely that we will find people working from a "single vision." Few people hold uncompromisingly to any one or another of these belief systems or, in all probability, to any other *simple, consistent logic of belief.* Pure belief in a single reality can be found only in the worlds of the philosopher and in the minds of people a clinical psychologist would label "insane." Further, as I elaborate in the next chapter, *one cannot do anything wholly from within one reality.* One of the great attributes of *Homo sapiens* is that we have available a variety of modes of thinking. Whether the variety rises from our triune brain, the imprinting of behaviors on our unformed infant characters, or the chaotic responses of our 10 billion brain cells dancing to celestial music, we demonstrate a multiplicity of personalities that constitute the human experience. While we have rather little understanding of what separates the multiple personality structure of the schizophrenic from the open responsiveness of a fully functioning adult, we recognize that the richness of humanity derives from the complexity with which we respond to and affect our environments.

In everyday life, we use the assumptions of more than one of these realities. Some people will be strongly dominated by a single worldview, but the majority of those I have encountered and examined typically use the assumptions of two realities. The commonness of the dual commitment is evident in the ease with which we can associate them with common labels. For example, the ideal *manager* has qualities that are closely aligned with a joint sensory-social reality; the *designer* aligns with the unitary-sensory. In Chapter 5, I elaborate on these types in the discussion of different styles of leaders and followers and the processes of culture building.

CONCLUSION

Conflict, and thus issues, are founded in differences. The differences in belief described in this chapter are fundamental, being based in our beliefs about reality. There are no grounds on which we can resolve these differences. We do not have, at the moment, a meta-logic with which to select among the propositions of the realities described here—or among those out of any other set such as Pepper's, or Burrell and Morgan's, and so on. It is not possible to ascribe to one logic dominance or create a synthesis without a common ground. Yet it is obvious that we do resolve issues and the conflict that is inherent in them; we do go beyond illogics in daily engagements; we accept the anomalies, using various interpersonal agreements to ignore the differences that separate us. The agreements are on the tenuous grounds that we call the bonds of family, friendship, and culture. Certainly, most of our theories of power are needed to explain the ways we use to bully others into accepting our view of reality. The law does it civilly; war does it tragically. Neither can claim the solutions are logical; but, amazingly, agreements do hold.

Understanding the source of the anomalies is itself an important aid to resolving issues, if only because it warns us not to waste effort trying to develop a shared logic for our arguments. Seeing the anomalies in this form may have some impact for they are not mere philosophical oddities; they underlie the differences in beliefs that have led to most of our wars of words as well as those of violence. We need only look at the long history of the "mind-body" problem that for 400 years has been the source of unending arguments. This problem is immediately visible to us in the argument over the reality of psychosomatic illness and, even worse, psychosomatic cures of illness. Some, coming from a sensory-unitary mind-set, think such an idea absurd; others, of a social-mythic persuasion, don't bother to argue. They just go ahead and cure themselves—at least that is the way they see it.

A common response to my talking and writing about these alternative views of reality is that I am pursuing some sort of intellectual exercise, that I don't really expect anyone to believe that reality is anything but the way it is—that is, as they see it. Our beliefs are very important to our security, and I do not expect the readers to withdraw from their positions easily. So, aside from the fact that what I have described above is unfamiliar and certainly abstract, remembering the differences among the realities will be an uncomfortable task. For this reason, I use various repetitions to support your understanding. One such tool combines the major characteristics discussed above into a single chart, as is done in Diagram 1.3. A second is holding on to the paradoxical condition that we seldom work out of a single reality so we must continuously reflect within to see how we are combining the diverse worldviews. We insult ourselves and others by placing our thinking in pigeonholes, alleging "single vision." My purpose in developing this typology is to help us transcend typologies, to see the rich differences among humans, and, ultimately, to recognize that it is critical to respect these differences in the process of resolving issues.

I recommend that the reader review the entries in Diagram 1.3 by comparing any one of the characteristics across the range of suggested realities. As you do so, you may find many of the entries implausible. In that case, I urge that you think of other persons, dogmas, and cultures for which these implausibles may be the very stuff of reality. So, while empirical scientists will find the source in nature, most of them will recognize that billions of religious people see nature as secondary to the Logos or other Truth. Similarly, it is "evident" to scientists that the world is made up of many things, but they will also know that people do not recognize them unless they have some particular interest in them. That is both a physiological and a psychological observation; if people don't care, a thing has no existence for them.

Perhaps the most bothersome implausibility may be the denial of moral judgment to three of the four. Most of my readers are bothered by my saying that great leaders, spiritual as well as political, have been amoral in the sense that they would have no concern for other persons yet bear responsibility for all that is in their image. I think it is important to consider this possibility in understanding their behavior and in developing an understanding of the working of the charismatic personality—remembering, of course, that no one acts entirely out of a single reality.

Most important to this discussion is the awareness that change is a difficult issue for a large part of the world's population. I am claiming that few have a deep acceptance of change as something created by human beings. Among the pure forms of reality, only the social incorporates change. It is true that the mythic reality appears to call for capricious and unstable behavior, yet, unless a mythic person accepts the foreign notion (derived from the unitary logic) of continuity, he will see what is as the only thing that ever existed and thus believe he has never been involved in change. The unitary allows changes only in naming (classification) or interpreting. The sensory reality admits only change that follows from antecedent conditions. In the sensory view, change happens. *If we were completely knowledgeable,* there would be nothing unpredictable; all follows the imperatives of nature. In the next chapter, I try to make some sense of "change," developing a theoretic view of both change and the resistance to change.

II

A Walk with Philip Slater

This book and my ideas on meta-praxis are about the paths of intentional change. I commented in the Introduction that I have found traversing this path both heady to pursue and seldom successful, if success is measured according to images held before we set off on journeys of large-scale change. Both the anticipation of being a party to a valuable social outcome and the difficulties of achieving a viable outcome indicate how important it is to take a wise companion along the path. For me, Philip Slater, as he presents himself in his book *Earthwalk* (1974), is such a companion. His work provides advice and cautions to anyone who would embark on a change effort. I found his six "profound misconceptions about change" can guide my efforts in this work, so I offer them to those readers who have not themselves read or heard his advice. In contemplating the set, I realized that four of his misconceptions (2 through 5) point to the central difficulties one would experience in attachment to the four realities described in the preceding chapter and, in doing so, they indicate means by which the misconceptions are transcended.

SIX MISCONCEPTIONS

1. It is possible to have change without stress. Resistance to change is certainly one of the healthier instincts of human beings, at both the biological and the social levels. Continual change is not the natural setting of human life. We have not the wisdom to allow us to unendingly upset the rhythms and integrations that have been established in our biological and political bodies without causing serious stress on our systems. Slater (1974, p. 139) expresses the extreme condition that "the major cause of disease is change . . . *even if the changes are desired.*" His is not a proscription against change but a call for sensitivity, to weigh the costs of change against the advantages thereof.

2. *The social system in which we live is static and empty—a motionless container that must be filled with plans, programs, and energy—the fallacy of "positive programs."* Perhaps Slater's caution has been heard, for, in the last few years, there has been an increasing awareness of a "program's" environment, both the immediate situation and the broader culture. We recognize the dynamics of the settings, but there is a more critical part to this fallacy: ignoring the impact of our own initiation and creativity on those whom we would engage in change. Slater (1974, p. 142) sees the principal reason that positive programs fail is that "we imagine that we are always beginning anew with our bold new programs." The result, in simple terms, is that our egos get in the way. Paradoxically, we must let go of the very attributes we think we are most valued for, our *creativity* and *personal drive*, to make space for the programs and for the latent energy that emerges from those involved. The ultimate *mythic act* is such a transcendence of one's own generative energy.

3. *Desirable reforms can be brought about when those who oppose them are either outvoted or reeducated as to what their best interests are.* Democracy is not realized in the will of the majority but in the realization of the individual within the collectivity. So, "real movement occurs with the recognition of 1) the legitimacy of all feelings, 2) the conflicts present within each person, and 3) the realistic differences between people in the way these conflicts are internally arranged" (Slater, 1974, p. 145). Real change follows from "the acceptance of the validity within each." This is the requirement for the unconditional regard of which Carl Rogers spoke and wrote. And, again paradoxically, it calls for a transcendence of caring for a particular outcome or value. The ultimate *social act* is such a transcendence, a move from care to compassion.

4. *Social change occurs through some sort of cognitive process—a problem is isolated and diagnosed, a prescription is written, a course of treatment designed and executed.* Unfortunately, those who heard Slater's words concerning the context of change took such advice to mean that, to write effective prescriptions, we must expand our sciences, become better at forecasting, modeling, and specifying courses of action. That is, we must become more competent at describing how the world is and how it should be. The misconception is that we can do that at a distance—that is, play a game from the sideline with established rules for which we are not responsible. "We are not and cannot be outside our social 'problems.' We are inside them—they are the medium in which we swim" (Slater, 1974, p. 150). The competence of the outsider

denies the opportunities of the participant. We must also let go of our *sensory* competencies if the participants are to own the solution.

5. *To bring about social change, one must obtain power.* Slater presents one more paradox: Using power to attain a change sows the seeds for the reemergence of what has been changed. The use of power "springs from and helps maintain the motivational core of the oppressive systems in which we live" (Slater, 1974, p. 156). In presenting this paradox, Slater confronts the common assumption that one must go to the top of the organization or government to initiate change, suggesting instead that it may not be possible to gain a resolution that uses power that is itself part of the problem. This is equivalent to saying there can be no change from within a *unitary* reality. As both ancient spiritual leaders and today's transformation leaders have recognized, ultimate power is gained in surrendering what one has the power to enforce.

6. *Social change is linear.* Students of the arts know they must draw on the beauty and aesthetic inspiration in primitive and ancient arts as well as on the styles of the prior decade and the prior century. So, "a viable ecology requires that the past be recycled too" (Slater, 1974, p. 151). It is only the particular philosophy of evolutionary Darwinism that holds that the later practice is always better than the earlier. I need to bring along another sage, the cultural historian Jean Gebser, who, in his book *The Ever-Present Origin* (1985), reminds us that we continually draw on our origins—biological, historical, and personal—in forming the future. We repeatedly must *go back for a better start.* For such a trip, we may rely on myth and old stories along with our histories.

All these maxims need accompany me as I present this theory of practice and, as Slater warns, should accompany each of us along the paths of resolution.

2 The Dialectics of Change

When I began this investigation into the modes of resolution of complex issues, I thought it could be viewed as a question of strategy; that the fundamental act was to identify the appropriate modes of change to be used with the prevailing conditions. I thought the work could be framed as a form of contingency theory, fitting the approach to the situation. The illusion that this was a satisfactory approach broke down as it became evident that conflict, the processes of change, and beliefs about reality are deeply intertwined. The exploration became even more convoluted as I recognized that the processes of change themselves form a self-generating dialectic. I suppose if I had been a deeper student of oriental and esoteric thinking, I would have anticipated the deviousness of change efforts.

I came to see that all change efforts, even the successful ones, are results of alogical, or translogical, efforts, ones that we accept out of habit. Our cultures create blinders that block from our vision the processes we use to effect change. My explorations have had to get behind the culture's habits, to slip through the anomalies to get access to the illogicality and build a theory that recognizes the need to go beyond our conventional modes. It has been a "crazy-making" task, unendingly requiring me to suspend judgment and reject comfortable appearances. I came to understand the warning voiced by the biologist and system theorist, Gregory Bateson (1972, p. 305), that every effort at such work is dangerous, even psychotic.

But, as occurs often, what is once seen as psychotic becomes comfortable when we can construct a logic to explain that world. I have
not yet attained such comfort, but the material here represents a first
working version, a first transcendence, of the anomalies in our accommodations of the illogics of resolution. I have gained confidence in its
usefulness by the very fact that it does not imply a certainty beyond
the certainty that the ambiguity we are confronted with is in part *essential ambiguity*.[1] We can never know if we have a best solution or
even if we have taken the best route to the resolution of a conflict.

When the English philosopher David Hume tired of working on the
logical impossibilities of a classic cause-and-effect physics, he is said
to have walked out to the billiards table to play the very game that
epitomized the rules of that classical physics. At this point, I have
developed enough theory to walk back and forth between the
phenomena of this translogical world and ordinary descriptions and
relate these for the reader. I am, and the reader should be, continually
suspicious of my language, aware that, in every statement I make, I am
biased by the mythic and social reality from which I most easily speak.
New theory requires new language, and the deeper the change called
for by the theory, the longer it will take for an adequate vocabulary
and syntax to be established.

The exploration of the illogics of change led me far from the daily affairs of conflict resolution and change with which I began to a more philosophical inquiry. I found this redirection profitable to a degree I could
not have anticipated for I uncovered an elegant model of change processes and entered a translogical domain that seems to approach the territory Gregory Bateson labeled Learning III. The brief discussion of his
theory below will relate my view of change theory to Bateson's somewhat more familiar model. From there, I go into new territory.

The theory I present is based on two ideas:

1. Strategies for resolution can be mapped as transitions through the
   space of alternative realities; that is, changes are created on phenomena of one reality by operations defined in a second reality.
2. These changes flow along either differentiating or conventionalizing
   paths according to various strategic considerations.

A *path* is a progression in the use of worldviews and their logics in the
pursuit of a resolution of a conflict or change. The concept of "path"
grossly elides the details of such processes, but the idea indicates the
general direction of development. Diagram 2.1 shows an example of
such a path. It begins within a unitary position and moves through a

Diagram 2.1 Paths of Resolution

minor engagement with data and a more significant encounter with value issues, an allocation of goods (sensory), and a return to an approved solution. To solve a problem requires the use of logics from at least two different realities—one reality *describes the given world,* the other *directs the change.* The resolution of major issues is likely to require a complex interworking of many such sets of two or more realities.

With deep consideration, it appears to me that our consciousness of reality is created by the act of confronting one reality with another. I know that the moon is not made of green cheese and I am not the King of Hearts only because some other people *did something,* some others acted in a way that changed the world—in these cases, by walking on the moon and by noticing that I had no crown. The ideas developed here indicate that there is much to explore beyond the conventionalities of our current view of reality.

This approach to change and conflict takes as fundamental that any change will induce conflict. I assert that we must account for the occurrence of resolution rather than for the presence of conflict. *In the conscious world of mankind, conflict is primary; resolution of conflict is the province of culture, managed by learned accommodations and social conventions.* This assumption is central to the meta-praxis. I will develop it further here and in later chapters.

In this chapter, I begin the presentation of this theory by outlining the levels or orders of change, following the model of learning offered by Gregory Bateson. Next, I present concepts of conflict, problems and issues, which provide the setting for the theory of resolution. Finally, I discuss the two directions of change and the need for concepts of two or more realities to be used in every change and resolution effort.

COMPLEXITY AND ORDERS OF CHANGE

Orders of Learning

To understand what is involved in making a change, we need a language of alternative forms and degrees of change, one that deals with both the complexity and the depth of the change. Gregory Bateson (1972) provided a descriptive model in the analogous field of learning, which is itself a form of change. His models, or orders of change, range from the simplistic habit formation—Learning I—to changes in the evolutionary processes of human species—Learning IV. In the past few decades, we have come to recognize that, to effect intentional changes in society and in our personal lives, we must go beyond new stimulus-response patterns to "learn about learning." Much of the work in social and organizational change is now focused on the second order of change—equivalent to Learning II. But, with the failure of the assumption of a monological culture, we now can recognize that we need to deal with a further level of change that I propose is captured in Bateson's ideas for Learning III.

The simplest order—*first-order change*—consists of reformations that occur with no change in the meaning of the context. In studying learning, we are concerned with memorization and rote learning (in first-order change); we consider any simple habituating, that is, learning the skills to walk, eat, drive, work, and so on. These changes, which are basically pattern forming, occur without reformulation or conceptualization of the content. We learn to walk typically without employing ideas about movement; we work by trial and error, though there may be some ideas gained by watching others walk. The great majority of all animal (including human) behavior is first order, that is, makes contextual changes that are so minor that we normally would consider them trivial. Because such acts do not call on conceptualization, *they raise no questions of reality.* Learning I precedes the need to ideate or to conceptualize; things just happen with more and less difficulty. I judge first-order changes to be local, neither inducing conflict in themselves nor significantly contributing to solution of issues.

Second-order change involves the creation or change of a context. It presents new images, defines (bounds) new concepts, or intrudes into the space of existing concepts, for example, by forming classes, labeling objects, and organizing acts. Second-order changes produce and use mental constructs that depend on a sense of reality. For some belief systems, these concepts represent evidence of real things, relations, or qualities. For others, the concepts are symbols invented for the occasion. But, whether conceptualizations are thought to be discovered, revealed, or invented, their use allows us to restructure the world in small and grand ways. Naming a person, place, or phenomenon gives continuity. Naming establishes similarities; naming a green object in my garden "a fern" gives me power to learn about it by comparison with other objects I have already studied. On the other hand, I may find it does not fit the existing category "fern," so I become aware that I need to form a new concept.

Second-order change is accomplished by using one reality to modify representations in another reality. For example, we can symbolize a *sensory* perception by forming a concept (from unitary reality). Naming a green thing a "fern" transforms its status to an idea; unnamed, it remains simply an ephemeral sensation. Similarly, *social* feeling can be empowered by a *mythic* act; by an act of creating an idea, a person gains ownership of an idea. Again, a mythic image, a dream, is reified by constructing it with material of the *sensory* world—if one does not so materialize a dream, it fades, as did the Cheshire cat until all that was left was a smile. In general, only through the cofunctioning of two (or more) realities can we reify symbols and thus make second-order change. One cannot use, for example, a sensory perception to form a new concept of a sensory perception, and no sum of sensory impressions or of unitary designs alone will ever get a bridge built or an illness cured. What constitutes a second-order change may vary among people. Those with a very limited experience with categorization, which in the West is usually equated to a limited education, may easily find novelty and thus would call on second-order learning frequently as they moved into changing world scenes. Those we call sophisticated may find almost everything as expected; everything has a name, so creating categories is needed less frequently.

Since its introduction by Gregory Bateson in 1942 (see *Steps to an Ecology of the Mind*, 1972), the idea of orders of learning has been widely developed. Following Argyris and Schön's (1978) concept of "double loop learning," a great many other writers have recognized that most interpersonal and societal changes are second order. Levy and Merry (1986) list various authors who label second-order phenomena "morphogenesis," "policymaking," and "root," "revolutionary," "radical," and "transformational" change. The range of changes that are logically second order is extremely broad, from adapting a class of ideas to include a new example, to forming a society, but all such changes participate in the basic processes of concept formation, adaptation, and propagation.

Operating with a meta-praxis parallels *third-order change* in requiring thinking beyond our current logics. I see Bateson's "Learning III" as an introduction to what a suprachange beyond the second order might look like. Bateson suggests that Learning III is learning about the concepts that are used in Learning II. Third-order change would form concepts and values across the range in which the changing/organizing/synthesizing mechanisms of second-order change operate. In particular, as Bateson (1972, pp. 301-305) suggests for this next level of learning:

> In transcending the promises and habits of Learning II, one will gain "a freedom from its bondages," bondages we characterize, for example, as "drive," "dependency," "pride," and "fatalism."
>
> One might learn to change the premises acquired by Learning II and to readily choose among the roles through which we express concepts and thus the "self."
>
> Learning III is driven by the "contraries" generated in the contexts of Learning I and II.

Berman (1981, p. 346) defines Learning III as "an experience in which a person suddenly realizes the arbitrary nature of his or her own paradigm." This is learning itself, but more important is the learning to work from spaces beyond our habitual bondage. We are most likely to have touched this level in a sudden understanding of a person who is very different than ourselves, something that might occur on an occasion when we share in a deep tragedy with others. We can induce awareness by engagement with typical behaviors of another worldview.[2] For example, holders of a social reality might confront the sensory and unitary realities via a long solo retreat into a natural wilderness. Or we can grow in appreciation of other realities by deep exploration and cowork with people of other realities. We can gain access to Learning III via the anomalies of Learning II that become apparent as we try to place a practice, a body of knowledge, a social custom within the alternative realities. Learning III operates beyond the logics of the learning processes and schemes for categorizing, unconstrained by the groundings that have made life both secure and problematic for prior millennia of human life.

Meta-praxis uses third-order change processes that build from Learning III, articulating both the setting for change—the realities—and an approach that goes beyond second-order conceptual thinking to narrative logics by which to follow strategic paths. As "learning" is a form of change, so Bateson's descriptions for Learning III mostly carry over to third-order change.[3] Learning III and meta-praxis lead, however, to different images of "transcendence" that come from multiple realities. Bateson and his interpreter, Maurice Berman (1981), however, suggest that the transcendence necessary for Learning III leads to a holistic (unitary) worldview in which all subject/object dichotomies have disappeared—

a conclusion they find discomforting. In addition to giving access to unlimited choice, Bateson and Berman suggest that such freedom produces disconnection from reality and thus openings to the darker side of humanity. My view of multiple realities leads to an entirely different opportunity. Rather than seeing all-as-one, this meta-praxis respects differences and provides a systematic way of using the differences, following paths of diverse belief systems appropriately. I understand that third-order thinking, as in this meta-praxis, will give the freedom and space in which to *choose the realities* required for resolving conflicts.

I return to the concept of third-order change in the final chapter. Now I introduce another complexity that must be recognized in establishing a theory of resolution.

CONFLICTS, PROBLEMS, AND ISSUES

Conflict is induced in every consciously chosen change. Of course, in the vast proportion of events, conflict does not surface. As I define it, conflict arises in the confrontation of inconsistent logics on the occasion of selecting among alternatives to effect a change. Conflict results regardless of the degree of differences experienced. On every occasion when one's belief about reality is disturbed, conflict is an inherent consequence. The disturbance may be between logics that are used in a choice process by a single person or by two or more people in formulating and resolving an issue. The awareness that we are making translogical choices would in itself lead to conflict because we lack a *logical* path of resolution. Human beings, however, have protected themselves against unending disturbances and strife by developing modes of accommodation that, taken collectively, form the *culture*. In some cases, we call this accommodation *rationality*; in others, *respect*; and in still others, *habit*.

Culture, in the form of habits, conventions, and expectations, allows us to ignore the illogics of our actions and assert that the absence of an overarching logic "means nothing." The existence of cultural patterns reduces most conflicts to such a degree that we ignore them, so we tend to think that conflict is a special, though important, failure to manage differences in worldviews. This view is useful in our daily lives but is an error in constructing a theory of change and processes for resolution. *Because conflict is present in every process of intentional change, all methods of change must deal with conflict, in some cases trivially, in others centrally.*

The notion that some problems are solved and issues are resolved through developing a shared value system is an obscuration, a mask made up of accommodations that allow us to ignore conflicts. Fortunately, in the times of a strong and pervasive culture, in the vast majority of human interactions, the accommodations hold. The manners of a society allow us to ignore the meaninglessness of behaviors; for example, those that order our manners in a crowd, on the highway, in daily commerce, in family conclaves. Even in these rather stable areas of our lives, however, we recognize that conflict is just beneath the surface, particularly in the intensity of urban living and in times of rapid change. The random "freeway shootings" in Los Angeles in recent years attest to how fragile the accommodations of our culture are.

Treating conflict as ubiquitous casts a particular shadow on humanity and the value of consciousness. It implies that, in becoming conscious, we have invented new ways of warring among ourselves that the animal kingdoms do not share.[4] We do not just war over scarce resources and opportunities as we see among lower forms of biological life but also over issues of god, authorship, fairness, and so on. It appears that humanity is in a particular stage of its evolution in which, along with consciousness, come the conflicts that flow from multiple constructions of reality.

Fundamental to my theory of change, then, is the premise that conflict is ever present. This conflict arises from the invention of different approaches to defining reality, which, in turn, induces questions of how to limit, or bound, the application of these realities. When we agree as to what "is real" and about the conventions of dealing with ambiguities around reality, the problems we face are simple. When we are less capable of agreeing on what is real, the problems become complex. The complexity of achieving a resolution is thus a function of the variety of realities used by the parties to that resolution. The variety places strain on the ability of a culture to accommodate differences.

When we recognize that a difficulty is well bounded and formulated, and that we have the requisite resources to solve it, we tend to think of that difficulty as a *problem*. Electronics engineers could at one time solve their design problems on a "breadboard," nicely isolating them from extraneous influences. Playing chess presents the player with similarly restricted problems—well formed though not easy to solve. Getting a homeless person an evening meal may solve a problem of the moment, but it does not resolve the issue of poverty, poor mental health, and income distribution that combine to produce "homelessness." Homelessness is not a well-bounded problem; attempts to solve any aspect of it spill over into other areas of social concern. A free meal regularly offered to the street folk in Los Angeles drew increasingly large crowds that compounded the difficulty locally and created other dislocations at least as grievous as the one on which the meals program had focused. Applying a local or partial solution in such situations will typically produce greater difficulties in the surrounding environment. We need to treat the unboundable, supra-problems differently. They are issues, not problems.

An *issue*, as defined in Chapter I, is an unbounded, ill-defined, overwhelming complex of problems. Homelessness is, in the minds of most Americans, an *issue*. As I observed earlier, the word *issue* itself expresses a sense of outflowing, uncontainable at a point in time and space. To dam it in one place is to invite overflow into another. If attempts to resolve an issue are not to create more problems than are solved, an issue must be approached as a whole with strategic awareness of capabilities, recognizing that neither the content of the issue nor the process of resolution can be contained by well-bounded constructs. Problems and issues are not definitively separated, but everyone knows the difference between a "breadboard" problem and the issues in "the South Bronx." Yet, in practice, we spend much effort attacking issues such as urban redevelopment as though they were first-order problems, resolvable by a mortgage rate reduction, or, as second-order issues, resolvable, for example, through eliminating interracial strife. We fail to recognize that the majority of the issues facing humanity cannot be resolved by views and approaches limited to these two orders.

I argue here that the logics on which we have traditionally based strategic approaches to problems are not sufficient to resolve the issues and conflicts that arise in poorly defined or weakening cultures. What worked well when the culture was well established may not be sufficient when its fabric comes apart. It is a sad joke on humanity that, in the waning years of the Age of Rationality, we still expect to find algorithms that will create peace on earth. We could not, as the CIA is reputed to have tried in the past 30 years, "resolve" the cold war with the theory of games using data from econometric models of the Soviet economy. It is easier to solve the problem of getting a space ship to fly by Neptune than it is to eradicate the Colombian drug lords. The trip to the stars requires myriad problems to be solved, most of them neatly bounded by the deterministic realities. While all the difficulties in the space program are not purely scientific, the interactions of the difficulties can be mostly decomposed into separate "problems" (according to Feynman's 1988 recounting of the *Challenger* disaster). Eliminating the drug lords, however, requires dissolving an immense psycho-socio-political knot and resolving issues at every level of human existence. Similarly, homelessness and world peace are issues that are beyond the problematic. If we approach a mess such as the drug issue, or homelessness in America, or starvation in Ethiopia, as a problem or a series of problems to be solved, our efforts will almost certainly create equivalent messes in their wake. Resolving these and all other issues requires that we develop strategies of change based on an understanding that change is itself a generator of difficulties. We will never transcend the self-generating effects until we have recognized them and can learn ways to work at a new level, the level I identify with *third-order change*.

To find ways of working at a new level requires that we know what the processes of solving and resolving are. In the following section, I introduce an approach that has ancient roots but is not commonly considered by social scientists or activists. It allows me to develop a strong theory of change, the value of which will be tested in its applications.

THE TWO DIRECTIONS OF CHANGE

Our "realities" are the flowers of second-order change. Symbolizing a mental image, a sensory impression, or an event—as we do by naming them—constitutes a second-order change because it gives reality to a perception. Such changes can occur in one of two directions: *conventionalizing* or *differentiating*. An organizing, or symbolizing, act may form a convention by naming the image, thing, or event, placing it in a class; for example, "identifying" the species of a newly discovered bird. Or it may create a difference by separating out, distinguishing, something that had been an element within a particular context; for example, creating a new invention such has the motor car, or a school of art such as cubism or the Bauhaus. These two forms of symbolization, that which conventionalizes and that which differentiates, represent the two *directions of change*, toward or away from an existing symbolization. Conventionalizing moves toward a more monistic position; differentiating moves toward a more pluralistic position (Diagram 2.2).

Conventionalizing symbolizations form cultural "sets" like sentences, equations, tool kits, suits of clothes, and city streets. As a way of resolving issues: "Conventional symbolizing bestows order and rational integration upon its disparate context."[5] America, according to the contemporary anthropologist Roy Wagner (1975, p. 49), is a conventionalizing society, one that dominantly solves its problems by forming generalities, models, and classes and systematically organizing empirical knowledge to gain power over ideas as well as resources. For example, the fascination with personality tests that tell us who and what we are like, identification with celebrities by printing their names and faces on our T-shirts, the commitment to population statistics, the devotion to quantitative models of social phenomena all represent conventionalizing drives. This drive has led to a melting pot image in the United States instead of one of multiculturalism. Americans have

Diagram 2.2 Conventionalizing and Differentiating

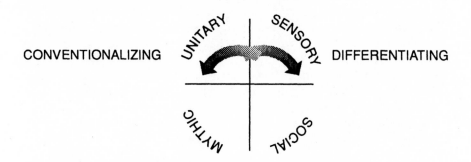

tended and still tend to identify with symbols, as evidenced by their attraction to fashions—in clothing, music, child raising, health, and management practices. The drive is particularly evident in our efforts to change, whether in the individual's wish to lose weight or in the industrialist's need for improved quality and production. In their drive for conventionalization, Americans rush to conform to new styles, names, and behaviors, reducing symbols to conventionalized signs, many of which soon fade from our consciousnesses.

The opposite drive to differentiate leads to the invention of new symbols, concepts, metaphors, and relations. Pure initiation is the extreme form of differentiation. The unique experiencing (sensing, imagining) of people, objects, and places of everyday life creates symbols that stand for themselves, individuating a person and carving out of the universal soup new islands of meaning. Such events occur in microscopic ways millions of times a day when insights "pop" into a person's head. Perhaps the most common insight is noticing a difference or making a discrimination—that two birds are not alike, that the sun rose earlier this morning than last week—and, a little less common, the generation of a pattern. An elegant example is the invention of perspective drawing, the creating of ways to give the viewer the impression of depth in a flat drawing. We can find whole catalogs of differentiating ideas/changes in the inventions of Ben Franklin, Thomas Edison, or Edwin Land of Polaroid.

We experience differentiating changes arising from initiatives that ignore and/or destroy the conventions. "A differentiating symbolization specifies and concretizes the conventional world by drawing radical distinctions and delineating its individualities" (Wagner, 1975, p. 44). Deep differentiation is a generative process that transcends the separation of observer and observed (the subject-object split) to create new wholes. Whereas a conventionalizing society focuses on placing its members into established classification, members of a differentiating society focus on being unique, on not being part of an industry or association. The Walt Disney Company, a perfect example of an institution that has taken a differentiating approach, has been successful during the past 60 years whenever it has found solutions beyond competition. The Disney Company, however, counterinvents the conventionalizing industry. Its differentiation provided the theme park idea that leads others to conventionalize, thereby creating the very competition that Walt Disney had transcended. As we shall see, it is common for solutions to create situations by counterinvention that may be as problematic as those that have been resolved.

The Innate and the Intended

Change takes place in the movement from a position in reality that is assumed to be the basic reality in the direction determined by the reality of *intention*. The *innate* arises within (is defined by) the reality that the person or organization takes as given; the *intended* uses the logic and constructs of the reality toward which one moves by choice. Thus the two (or more) realities that are present in effecting a change or solution play distinct roles—one defining, one directing. Perhaps a third reality is called on for evaluating. For example, the innate elements of a problem may be a plot of land and some building materials; this is stuff recognized within the sensory reality. The intended element is a plan for a house (a unitary notion). The problem is solved by finding ways to execute the plan with the stuff available. In another instance, the innate is a belief about the morality of a position such as withholding a new drug from distribution to those who could potentially benefit from its use—set in the social reality. The intended would operate within the sensory world to allocate a good or opportunity properly among the involved people, in this case, allocating the drug to those who can use it with the greatest overall benefit. The intention keeps moving from the given condition onward to the solution. The intended *takes control* over the innate, leading from the problem to the solution. Wagner (1975, p. 44) comments that the necessary control "is provided by the sharp and binding ideological discrimination made between [differentiating and conventionalizing.]"

The control directs the resolution, selecting outcomes to achieve the intended. To attain a clear, full resolution of an issue, we must carry through an effort in a consistent direction, either conventionalizing or differentiating. (This dictum is central to the grand strategies of change that are introduced in Chapter 4.) A differentiating control will separate out an entity, making it distinct. This is a form of *reframing* (Watzlawick, 1974). For example, creating a new market for a product; we create a demand for an idea such as TV by establishing it as a unique service (differentiated). In contrast, a conventionalizing control forces the situation to be viewed within the existing structure. "Conventionalizing" conserves the existing base of principles and classifying rules. To continue the example, a governmental agency regulates TV broadcasting to ensure that it does not violate civil rights. Choosing the "wrong" direction interferes with a resolution. For example, calling the newly invented automobile a "horseless carriage" conventionalizes the idea and inhibits differentiation.

To effect a change, control must be established in a reality different than the one in which the "givens" have been established. The given in a problem of setting a price on some article, for example, is the sensory reality of that article; the price is found by a differentiating evaluation of goods, that is, by a comparison of values in a space of social reality. Conversely, in the problem of marketing a product, the social reality may be taken as implicit and the solution is the assignment of values to sensory objects or opportunities. This path conventionalizes the goods.

Every attempt at resolution needs to be described in terms of the realities imposed on the situation by those involved—the reality that is accepted as implicit and the reality that controls the process of resolution. This specification, in turn, implies the differentiating or conventionalizing direction of the change. The choice to differentiate or conventionalize establishes the controlling direction in a situation and thus is a *political* act. Typically, a differentiating choice is viewed as a move to the left, and a conventionalizing, a move to the right. It is important to acknowledge that choice of routes to a resolution is political.

We will not be able to sustain a change if our direction is ambiguous. There can be no second-order change without the intention that sustains the direction of change, whether the initial direction is conventionalizing or differentiating. To see a work of art done in the manner of cubism as poor representation—that is, according to a "conventional" criterion—is destructive of innovation; conversely, failing to see psychotherapy as a form of spiritual healing obscures the usefulness of traditional knowledge. To maintain the direction, we must put blinders on our awareness of the inconsistency inherent in using one logic to set the context and another to judge the appropriateness of a change. It is difficult to hold on to intentionality if we allow ourselves to keep seeing the world through a multiplicity of realities. Blindness and courage both serve intentionality. Without cultural constraints, we would be unable to maintain focus.

Our habits of speech lead to ambiguity in efforts to resolve issues because they do not discriminate between directions of change or among realities. These failures lead to confusions about what the "cause of things" are and thus to miscommunication. For example, two parties may take the sensory reality as given, but one may conventionalize toward a unitary world and the other differentiate by setting values in a social logic; the unitary theory (e.g., that classifies an event) may be "meaningless" in the social reality. The current exemplar of this divergence is the abortion conflict. The fact of pregnancy is accepted by both sides as given. One view, out of the unitary, decides the argument in the context of principles, specifically, "thou shall not murder"; the other takes it in the social context of human suffering over the anticipated course of life of parent and child.

The confusion over the phrase *the cause of things* is compounded by the possibilities for confusion not recognized by many in current society. Even if recognized, the idea that we are working from multiple realities is unfamiliar and highly discomforting to many people. As pointed out in the first chapter, we cannot even describe the mythic's causality except by taking it on. It is almost as difficult to acknowledge that something does not exist unless someone "cares" about it (social reality) or that some idea is immutably true (unitary). Once we recognize that differences in the construction of alternative realities imply different causations, our ordinary syntax becomes suspect. Our familiar use of *cause* and *effect*, which comes from deterministic realities, leads to paradoxical reversals. In the deterministic worldview, the innate or primary qualities of the situation set the "cause" or motivation of the action; in the social reality, the intended outcomes "cause" the outcome; and, in the mythic, cause and effect are one.[6] These confusions are part of our daily communications, and they proliferate contentions unless there is agreement about how we will use causal language. Again, reflect on the misunderstandings that follow from questions that ask "why?" "Why did you do that?" The sensory says, "*because* I was tired." To which the social responds, "*because* you didn't care."

Counterinventions

These two directions of change, conventionalization and differentiation, do not act in simple opposition. Each, in the extreme, acts to produce the same effects, inadvertently, as the other does overtly: Each direction *counterinvents* the other. Thus a differentiating act, by individuation, forms a new base for collectivization. For example, a stage or film success that is strikingly different than the contemporary lot of

Diagram 2.3 Counterinventions

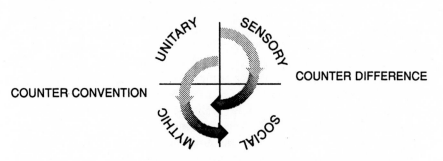

plays or films may set off a spate of sequels and "takeoffs" that are received by how well they follow the source production's plot and style. Conversely, a conventionalizing solution eventually leads to differentiation as we partition a whole according to color, size, ethnic background, skill, or other qualities. For example, "classless societies" quickly invent categories that differentiate individuals according to how well they are accepted in the hierarchies of state, and these classes begin to have "a life of their own." Even in George Orwell's *Animal Farm*, the pigs became a class of their own as the "most equal among equals." These countermovements are illustrated in Diagram 2.3. As illustrated, the differentiating movement creates a whole, and the conventionalizing leads to pluralistic identifications. These are illustrated in the top portion of the diagram with the shaded arrows. The direction taken in the first stages in each of these cycles is countered in its completion, as noted in the solid arrows in the lower portion of the chart. Roy Wagner (1975, p. 51) summarizes:

> Order and disorder, known and unknown, conventional regularity and the incident that defies regularity, are tightly and innately bound together, they are functions of each other and necessarily interdependent. We cannot act but that we invent each other through the other.

Wagner here lays out the communion of opposites, articulating the balance that characterizes biological life. Any effort to make changes defies this balance, so becoming aware that one cannot invent something without counterinventing its opposite is deadly to one's intentions. Wagner claims that "to see the whole field at once, in all its implications, is to suffer a 'relativization' of intention, to become aware of how gratuitous a part it plays in the design of solutions." To attain a solution—whether by a conventionalizing or a differentiating approach—we achieve an imbalance by momentarily restricting our vision. We establish one aspect of a situation as given—that is, as the innate set of facts, symbols, meanings, or principles—and the other aspect as that toward which we *intend* as the outcome of the change effort. I find it to be a strange proposition that we have to become less aware, less conscious of our surroundings, to focus actions and perform with courage, as will be discussed in Chapter 6. Yet only by hiding from most of the realities can we tolerate the unlogical aspects of our actions. Without the courage to blind ourselves, we relativize our reality beliefs and therefore block both the identification of solutions and the implementation of change. So Hamlet stood frozen to deliver his grand soliloquy, "To be or not to be . . ."

If we allow ourselves to think along both directions of change, we become caught in a circular dialectic: The drive to conventionalize eventually counterinvents differences as the whole is fully articulated, and the drive to differentiate creates new wholes (images, metaphors) that come to replace the conventional. The more successful we are at changing, the more certain it is that we will arrive back where we started. The history of revolutions of the left that end up with governments of the right sadly provides evidence for this paradox.

The natural tendency to counterinvent interferes with our ability to focus our intentions on creating changes. When we differentiate, a counterinventive convention interferes with ("intrudes on") the intentions, hinders the formation, of a new concept. Thus, for example, conventionally trained people in the biological sciences may have trouble seeing freshly a natural phenomenon they have studied. Their training provides a "mask" through which they classify the biological objects they encounter. I have a sharp memory of "killing" (intruding on) a wondrous new image by masking over the image with a name. I had come upon a beautiful fern plant emerging from its winter dormancy, and its botanical name blurted into my consciousness before I could appreciate its uniqueness. My conventionalizing denied my recognition of it as a unique (differentiated) being. I reduced it to its "sign" in the catalog of biological species. To be fully captured by that experience, I would have had to forgo the conventional naming and create new words, qualities, relations by which to give it meaning.

Conversely, when we conventionalize, we also note the ways in which a thing is different. When we counterinvent we tend to give identity to the part as we try to put "stuff" into its proper place within the conventional scheme. The very act of defining what stuff is in conventional terms can lead us to see its uniqueness. We have seen repeatedly in history and daily life how the clear classification of a person as a deviant has led to the person recognizing himself as unique, beyond the conventional scheme—thus the birth of a revolutionary. We hold

Diagram 2.4 Counterinventions in the Evolution of an Organization

Change	Counterinvents (produces a crisis of)	Direction of Counterinvention
Creativity	Leadership	Diff. → Convent.
Direction	Autonomy	Convent. → Diff.
Delegation	Control	Diff. → Convent.
Coordination	Bureaucracy	Convent. → Diff.

back the generation of uniqueness by subscribing to a discipline, establishing and living by a code. Such training allows us to properly classify and maintain accounts, follow laws, and observe objectively.

Counterinvention will occur naturally on the occasion of change. The widely reputed theory of organizational growth proposed by Greiner (1972) illustrates such counterinvention (see Diagram 2.4). He proposed that with each type of change is associated a type of crisis. For example, if an organization attempts a change that increases the strength of the *direction* it imposes on the members, it will generate a crisis around needs for *autonomy* unless supportive conventionalizing processes accompany the change. Or an effort to delegate authority will build a counterforce to increase the control by the central authorities.

This dance of counterinvention has a peculiar effect on our drive to make changes. Recognition of the counterinvention process not only makes us aware of the need to understand the total process of change in a system. It also surfaces some of the puzzling phenomena of change: an explanation of the familiar phenomena of backlash as the appearance of counterinvention; an appreciation that "trying" itself may increase the difficulty of solving a problem, surfacing additional sources of conflict; and an understanding of the frustration that radicals feel when they have pushed their revolutions to the extreme, only to find themselves in "the camp of the enemy." Ardent individualists, if successful, will find themselves in the camp of conformists to *their own* position, and the radical monists may find themselves supporting differentiation. It is not surprising that, as Bateson warned, full engagement in third-order change may be schizogenic.

CONCLUSIONS

The motivation for this investigation was to find ways to resolve issues that arise in a time of increasing interdependence of human affairs.

Social scientists and activists have expected we could define the issues and find their resolution through understanding the complexities that have increased at every level from the interpersonal and organizational to the political. It seemed that the common characteristic that transformed problems into issues was the appearance of *turbulence in the sociopolitical field,* which Emery and Trist (1965) identified as a major new factor in managing affairs in the last half of the twentieth century. My search took a different direction, however, to arrive at the unexpected conclusion that issues originate in our diverse conceptualizations of reality. I do not deny the familiar explanations in terms of complexity and human foibles. Rather, I contend that the issues of the day cannot be resolved in such terms alone. Recognizing turbulence will explain the origin of issues; it is not much help in resolving them.

The search has lead me to the beginnings of a theory of change, toward a praxis that assumes conflict is fundamental, in opposition to our current logics that are based in syntactical rules created in an era in which conflict and change were treated as anomalies. My search has identified a way of understanding the *multiplicity of worldviews* that we will use to resolve a conflict and has led to the general notion of paths of change that must be traversed in the attempt. Bateson's work provided the concept of *orders of change* required to deal with issues as well as problems. Wagner's work provided the basic *direction* to be taken on these paths and the awareness of the paradoxical but familiar efforts that arise to counter the processes of change.

I have treated these concepts rather more briefly than I think they deserve. But to treat them fully here would take the reader away from the central purpose of laying out the elements of a meta-praxis. The whole work must be seen as a preface to a new order of understanding the ways in which we may resolve issues and conflicts; that is, to clear up the messes made in prior change efforts. The current form provides the foundation for the tactics and strategies needed to resolve issues, for confronting the illogics and paradoxes of change.

In the next chapter, I continue building the foundations of paths of resolution by displaying the modes of change that form the steps along these paths. The discussion of the paths takes us back to a consideration of the role of culture, because, in exploring these paths, I find that they have an ancient heritage, calling for us to explore the relation between our sciences of resolution and the deep cultural insights carried by myths. Until we get to understand this relation, we must proceed as did Alice "through the looking glass." She could find no rhyme or reason for her path but just kept going on, as was her habit.

III

Six Games of Chess

Drawing by A. Paul Weber

Tamara Bliss's study of the games played by citizen advocacy groups with corporations led us to articulate these six boards—four competitive and two noncompetitive—where I had not noted this distinction. Her dissertation (1996) is an example of the ongoing extensions of the alternative realities model.

What is the game you play out there in the real world?
It isn't checkers or chess. It is much more complicated than that sort of game.

How can it get more complicated than chess?
Well, out there the rules aren't set. People make them up as they go along. That is the game of politics.

If they make up new rules, I am not sure I'll want to play.
Now you're talking about another game. It's about how you want to spend your time. That is a game of economics.

Then I'll create my own game and get others to play with me.
That's something else, not quite a game. The play gives meaning to our endeavors, and the prize is a coherent culture.

Resolving complex issues is more complicated than chess, politics, ethics, or creative leadership. Complex issues require some conscious mixture of skills and courage, humor and humanity, and persistence. To help you see how we achieve resolutions I introduce an analogy, viewing the process as a set of games within games. Chess provides a peerless image, for it has been widely used to help us understand how we humans play "for real."

Consider what a player faces when making a move on a chess board. The player must know the rules of chess: what moves are allowed and which are excluded. He must recognize that he and his opponent have the same basic information about the game. They are both constrained by the same set of rules and share the same objective of winning. They agree to play the same game. Both players consider how their opponents will strategize and what tactics will be successful. They each assume the same long-run objective: to checkmate the opponent or force his withdrawal. Chess allows us to think of issues in white and black, right and wrong, winning and losing, guided by the rules of play. Each player knows from prior experience what moves "work." Each must also pursue an overall strategy as well as sizing up the opportunities available at the moment.

In the long tradition of chess, a vast number of alternative strategies—programs of offense and defense—have been explored, evaluated, and stored in memory for use against each opponent. Any change in the rules would reduce the advantage achieved through analytic skills and long practice. "The player is trained not only to anticipate every future possibility, but to control the future, to prevent it from altering the past" (Carse, 1986). The player with the superior analytic ability is usually the winner. This is true in chess, but not so in other games out there in the real world that are much more complicated. For out there, the rules aren't set.

Drawing by A. Paul Weber

Envision a chess game in which there is a second board. On this board, the play of a piece will change the rules by which the game is played on the first board. For example, a move on the second board could add squares to the playing board or allow you to trade a piece captured by the opponent for a lost piece. On the second board, the game is designing the play of the first board. Such redesign in the rules of play are common in formal games. For example, basketball added the three-point shot, and auction bridge added the contracting process.

Play on the second board is a solitary decision where one person or one group makes the rules. In the games of commerce, deregulation of industries creates new games where players change the rules to "rig" the game in their favor. A dramatic example of such play in the business world is the development of the various forms of leveraged buyouts. For example, using "junk bonds" has radically changed the rules by which executives manage a firm's assets. T. Boone Pickens was the hero (or an Antichrist) of this extended game.

Play on the second board is the game of the authoritarian, autocrat, or even fascist dictator. It belongs to those who wield power, direct force or cleverness, cunning and surprise. Almost every war starts with moves on the second board. Hitler radically changed the rules of war by bombing civilians. The Vietnamese changed the rules of war by conducting guerrilla warfare, using tactics learned by the Americans in their wars with the Indians and reinvented by Lawrence of Arabia yet ignored by Western war rule makers who have been formal, technologically oriented strategists with a proclivity for playing chess by the rules. Play in the second game is based on the power to establish the rules by which the first game is played. Its moves control boundaries, structures, expectations, and moral precepts.

Now expand your vision to a third board where two or more people can play at rule making. This third board is the site of competition for power, the setting for establishing what is right and what is ethical. This is the game of politics played by lobbying, cajoling, proselytizing, and using other unscrupulous methods.

Sometimes, power plays made to change the rules of the third board are explicit; for example, writing legislation so that only one company can possibly win a "competitive bidding." This occurred when a particular company rigged the law so they would be the exclusive legitimate bidder to wholesale the California lottery tickets. But most often, plays are more subtle, and sometimes they appear to be a normal move on the first board. We experience the play as if the two games are collapsed onto one board when a particular move has both operational and strategic consequences, affecting the first and third boards.

When the impact of the political game has been absorbed and new rules accepted, the game reverts to the first board, and the analytic minds focus on operational gaming in accordance with the newly defined situation. Politics reestablishes "business as usual." However, third board games are not concluded by a win or a draw but continue as long as there are players in the field. You win at politics by keeping the opponents playing by the rules that favor your interests.

If you can't "load the dice" on the third board, you can buy a victory on the fourth, for "every one has his price." Games played on the fourth board are played in the marketplace and within relationships where we exchange money or favors for goods and opportunities. In the most elementary form, the game is "bartering," through which we acquire resources to play on the first board. You win by bargaining for new stakes. I can buy a piece—say, a fullback or a company—to put on the playing board. The fourth board evaluates what matters and then assigns resources and responsibilities.

Games can be both competitive and collaborative. We characterize the games on the previous four boards as competitive. They are games played against other people, against nature. On the ideal first board, "some win, some lose." On the second board, the success of leaders may or may not benefit those who play their game. In the politics of

Drawing by A. Paul Weber

the third board, and in the exchanges of economics on the fourth, we move from simple competition toward exchanges that can benefit everyone although each player still thinks in terms of winning. There is another class of games, collaborative games, that are played on the fifth and sixth boards. These games give meaning and opportunity to the players and those they entertain.

Games of the fifth board lead to new ideas, new activities, and new products. There are fundamental acts of creation, originating that which is to be. The magical play transcends rules, boards, and teams to make new games and enterprises. The play of fifth board games can produce little everyday innovations and great advances in science, technology, and the arts through which emerge new games of the first board. Change on the fifth board frequently affects play on other boards. Great moves such as Gandhi's elevation of the nonviolent confrontation changed play on the third and fourth. It is the fascination with play on the fifth board that characterizes the evolving play in modern societies.

Sixth board play creates meaning, image, and opportunity within the community or institution. Creating games engages a community in a collaborative effort. Setting the rules and values given to pieces, positions, and outcomes adopted by the players gives to their relationships with each other. Play on the sixth board is the telling and retelling of a core story, often one of how everyone pulled together to create the theme of the group. Stories of the sixth board sustain our culture; it wins in the creation and acceptance of a myth.

Altering play on the sixth board can change the whole purpose of societal games. For example, Rachel Carson's *Silent Spring* (1962) changed our position on the environment so that we no longer viewed nature as an enemy to be conquered but as an ally with whom we must cooperate. Former President Jimmy Carter's *Habitat for Humanity*, where volunteers build homes for low-income families, is a classic example of how sixth board play can repeatedly create images and meaning within the community. Because everyone participates in the physical and emotional rebuilding of the neighborhood, people feel connected to the project and the commitment to maintain the positive community image. By cocreating ideas or images that reflect new shared values, the game can permit everyone to win. From these efforts emerge new meanings that are often incompatible with existing games, thereby moving the players into new situations in which the old problems and their solutions have become irrelevant.

In stable times, the play of games tends to be controlled by those who like rules and principled, structured behavior. Consequently, there are fewer occasions for games on the fifth and sixth boards. In recent decades, rapid changes lead us to play the more open games. For example, for the first time in nearly a century new moves are being introduced that take the corporate world beyond profit maximizing (first board) and personal power (second board) to question the purposes of conducting business. Similarly, our concern for endangered species changes the technologies and regulations of our commercial life. Play on the sixth board includes the awareness of community, environmental, and world issues such as terrorism, overpopulation, and loss of genetic and cultural diversity. Many of us now ask *why* we play as well as *how well*.

We are continually asked to choose the boards on which we will play, when we use them, and in what sequence. Few problems can be solved on a single board, and confronting every issue will require us to play the *game of games* in which we must decide by what criteria will we select rules for play? We must decide on what boards and in what sequence do we search for resolutions of social ills and international strife and hold our Gaia in animate balance?

THE MASTER
GAMES OF CHANGE

	Board	Game	Objective	Mode of Change
Competitive Games	1ST	Same Game	Expert action. Play most competently within the rules.	Analytic
	2ND	New Rules	Set policy to gain advantage for play on the first board.	Assertive
	3RD	New Values	Working the issue politically & ethically.	Influential
	4TH	Market-place	Assign values & motivate involved parties to effectively use resources.	Evaluative
Collaborative Games	5TH	New Games	Explore opportunities, create new games & make novel things work.	Inventive
	6TH	New Culture	Display vision enhancing spirit, meaning & opportunities.	Emergent

3   Modes of Change

The metaphor of the multiple games of chess provides one way of understanding the absence of a general theory of planned change. The vast majority of theories of change are expressions of play on but a single board, taking the other modes of play as given. Many are technical; that is, first board play, growing out of the hard sciences, economics, game theory, and social or engineering design. Others are political, strongly based in second board play, though most great strategists have also been knowledgeable tacticians. A few grand theories have been from the fifth and sixth board—Gandhi's nonviolent approach arose out of both. And we are plagued with the highly creative, fifth board—work that, like the most banal of science fiction, charts a future with no reference to the social and political efforts on the middle boards. This view of planned change is suited to a simplicity that few of us experience today. The complex issues require a strategic path calling for play on two or more boards. To identify and construct paths for the resolution of conflict and complex issues, however, we need first to establish the building blocks of such paths. These are the methods of solving the discrete problems that face us in both daily engagements and grand change efforts.

PROBLEM SOLVING IS IRRATIONAL

Problem solving is a characteristic activity of Western man. Whether one's profession is hunter, homemaker, student, farmer, physician, soldier, shopkeeper, engineer, or teacher, the daily challenge is *solving problems*. We are trained and habituated to approach the world as a series of problems among which we must choose those we will attempt to solve.

Problem formulation is paradoxical, for a situation is problematic only if we know that there is an existing criterion for that which is nonproblematic. We cannot detect that something is "wrong" unless we know what the criteria are for "right." The solution must, in principle, exist, though it need not be attainable. The condition of knowing that something is wrong implies that *what is* differs from some pre-established criterion of *what is right*. A problem may be a statement of an awareness that data of one's experience do not match well to a principle or "truth" that exists in the ideal state, that is, in the unitary reality. Alternatively, a problem may arise from sensing that an *unfairness* exists in the allocation of some valued entity or opportunity, again a comparison between data and a preexisting condition. The problem then is a construction that notes a difference between data and a criterion. *Problem formulation,* or, as it is variously labeled, *problem sensing, finding, naming,* or *identification,* is the associating of a set of data with a criterion, a truth, or an evaluation process.

In daily problem solving, we limit our formulation, and thus our scope of play, to a simple game that is played on the first board level. For example, the problem solver might approach situations using technical skills characteristic of first board play, accepting the rules and evaluations that have been established on the second and third boards. Such a focus serves us well in managing the unendingly repeated problems of human life. It is often simpler to tell a doctor, a policeman, or a clerk what they ask rather than challenge the legality or ethics of the question. That is, we work within the convention, accepting the irrationality of using rules and values and data without reference to the realities from which they derive.

But this limited response is not sufficient for coping with the deeply entangled conflicts that increasingly dominate the globe and intrude into our daily rounds. For these, we need a variety of responses as great as the complexity of the *issues*. Furthermore, we need a strategy for employing all the various modes of problem solving that arise within the different realities. Problem solving leads to the solution of problems, avoiding issues by delimiting the scope to first board play and to elements in a strategically designed path of resolution. Building a program of change on problem solving is equivalent to the approach of a hack writer who strings together tragicomic episodes with bits of sex and violence to form a soap opera. There is excitement, but the story never gets anywhere. (I sense that many managers, like the authors of soap operas, design their work to make sure it will drag on for years without any need for deep resolutions.)

One of the important roles of culture is to define and limit the ways in which phenomena, including problems, are framed. That is, culture provides the disciplines for our dialogues and developments. Thus there are whole classes of choices that are made within the rules of a given discipline. A few disciplines claim an internally consistent foundation, based in the premises of a single reality. The epitome of such disciplines is mathematics. Within mathematics, a problem can be well formed according to the discipline's own rules of discourse, explored with its logic, and tested against an integral criterion.[1] There are other disciplines that approach the well-defined codes of mathematics. Examples include the play of games and sports, the roles imposed on members of organizations, various sets of administrative regulations, and a variety of pseudogames such as military strategies and war itself.

No matter how well formed these disciplines and their domains may be, making changes in them, taking any action, requires the assertion of propositions *from outside of the reality* within which the discipline has framed the problem. Acts of designing and effecting change are outside of the logical schema of any one concept of reality—as defined here.[2] Even the choice of a chess move requires reference to the rules and purpose of the game that depend on the logics of the second and third boards.

"Real problems" are not solvable within a single reality, any more than a chess game can be won without reference to rules. A solution to a problem becomes meaningful only when its elements are juxtaposed to another reality. For example, the definition of the sensory reality does not provide for any inducement for change. Forming a solution implies a choice, and therefore a reason to change, that can only be found in another of the realities. Some degree of intentionality must be introduced to solve even the most down-to-earth problem. Similarly, created symbols (from the mythic reality) or designs (from the unitary reality) do not contribute to solving a problem until they are concretized in the sensory reality. Einstein expressed this argument in his oft-quoted "to the degree it is real it is not mathematics and to the degree it is mathematics it is not real." I convert this to the general proposition that *to the degree that it is "real," a change is not logical; and, conversely, to the degree that it is logical, it is not "real."*

Every intentional act encounters antinomies, *logical inconsistencies.* So every means by which we attempt to solve problems is also alogical and therefore potentially conflict inducing.[3] Through habit and covert assumption, however, we operate with these problem-solving modes, civilly, until an issue arises that will not let us ignore the realities that we believe are being violated. We need to learn to manage these conflicts strategically, by incorporating the modes of change into paths of resolution. That is the function of a meta-praxis. But before I discuss the strategies, I need to present a coherent image of the modes of problem solving that are the elements of a general strategy.

THE MODES

Modes of change are the classes of tools or methods used to achieve a change or a solution in a particular situation. As I have defined them here, a mode of change requires involvement with two or more realities. The assumed reality provides innate structures that are taken as given; in a second reality, we establish the focus that organizes or controls movement toward a desired outcome. Thus all the modes of solving problems, or resolving issues, are composed from elements of two (or perhaps more) realities. One way of identifying and building a science of the use of problem-solving modes is to explore all the ordered pairs of realities. In this simple schema of alternative realities, the pairs of realities form six modes (that is how many pairs we get taking four realities two at a time), and each comes in two varieties, depending on which of the pair is taken as the given reality. For the most part, these modes are recognizable as familiar everyday problem-solving approaches—for building things, agreeing upon a value, doing arithmetic, deciding whether a person is guilty of a crime, delivering a product to market, and so on. I have graphed the basic six on the map of realities and described them briefly in Diagram 3.1. While there are an unlimited variety of tools and methods used in solving problems, I find that the six pairs are sufficient to illustrate the approach I am taking.

This list appears to span the range of modes that are in common use in the Western world; however, the list should not be taken as definitive. As already demonstrated, these modes are themselves typically used in combinations—I could unendingly catalog these combinations. (I presume there are entirely different schemes for identifying modes that have not been made visible by this scheme of classification.) One of the major values of developing a scheme such as this meta-praxis is to aid the search for new or unrecognized methods and, eventually, as Paul Feyerabend (1975) suggests, to go beyond or *against method* as is done in the development of third-order change.

I limit my exposition to these six major modes of change that form the elements of the paths of resolution developed in later chapters. The descriptions I present are brief, aimed at connecting these modes to definitions that are already familiar to most readers. My purpose is to provide sufficient description to allow the reader to understand the part each mode plays in the larger context of resolving complex issues. A handbook of the techniques of problem solving organized in accordance with this typology is to be published shortly after this volume has been published. To include such an exposition would have been burdensome in the first presentation to the reader. Here, I present only a discussion of occasions on which to use the various modes and, by implication, provide a cautionary message on the dangers of using them without consideration of the context within which the overall issues are set.

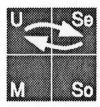
ANALYTIC MODE

> The dimensions of the chess board, the character of the
> pieces and the rules of the game constitute the context in
> which the chess pieces [of foreign affairs] are moved.
>
> —Graham Allison[4]

Everyone who has ever made an articulate, educated effort to change anything has experienced the analytic mode. We carry out such efforts in the sensory and unitary realities. Analytic changes are those made by seeing the "cause of things" and then setting those causes so as to make the changes occur. The analytic mode is used any time one makes a decision or solves a problem by combining some theory, no matter how simple, with some set of observations to attain some change. The analytic might be called "planned action," for it depends on creating some plan or design. For example, one is in the analytic mode when one solves the problem of what to do next by making a list to accomplish a task. So one uses an analytic method in designing and manufacturing a gadget that would increase a company's sales, in forming an annual budget, or in scheduling a vacation trip.

The analytic mode is defined as the process by which a *design* is created that "solves a problem." The pure concept allows no action, no creation of anything, for that would call for free will—free will is not

Diagram 3.1 Modes of change

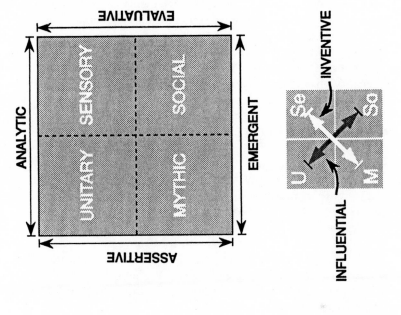

THE BASIC MODES OF CHANGE

ANALYTIC: change achieved by imposing policies that have been developed by testing an idea, formally or casually, against empirical data—theory applied through data. Actions derives from unilateral authority. The Analytic is often accepted as defining 'rational action.'

EVALUATIVE: change achieved by developing evaluations and rankings among empirically identified alternatives. Action follows from communications involving values. Power based on market and democratic sources, guided by 'rational' choices.

ASSERTIVE: change achieved by a leadership of either a charismatic, personal expression (based in the mythic) or an agent of authority (based in the unitary). Results are meaning making.

EMERGENT: change achieved through creating and accepting a new idea that may have originated with an idea leader or emerged from the involved group.

DIAGONAL COMBINATIONS

INVENTIVE (MYTHIC-SENSORY): change achieved through the material realization of a new (creative) idea. In a pure form there is no recognition of values or social truth, though the idea may attain acceptance for its 'value.'

INFLUENTIAL (SOCIAL-UNITARY): change achieved by acceptance of new values, either through the imposition of a 'truth' by an authority or through the adoption of a value by a population. The pure mode takes no account of data.

85

part of the formula. Rather, in the belief system of the analytic, the articulation of the plan *produces* its execution. The plan includes those elements we typically call the *motivations*. From a deterministic worldview, the psychological concepts related to drive, such as pay, motivation, incentives, and encouragement, are simply elements of the causal description of the situation. From the viewpoint of the analytic mode, "paying people to work" is equivalent to gravity "exerting a force on a body." It is part of the givens of the situation; motivation is *innate*.

In the analytic mode, then, solving a problem means laying out a trajectory that *of course* will be realized, subject to error in the plan. There is no *doing* in the analytic mode, no willful, no conscious action. A plan, whether as simple as turning on a light switch or as complex as building a new city, is instigated. It is observed, and perhaps a redirection is specified. Change is brought about by defining a situation. When properly defined, the "change" will, of necessity, occur. The changes occur in "reality," that is, within sensory reality. This process is a formally ritualized conversion of sensory data to realize a theory, and its necessary future state we call the *outcome*.

Of course, this description is not how we experience a person analytically solving a problem. We think of some person willfully choosing to create a solution. But the lawful base of the scientific worldview makes no provision for such choices. We simply ignore the paradox that speaking of the willful action of making something happen violates the rules of efficient cause.

Those who use the analytic mode out of their natural acceptance of a unitary-sensory world are concerned with establishing validity via testing an action's truth empirically. As Max Weber (1947/1968, I, p. 5) said, the means must attain ends with "the highest degree of verifiable certainty." So a pure analytic approach calls for a purity of results, for which many engineers, financially oriented professionals, and planners have been noted.

In this sense, either the unitary or the sensory reality must be assumed, that is, given. If the unitary reality is given, the process supports the maintenance of theory; there is a tendency to see objects and events within the sensory reality only as they are reflected in a theory. Analysis designs our experience according to a theory of the world we hold in our heads. One can see this, for example, in Freudian psychoanalysis. Conversely, if the sensory world is accepted as given, the focus of the process is on finding a theory that will explain the data. Here analysis conventionalizes the observation. For example, we induce a psychology from observations of behavior. (Diagram 3.4 summarizes the *given* and *controlling* effects for the analytic and the other five modes.) The elements of the analytic mode are these:

1. *A theory of the situation and the data, linked by rules for matching data and theory.* Instrumental rationality (per Max Weber in *Economy and Society*, 1947/1968) is worked out in the use of the two deterministic realities: the sensory and the unitary.

2. *The implementation process.* Using a series of problem-solving modes requires a knowledge of the situation, that is, of sensed data. This requires a systematic way of counting things in the sensory world according to the classifications established by the theory in the unitary world. In an economic setting, the analytic mode defines the world in terms of the history and current state of prices, qualities, and quantities of goods together with the demand parameters of the consumers.

3. *A method of linking, that is, a measurement theory* through which each sensory impression is given a label or characterization in the language of the theory. For example, measurement provides a stable linkage between the sensed qualities of a good and its price relative to alternatives, or the fit between a hole and the screw you will select to put in it.

4. *Identification of a difference* between the received data and the optimal set of characteristics indicates an error, a condition that calls for something to be redesigned, reperceived, or reselected.

5. *The basic assumption of rationality.* That is, given the correctness of the model, any set of "rational" (and conscious) people will move the system from an inferior to a more desired state. The critical condition for such movement is that there is sufficient motivation (goals), that is, "potential" for change, actually to drive the system from the inferior state to the desired one. Any failure is attributed to an incompleteness in the understanding provided by the model. Errors are not a product of moral failure; there is no concept of guilt, only of mismatch. The model was simply incomplete, or the measurement did not follow the established rules for linking data and theory. Any claim of irrationality on the part of the human component of the system is paradoxical, for the analytic mode does not allow for irrationality, only imperfect theory or observation.

The analytic approach accounts for values and individual choice by recognizing that the individuals and groups in a situation may have value measures. This view does not require intentionality. As recognized in game theory, any formal game with competitive objectives can be reformulated into an optimization problem, so choices can simply be treated as system responses stemming from characteristics of the situation.

This description is of the pure analytic mode. It may appear free of internal contradictions because the theorist and empiricist see no limitations on the possibility of understanding the "real world." While we may never experience anyone working entirely with one pure mode, it provides a conceptual setting through which to define a situation "rationally." The most powerful example of this use is the scientific method, but analytic reasoning also is used in formal rhetorics (e.g., Toulmin, 1972) and with a bit less rigor in strategic planning analyses (e.g., Mason & Mitroff, 1981). By gaining awareness of the pure form, we can identify "the irrationalities" that must be introduced to adequately understand a change process as well as to see more clearly the insanity that follows from working within a narrowly defined pure rationality.

The analytic mode requires that there be a well-established truth system—a traditional cultural or strong scientific confidence—to assure the problem solvers that the plan is "true." The truth, and/or its proponents, must have authority with the stakeholders to the problem. The analytic game is played on the "first board" with a belief in the rules by which the game is played. One can think of it as a competitive game or a game against nature with no element of personal force or leadership in this model. Leadership and process are one concept. A critical element of the authority of this mode, the glue that holds the separate unitary and sensory thinking together, is a measurement process.

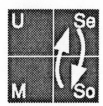

THE EVALUATIVE MODE

The evaluative mode, which involves the sensory and social realities, is the prototypical problem-solving mode in social situations and in the management of daily economic and domestic affairs. It is the mode that has become popular in contemporary U.S. democratic culture. It operates by assigning value to goods and to alternative courses of action. The objects or goods reside in the sensory reality; the values, in the social. Choices are made by allocating values among resources—time (attention), energy, and material goods—either singly or in conjoint decision with others. It differs from the analytic mode in that the alternative allocations are established by the participants' values rather than deduced from theoretic premises. Solutions are judged by the degree to which they provide *fair* allocations. Participation is a game of the fourth chess board.

The assumption of the evaluative mode is that a solution *fairly* allocates values *among* the participants in the problem. A solution is achieved when those involved in the problem agree on the allocation of values. Such decision making could be done analytically if the values were a measurable quality within the sensory reality. But values and facts are logically incompatible; even in practice, an opportunity will be considered to have different values by all those who might use it. The complexity of such problem solving is highlighted in the division of property of a deceased elder among the family members. The values the legacies take is affected by the act of being given to one or another family member. That is, the value of a good follows not only from its intrinsic qualities but from the comparative value of the object as seen by the other members of the family as well as from the sense of the fairness of the distributions and gifts that the deceased has made to others in the family over the years. Such a distribution problem is clearly a pluralistic exercise.

The elements of the evaluative mode are (a) framing and reframing that determines what aspects of a situation and its environment should be valued; (b) valuing, that is, assigning values to opportunities, states, and people; and (c) gaining acceptance for the proposed solution. More detailed descriptions follow:

1. *Framing establishes the aspects of a situation that are to be included in a problem definition, deciding the factors and the set of people or organizations whose values are to be taken into account in the decision.* The bounding of a problem is done heuristically as there is no general theory or rule—within the sensory and social realities—for setting the frame on a problem. Reframing and the initial act of framing are essentially acts of will, of visioning or revisioning boundaries and choices achieved through negotiating, considering, building empathy, and so on. Reframing changes the set of alternatives that are considered as solutions. Reframing changes the problem definition; in some cases, the problem disappears.[5] (The famous connecting-the-nine-dots-in-a-square problem is a simple example of making an impossible task trivial by changing the problem's frame.)

2. *Valuing is the reification of feelings.* It converts feelings into objectified and comparable onta. It is a fundamentally subjective, interpersonal process that cannot logically be reduced to an objective process. That is, one cannot set up nonsubjective scales on which to compare one person's values with another—we cannot make interpersonal comparisons of utility according to any set of consistent logical rules.[6]

Also, as illustrated in the legacy example, values are dependent on the frame in which the problem is set.

3. Gaining acceptance is the process of getting the values of those involved mutually agreed upon so that people will accept the solution; that is, do what they said they would do if they were rewarded accordingly. The process is complicated because the values are dependent both on the proposed allocation and on the statement of the problem. Changes in either aspect interfere with a solution's acceptance. Therefore gaining acceptance may require repeated revaluation of alternatives—negotiations— to gain approval.

All three processes are interdependent—no one can be achieved in isolation from the other two. If the participants take the sensory reality as given, the issues are primarily ones of evaluation, of what an object or opportunity is worth; if they take the social as given, the questions arise about what a fair allocation is. The practice of evaluative problem solving thus differs importantly depending on whether the participants are focusing on the social or the sensory reality.

For decision makers who hold the social reality innate, values are entities almost like nearly freestanding numbers, such as money values, that can be plugged into a formula in a way that allows decisions to be made independently of those involved in the problem. This is the typical assumption of economics; once prices (or supply and demand functions) are identified, the problem is reduced to an economic allocation. Those who take the sensory reality as innate must derive values from the situation as defined by the boundaries and by the other people who are included within the problem definition. Where we assign control in the social reality, the problem solvers have a need to consider the frame of the problem, the feelings of those involved, and the opportunities to reassign values to parties in such ways as to increase the apparent resources available for the problem's solution. Thus the process of resolution may involve continuing negotiation around boundaries by active intervention. Problem solving becomes a *communication* in which the involved individuals participate in the dialogue between the valuing process and the allocation process.[7]

The variety of ways in which we participate lead to quite different modes of change. All involve social and sensory reality, but, with the varying placement of control, the methods range from the near analytic to the primarily value definitional.

Diagram 3.2 presents the range of styles in the evaluative mode. The *allocative* extreme places the emphasis on collecting evaluative information much as though it were sensory data. Values are assumed to be independent of the situation and the time; they are to be provided

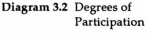

Diagram 3.2 Degrees of
Participation

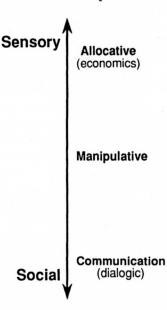

by the participants as data during an initial step of the problem-solving activity. Thus, for example, values can be obtained from the participants by studying markets or by running surveys. The values are then inserted into decision-making formulas. This is a favored approach of U.S. social scientists, human resource practitioners, and technical managers because it mimics the familiar analytic mode of the sciences, both in the structuring of the problem and in the repeatability assumed in experimental design. This style assumes that participants will accept a solution, "of course," if their values have been accurately identified. If the people do not act as the decision model predicts, the elements may be repackaged, as the failure to carry out the solution is evidence that the values—thus the motivations—were inconsistently formulated.

The *manipulative* variation recognizes a significant degree of interdependence between the way the problem is stated and the values assigned to the elements. The boundaries of the problem and the values to be considered may be set more or less participatively, even democratically, say, through a group discussion. Once established, however, the problem solution would be worked out using experts or a manager to analyze the alternatives and set the allocations. In the most democratic form of this variation, the stakeholders themselves both frame the problem and assign the values, thus appearing to fully participate in the process. There still is a separation between the valuing and the action, however; the parties are *representing* themselves rather than being immediately involved. The manipulation occurs in the working back and forth between the values and the feasible solutions. This is the typical negotiation or arbitration situation.

The *communication* extreme assumes the integrity of the person as valuer and actor. Problem solving is therefore fully within the hands of those involved. This style keeps open the valuing process because it is interdependent with the proposed solutions; if the frame of the problem is changed, the participants recognize that the values assigned to the elements and outcomes may also change.[8] The acceptance of the participants' immediate involvement may improve the ultimate quality of a solution but it may also seriously interfere with attaining closure. Those people of a social reality recognize that a dialogue will never mean exactly the same thing to any two people. Each person has a different context and history through which to filter communications. But even more significant in an evaluative process, differences will emerge from the way in which participants experience themselves and others, from the support they sense, and from the effect the words are having on others. With such emphasis on the valuing processes, the credibility of established values and attitudes is noticeably weakened, thus making the whole problem-solving activity unstable. In the extreme of subjective *I-thou* relations, with unlimited symbolic interpretations possible in every communication, problem solving can become a nearly unattainable goal. In this extreme, the paradox of working jointly with definitions of objects that come from the sensory reality and those that come from assignments of values from social reality becomes particularly obvious.

These three variations of the evaluative mode span the participative and collaborative problem-solving techniques that are widely taught in Anglo-American cultures, techniques that use various styles of leadership, ranging from a task to participation to an integrative orientation. An immense body of literature dealing with this mode has emerged as the participative ethic has come to dominate U.S. business and social relations, informing us of which "style" should be used in any particular situation. I argue, as do many others, that the choice must be made with a strategic view of the issues within which the problem is embedded, but also that a evaluative solution will seldom resolve a complex issue when used alone.

 ## THE EMERGENT MODE

The emergent mode uses the social and mythic realities. It operates through the cocreation of ideas—symbolization—and opportunities of the people involved, making possible alternative actions and outcomes that are not seen given the prevailing sensory definitions of reality. Emergent solutions produce change by facilitating social inter-action. They are most useful in creating and/or revaluing ideas to transcend conflicts and apparent resource limitations. The processes involved are social and psychological because this combination of ap-proaches to reality deals solely with the realm of symbols, ideas, and values. Nevertheless, the characteristics of the outcome are active—"empowering," "enabling," "creating," "expressing," also "innovat-ing" and "discovering"—not of physical things but of ideas.

This mode has become widely recognized in recent years as a mode of social invention. It is currently seen to be particularly important in creating high-performing organizations—in creating visions that lead to "organizational transformation" and to empowering those in disad-vantaged communities. It is central to the efforts to create "excellence" in U.S. industry. The creative solutions primarily lead to new valua-tions of alternatives. They call for "plays" on the sixth board that open opportunities for new valuations on the fourth board. The civil rights and antiwar movements of the 1960s succeeded to a great de-gree through the publicized "sit-ins," popularization of revolutionary songs, and images of the peaceful march in protest—creations that placed the actions beyond conventional expectations.

The emergent mode facilitates the articulation of feelings and ideas, moving them from the private, even unconscious, realms into a public consciousness to change feelings and attitudes toward others—trans-lating from mythic ideas to social expression. Its methods increase the impact of one's ideas and provide the user with confidence that it is possible to "make things happen." In some cases, this is done by creating new meanings, symbols, and metaphors that radically reorganize one's perceptions of the issue, leading to a "reframing" of the issue. In many cases, negotiations between aggrieved parties are achieved by "putting things in a new light" that results in a party recognizing that it is not being threatened or devalued. Or reframing may occur through coming to see that certain valued resources have been removed or added to the problem, thereby directly rendering a solution. Reframing may allow the parties to see a situation as an opportunity whereas they had rejected it when it was seen only as a loss. Opening future possibilities makes avail-able new resources as expectations generated by the new ideas are of value to people who may hope to benefit.

As in each of the modes of resolution, there are incomparable but intertwined dual logics that make up the process: In this case, a logic of creating that thrives on novelty and a logic of acceptance that em-beds an idea in the familiar. These logics call on two fundamentally opposed psychodynamics, one idiosyncratic, the other quintessenti-ally social. The more powerfully idiosyncratic is the idea, the more difficult it is to gain acceptance, thus the need for a *facilitative leader* to build cocreative solutions. The stronger the social reality among those involved, the greater the need for mythic creative contributions from the leader.

The elements of the emergent mode are as follows:

1. *Processes for evocation.* The processes pull out of the unconscious ideas or combinations of ideas that respond to the issues. The prime methods are metaphoric and assertive, aimed at opening those involved to expression of ideas that have had no conventional verbalization or that are normally obscured by fear, habit, or a lack of awareness of the ideas' relevance. Thus the methods use visioning, storytelling, archetypal myths, graphics, word play, music, and other nonverbal means to evoke and articulate images that can eventually be developed into solutions.

2. *Dialogue.* Facilitation encourages symbolic communication as also is developed in the most communicative participation. The distinctness of every person's message is respected as a contribution of a person, not an abstract construct that must follow a logic. Exchanges are *I-Thou*, in the Buberian sense, through which each person feels both self-creating and appreciated. Effective dialogue creates psychic space for mutual creativity and thus solutions that are not limited by a logic of exclusion or by the conservation laws of the sensory world.

Work with the extremes of creating oneself and being created by the other provides both the sense of membership that supports group action and a sense of self-valuing that supports acceptance of a person's own creative capability. Emergent processes create changes that lead to resolution by affecting motivations, attitudes, trust, empathy, friendship, appreciation, engagement, hopes, self-esteem, and vision. (See Coopperrider & Srivastva, 1987, for more on the "generative and appreciative" approaches.) The power of the emergent mode is in part a function of the degree to which it taps archetypal human processes and needs. It is easier to build trust when we "know the story" consciously as part of our cultural heritage or when it echoes the collective, unconscious "memories" of childhood and prior times (McWhinney & Battista, 1988).

Emergent solutions are as distinct as possible from the more familiar and comfortable analytic solutions. They provide none of the grounding of the deterministic modes, no sure logic, no empirical data to back the arguments. In their place, emergent solutions confirm the efficacy of those involved in effecting the solution. They attest to the possibility of achieving what one envisions. In that way, they are empowering to those involved in creating the solutions. Whereas analytic solutions confirm the general belief in the culture's values, emergent solutions create a *quickening* sense of identity and, on occasion, open up new resources. Emergent solutions have the feeling of being creative; they are not so much images that are new to a society but fresh formulations of positions through which the participants sense they can make something work, move a position, or, most commonly, change the values held by the parties to the solution.

 ## THE ASSERTIVE MODE

At the base of assertive methods is *authority*. Solutions are created by the imposition of a rule by a person directly or indirectly acting through an institution, that is, out of the mythic or the unitary worldview. The solutions deal with issues of law and regulation; they work by establishing a truth (arising out of a mythic reality) or interpreting an existing belief system (typically coming more from the unitary worldview). The law may deal with matters of religious belief, civil behavior, or, less formally, with all social manner and behavior. The assertive mode deals with changes in the *principles* that constrain behavior, separating the acceptable from the unacceptable. It replaces the confusion of possibility with the clarity of a single true position. It is second board play, a visible personal politics setting the principles of conduct to eliminate problematic behaviors or to reinforce desired ones.

The assertive mode bears on situations as disparate as charismatically empowering an exploited community, deciding the age at which a fetus becomes a human being, setting tax liabilities or the true version of a catechism, and gaining acceptance for a mathematical theorem. A problem is solved, assertively, by a person or organization that provides the people involved with the confidence that defines some part of their world, eliminating all but one from among many alternatives. By holding aspects of the world constant, imperative solutions prevent problems from arising in the way that precedent law enables normal social and economic commerce.

Assertive solutions routinize, creating rules on the second board for games that are played on the first board. In ordinary problems, the authority is gained by the need of those involved to have predictability. Ultimately, and in deeper problems, the power of assertive solutions is to give one access to immortality—membership in an eternal order—or, more immediately, to avoid actions that are likely to be damning. This ultimate concern appears dramatically in the behavior of "old revolutionaries" who for decades have held on to the truths they bore in the battles of their youth. This cramped cry for the leader's immortality ruled in Shiite Iran, in the Soviet Union, and now, as in the past, in China.

The elements of the assertive mode differ significantly between those in which the unitary position is the given and those in which it is the site of control. They are as follows:

1. *A set of principles.* If the unitary is the given reality, the principles are the givens and constitute the "unity"; if the mythic is the given, the principles are whatever the mythic source asserts them to be.

2. *Monistic structure.* All elements are of a single system devoid of the instrumental relations in the social/sensory methods. What is called *change* in a sensory reality is an expression of the system at a different time where *time* is an artifice used to order daily affairs. Everything follows from one consistent set of assumptions.

3. *Denial of alternatives.* The height of the assertive mode is the assertion of one truth, thus forcing the condition of "consensus." This is a major tool used by mythics to resolve apparent internal contradictions within a system either by a creative interpretation or by establishing new principles. It is difficult to tell which is occurring in closely defined fields such as mathematics and logic.

4. *Rules of interpretation.* What appears as novelty is only an unfolding. Bach composed music from within a given cosmic order; the Bach-imitating computer takes Bach's rules as given and derives new interpretations, without originality, though perhaps giving pleasure. So a mythic mathematician may create a method of computation or proof that is outside of the axiomatic system yet generates only elements that are consistent with it. Both mathematics and formal music produce resolutions by assertive modes.

Though not as prominent in contemporary Western society as they were in earlier periods of high religious and political conformity, the methods of authority still manage a large part of our daily experience. With the rejection of religious beliefs, administrative law, social rites,

and ceremonies and, conversely, with the attraction to material gratifi-
cation, moral argument, and democratic institutions, the assertive
mode is despised. Our society seems to have little respect for authority that is not enforced by material rewards and deprivations. Even
topics that were once decided assertively, such as ethics, are discussed participatively. Large segments of our population—particularly those dominated by sensory and social realities—are now
uncomfortable with the assertive mode. Like the habits that dominate our behavior without being noticed, however, authority orders
our lives. There is always a need to set answers to problems that cannot be solved by reference to science, pragmatism, or moral debate.

The assertive mode approaches a problem with the assumption that
the principles on which the society, organization, or issue is based are
true but that an inappropriate interpretation has led to conditions that
need to be corrected. Ideally, an assertive method does not imposes
solutions by force but by bringing to awareness a "known" solution or,
failing that, by finding someone who knows or will channel an
authoritative solution to a situation. The effort gets expressed in one
of two ways depending on which reality is given and in which lies the
need for control. When the "law" is assumed, the role of the mythic is
to embody, or manifest, the principles and thus impose charismatically
that law and its interpretation on the culture. This has been the route
of religious reformations such as those carried out by the many Protestant sects. Alternatively, a challenge may be mounted in the assertive
mode by a mythic leader who declares the current truths invalid
or misguided and intends to establish a new received truth. In this
case, the mythic's view of the truth is assumed and the intention is to
establish a new ideology. The common examples are religious and political leaders and demagogues who come into power to establish an
order or rite or to give rebirth to a cause or culture. Taking the differentiating direction in an assertive effort produces dramatic results,
for they are achieved through the imposition of personal power, a revolutionary charismatic, or the power of the awesome authoritarian.

An assertive "decree" is accepted at its declaration. Only heretics
fail to accept its "essential truth"; others may make errors that are corrected as quickly as they come into awareness. Those who believe
make errors; those who challenge the principles are wrong, evil, and,
ultimately, threatening. The punishment for denial of an imperative
solution calls for separation from the monistic world to be "rendered
unto Caesar" according to one's materialistic or moralistic deserts.

THE INVENTIVE MODE

It is through inventive methods that the greatest intentional changes in the material world are created in the interaction of the mythic and sensory worlds. The inventive mode solves problems by creating, initially, an image, then manifesting it in a technological or artistic form. By definition, inventive solutions are those that have a direct effect on the material world, that solve the problem by making something, or moving or destroying it, or, magically, by transforming what we think is not a solution into something that is. A solution can be as simple as a dab of color added to a painting or as complex as a water divergence project that would send arctic-bound rivers south into the steppes of Central Asia. An inventive solution can be simply finding a thing that satisfies the problem definition or a pure creative manifestation that transforms a mundane task into an occasion of wonderment.

The inventive mode is not played *on* a board; rather, the inventive play creates "the board" and/or the "play" on one of the "lesser" boards. That is, the fifth board is never itself manifested—the product is always to be found in a lesser board. Where the sensory reality is dominant in the mind-set of the inventor, solutions arise within the rules of current play, using accepted knowledge and customs. Such solutions usually come from the rearrangement of objects and ideas that are available but have not yet been applied in the problem situation. A solution to a problem can be found in a hardware store or a tropical garden as well as in a laboratory. Alternatively, many problems are solved by the invention of symbols that go beyond habitual and unconscious limits we have imposed on a situation. Systematic techniques, such as the synectics work of William Gordon (1961) and de Bono's (1996) development of lateral thinking, support finding the nonobvious.

The elements of the inventive modes are these:

1. *Metaphoric generators, the outcome of which are symbols, models, tunes, plots, and so on, that provide a coherence not present prior to invention* (McWhinney, 1991). Saying "metaphoric generator" does not explain much for we don't know their general characteristics, but it does point to processes we recognize as "creative."

2. Manifesting processes, tools, and crafts by which a symbol is realized in material form.

From the sensory view—taking the sensory as given—a created "thing" did not exist before. From the mythic view, the invention is a verification or expansion of self (if there were any doubt to begin with). Simple or bold, a pure invention is not created to serve a purpose within the mythic/sensory dimension. Like the Incas' wheeled toys and the Chinese firecracker, inventions, at the least, enliven their creators. An inventive solution is first measured by its immediate aesthetic impact, free of the intrusive judgments of the unitary and social realities.

The claim by scientists and artists that their work is value-free is correct to the degree that they use this mode in their creative work. Inventive solutions that arise in the mythic-sensory dimension carry no moral impact and suffer no constraint from any truth systems. Only in their integration into the larger world do they gain such attachments.

The location of control between the mythic and sensory realities makes a great deal of difference in the kind of creative outcomes that are presented as solutions. When the mythic is taken as the innate source, the work of invention consists of transforming the idea into the sensory reality—making the idea tangible, "making it work." When the sensory is taken as innate, the creative act makes symbols from a collection of data—*inducing* new concepts. This is the ultimate differentiating act that produces new conventions. Both can produce highly inventive solutions to a problem.

THE INFLUENTIAL MODE

The influential mode solves problems by changing or establishing the preferences that people hold through the interplay of value and principles in the social and unitary realities. At one extreme, a problem is solved by gaining concurrence on values through moral debate among a population; at the other, proselytizing enforces behavior that follows from an established belief system. In the interplay of values and truth systems are the games of politics. These changes in the culture solve problems by affecting the belief systems that are grounded in the habits, needs, fears, and expectations of a population. The changes affect questions of membership—who may belong and what commitments one must make in joining. Conversion and persuasion play on the third chess board to establish rules for play on the first. Conversion changes moral and ethical positions; persuasion establishes rules of behavior. The influential mode deals only with *nonmaterial* systems of concepts, which are the sources of meaning and the means of defining oneself.

Forming cultures has been a central process with all social animals, not just humans. Membership is a condition necessary for maintaining a species, acquiring resources, and ensuring safety. It is also a source of problems that arise from interindividual behaviors. The rules of behavior are clearly established among higher animals and among primates. We see evidence of adaptive problem solving around violations of rules and the qualifications for membership. For example, the traffic police recognize that they must accept that the normal maximum speed is set by custom, moderated by some safety conditions and the likelihood of arrest for being deviant. The legal speed is a fiction, but one that can be used punitively to control behavior when the police so choose. The speed limits are de facto unenforceable, so that they adapt by creating an operating limit that they consider normal. Such limits are adjusted by conditions, and the driver must be sensitive to noticing such changes within the gray limits. So it is with many of the laws of a society.

Within human communities, issues of membership and social behavior accompany any change in conditions. As a result, the methods by which cultures are created have been well studied and discussed from the earliest historical times. They become variously critical as a function of instabilities in a society. Conversion—or proselytizing from the Greek "to indoctrinate the stranger"—is the critical method when there are weak social groupings in the presence of a dominant, given culture. Persuasion develops via dialogue and moral debate about the social value system in a society lacking dominating rules. Politics is used to solve power issues among competing elements within a society; it positions a faction in society to absorb the losing elements. Within any macro or micro culture, the methods most used depend on the rates of change that are experienced and the degree to which a culture's values are under attack.

With the dominance of the American ideology, we learned well the tools of proselytizing for a democracy; they allow for a carefully delimited diversity and thus provide the setting for political solutions. The American culture, however, has remained relatively innocent of

moral discourse. Our inexperience is obvious in the awkward, sometimes violent debates over abortion and in our treatment of criminals.
In our current frustration with the inability to affect significant intentional change in organizations and communities by rational design
and economic incentives, we are coming to recognize that culture, values, beliefs, and morality have something to do with resolving issues.
In particular, the management of value issues is central to much of the
current methodology of conflict resolution, whether the conflict is resolved by judicial interpretation or by social negotiation.[9] The immate-
rial does "matter." The *rules of a game* are as real as the pieces with
which it is played.

The elements of the influential mode are these:

1. *Dialogue.* Above all, the modes of effecting influence are based in
discussion, ranging from the relatively one-way "proselytizing" dialogue, given the unitary position, to the moral dialogue, a social exchange aimed at establishing the meaning of *fairness, consideration,* and
all such terms of shared value.

2. *Dialectic.* Of all the modes, the influential mode most clearly ac-
knowledges internal contradictions—as dialectic solutions, they seldom produce resolutions. Resolution typically is achieved by
suppressing opposition, via influence, but allowing diversity in order
to maintain unity. When based in a unitary reality, the proselytizing
recognizes an alien belief system from which its advocates must be
weaned. As missionary movements have long recognized, it is wise to
allow only the totally devoted to go out among nonbelievers. In both
cases, problem solving requires the advocates to argue from the reality
opposite to their own. When the resolution is driven by a social reality, it is more likely that a synthesis will emerge based on a new set of
shared principles that may take on the quality of truth as the differentiating values become accepted.

The two involved worldviews, social and unitary, provide the usual
dual interplay of a form and process around two sides of the central
concept, in this case, *membership.* From the unitary side, the task is to
articulate appropriate rules of conduct without losing the shared dependence on the collectively maintained premises. From the social
side, the task is to form a common membership without losing individuality. Those of a unitary belief proselytize while differentiating;
the socials attempt to attain harmony with others by conventionalizing their differentiations. It takes acute observation to know in which
direction an influence process is moving. Movement in either direction expands membership; the social activist wishes to form values so

as to increase the number and variety of people who will join; the unitary organization expands membership by convincing others that its position is uniquely valid. An error in judging which is the dominant movement may result in finding oneself either "out," excluded from membership, or "in," with a loss of identity, when the solution is achieved. Vivid examples of the difficulty are apparent in recent alterations in the communist regimes of the Soviet Union, China, and Central European countries and increasingly visible conflicts within the ecumenical councils of religious orders.

"Critique" is a central feature of the environment across the whole range of influencing methods. Neither the social nor the unitary reality base provides a sufficient logic with which to make unequivocal judgments, so that, at the extremes, there are internal arguments. In those conflicts where some people take as given the principles and others the values, as in the current abortion issue, the arguments appear to be as much over the rules of solution as they are over the contents. When neither party can achieve a resolution, a natural fallback position is to change the rules of the game, hoping to find a set under which one can settle the issues attractively. This form of dispute is visible between the conventionalizing Catholics and differentiating evangelistic Christian sects in Latin America.

The range of methods based in the social and unitary realities appeals to a strange set of bedfellows—popes, fascists, judges, politicians, and humanists. They form a crew that has not been in vogue during the Age of Rationality, for they deal with the rules that society imposes on its members, at right angles to the rules of science and magic. The range is formally displayed in Diagram 3.3.

Proselytizing is a method in the extreme space dominated by the unitary. Successful proselytizing solves a problem by convincing the non-believer to adopt the premises of the believers, to let go of ideas and opinions that differ from the established norms. As with all influence methods, the solution does not require any action beyond the acceptance of a belief system—or the denial of its opposite. From the pragmatic view, it is hard to see that anything is resolved simply by a commitment to a belief; it is hard for the pragmatist to understand the importance of being free of alternatives to one's ideology.[10] Such a belief, however, is essential to the maintenance of membership. This is particularly evident in the role of the belief system in sustaining judicial integrity. If there are two or more competing value systems that must be maintained, the unitary mind has no means of resolution. This is the current situation in the U.S. courts in which there is an unresolved dialogue between constitutional principle and social and economic valuations.

Diagram 3.3 Methods in the Influence Mode

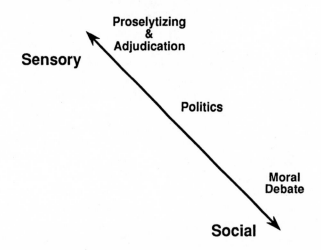

Adjudication presumes the membership of the parties and that the dispute is over interpretation and so should be carried out in a society's legal system and/or administrative apparatus. At the unitary extreme, the judgments are pure interpretation; problem solving is here a pure skill to be played out on the first board as we would play chess. The extreme form is common in minor administrative matters such as tax court in which the game is one of finding the most advantageous classifications of accounts. But even adjudication may not be free of sensory and social concerns. Evidence itself must be classified by an analytic testing method. But more central is the question of the source of the Truth from which the laws are deduced. If it is maintained that its source is outside of human control, the pure unitary methods are unassailable; but, if there is an opening to a humanistic foundation, questions of value enter. These may be settled politically or through moral debate under the cover of judicial procedures. We see examples of this concern in the discussion of such issues as tax equity and abortion. As Justice Sauter admitted in his interrogation for appointment to the Supreme Court, at some point, he would have to consider human compassion ahead of strict construction of the Constitution.

Political solutions are achieved by convincing portions of the population that they should become advocates for some cause or for members of some segment of society. These solutions are achieved by changing the relative attachment of the involved people to alternative memberships.

Typically, the methods used in politics are associated with *power*. However important power is in solving problems, it is treated here simply as a device for changing or redistributing memberships. *Politics* is designing or selecting the ground on which to dispute (or fight?). The specification of the grounds, in turn, leads people to play differently on the first board. That is, the political act changes the rules and the individuals respond, that is, *move*, according to their position, given the new rules. A clear example of this "play" is the annual meetings of the coaches and referees of a major American sport to assess and change the rules of their game for the coming year's play.

The *moral debate* is carried on to find a shared understanding that is acceptable to all who are party to the solution. Working from diverse positions toward resolution requires mutual understanding of the differences among the parties and an acceptance of how problems would be handled, given those differences. The solution to a problem is a rule by which particular allocations or constructions are to be accepted. The objective is to gain consensus in the evaluation in a way that allows the greatest degree of individual action. The paradox of the moral debate is the desire to have everyone adopt the same belief without coming to that belief by coercion. It shares with the other socially based modes the impossibility of interpersonal comparison of values, denying any *assurance* that a solution will be accepted. The moral debate has no end except in the acceptance of a "true belief." In practical terms, this means a judgment from a mutually accepted authority, perhaps in the judicial system or with a trusted third party as used in various formal and informal negotiation processes.

The moral debate is often used for "horse trading," that is, for negotiations in which a solution is found by trading off "goods" that are variously valued by the parties to the dispute. In almost any two- or multiparty dispute, there are typically a variety of valuings of the types of goods that are involved. The parties will differently value some aspects of the goods so that the total value varies depending on who receives the associated goods. Thus, by artfully distributing the goods among the parties, the gross value to all those involved may be increased. So, where there may have been a feeling of deficit among the disputants, a "win-win" solution can often be located.

The resolution of issues from the given worldview of the social reality is basically a *culture-forming* activity. The differentiating processes end up counterproducing shared values and common behaviors, that is, the prime indicators of a culture. The culture, in turn, is weakened by its efforts to expand its domain. It is interesting to note the swing from proselytizing to politics to moral debate as a culture's strength and integrity wane. This transition can be seen at the macro level of the American society at various times such as during the slavery debates that preceded the Civil War, during the Great Depression, and in the moral revolution of the 1960s. The Reagan years similarly led to deep moral concern over the micro society of U.S. business organizations. Indicators of the emergence of moral debate within the commercial sector can be seen in studies of culture (e.g., Deal & Kennedy, 1982), corporate politics (Culbert & McDonough, 1980), and efforts to proselytize for new unitary forms of organizational ethics (Adams, 1984). Such debates signify failures in the existing cultures. In these last decades of the second millennium, the failures may have accumulated into a "paradigm break" out of which will come new constructions of languages and logics that have been foretold by various mystical traditions and supported more recently by advances in thinking in the physical sciences.

The set of modes identified here provides a wide range of methods that could be used to solve problems, though I have provided no proof that the typology is exhaustive. Certainly the range is sufficient to establish the diversity of problem-solving methods and thus makes obvious the need for strategic selections in dealing with any issue of importance to those involved. The list also begins to show the importance of the relation between the methods and both the reality beliefs and the form of symbolization that a person, group, or culture uses in approaching a complex issue.

The set of modes discussed in this chapter are summarized in Diagram 3.4. This diagram is an expansion and fresh arrangement of the information in Diagram 3.1. In addition to the identification of the six modes, Diagram 3.4 distinguishes according to whether the problem solving follows a conventionalizing or differentiating path. One needs to go beyond selecting among the six distinct modes of problem solving, to choose tools that maintain the direction of change called for in the overall paths of resolution. For example, when our need is to *design* a project using tools from the analytic, it is critical that we notice that many analytic tools were made for *testing*. The selection will lead to a radically different outcome. If the task is assigned to people who hold a unitary worldview, they are likely to *test* rather than *design*. The result could be the rejection of a new idea before it is fully designed. A recent project initiated by the National Endowment of the Arts to show the contribution of integrated arts education began as a testing program looking for preestablished models that would prove the worth of the concept; thus, by design, it could not see new definitions of a solution.[11] As is typical, the bureaucratic approach tends to conventionalize, whereas the differentiating (design) approach is needed to find or create a solution. Conversely, in the selection of a mode to carry out a scheme such as an accounting practice, it is important not to use tools that support the establishment of new schemes. A differentiator

Diagram 3.4 Controlling Modes of Change

BASIC MODES OF CHANGE	GIVEN REALITY is located in the	INTENTION TO CONTROL acts in the	DIRECTED MODE differentiates -> <- conventionalizes
ANALYTIC: Achieved by imposing policies that have been developed with testing an idea, formally or casually, against empirical data, i.e., theory applied through data.	UNITARY	SENSORY	DESIGNING ->
Actions derives from unilateral authority. The Analytic is often accepted as defining 'rational action.'	SENSORY	UNITARY	<- TESTING classifying
PARTICIPATIVE: Achieved by developing value consensus in the relevant group based on empirical explorations. Action (allocation) follows from shared involvement.	SENSORY	SOCIAL	EVALUATING ->
Source of power is democratic, guided by a 'value oriented' relation to the data.	SOCIAL	SENSORY	<- ALLOCATING
IMPERATIVE: Achieved by a leadership of either a charismatic, personal expression (based in the mythic) or an agent of authority (based in the unitary).	MYTHIC	UNITARY	ESTABLISHING -> a new ideology
	UNITARY	MYTHIC	<- EMBODYING
EMERGENT: Achieved through creating and gaining acceptance for an idea that may have origin-ated with an idea leader or emerged from the involve group.	SOCIAL	MYTHIC	EVOKING ->
	MYTHIC	SOCIAL	<- ACCEPTING acceptance
INVENTIVE: Achieved through the material realization of a new (creative) idea. In a pure form there is no recognition of values or social truth, though the idea	MYTHIC	SENSORY	REIFYING -> manifesting
may attain acceptance for its 'usefulness.'	SENSORY	MYTHIC	<- INDUCING
INFLUENTIAL: Achieved through acceptance of new values, either through the imposition of a 'truth' by an authority or by the adoption of a value by a popul-	SOCIAL	UNITARY	ENCULTURING ->
ation. The pure mode takes no account of data.	UNITARY	SOCIAL	<- CONVERTING

should not be sent to do a conventionalizing task. And so, in each selection of a problem-solving tool, we need to consider the setting of the task, the proclivities of the individuals assigned to carry it out, and the direction of *control* that prevails in the organization or community. A lack of attention to *direction* as well as to the reality bases can disorganize a change process leading back into conflicts where flow had been established. As I will show in the next chapter, the power of a particular path follows from the proper, timely implementation of the appropriate methods.

CONCLUSION: MODES IN COMBINATION

> *And a fourfold vision is given me;*
> *'Tis fourfold in my supreme delight*
> *And threefold in soft Beulah's night*
> *And twofold Always. . . . May God us keep*
> *From Single vision & Newton's sleep!*
>
> —William Blake

The story of any important resolution of an issue will certainly include the use of all the problem-solving modes. It would be, as Blake suggested, a condition of supreme delight. If for no other reason in major endeavors, the variety of those involved will ensure that each mode has its champions. No matter how focused the effort toward a singular goal, it is likely we will see that a variety of methods must be used to effect a difference. Even the immensely elegant space voyages that glorify the achievement of the sciences (and thus the analytic mode) depend on the creation of a political climate (via the influential tools). The *Challenger* rocket disaster of 1986 attests to the need for a supportive social structure as well as high science. We must use complex responses to resolve complex issues. In times of great mission, the apparently simple and direct approach of a science or a charismatic movement may dominate an issue. A panoply of approaches, however, are still needed to cover the flanks. Every great crusade has had its bankers, peasant granaries, technicians, and apologists.

Recognition of the need for a complex response is not new, but there is little history of the success of complex responses beyond the momentary triumphs of highly focused military campaigns and a few battles against nature such as the capturing of Holland from the North Sea. A few "campaigns" against disease, poverty, organized crime, and religious manias have been won; but, more often, these evils have just run their course or the efforts to combat them have led to greater disasters than they averted, as is the case of the "green revolution" that destroyed the nutrition of the populations that converted to produce cash crops. In the light of the newly popular thinking about nonlinearity in human affairs and the related appearance of turbulence and chaos,[12] we have come to accept what we have always felt—that there is a sharp limit to the power of rational methods to achieve their intended results. It is clear that logics used singly lead us to worlds of insanity. It is distressing then to find that the *logics we would use to combine the worldviews* to be used in planning are similarly flawed— more accurately, missing their foundations.

The success of the problem-solving methods used in the scientific-analytic mode has handicapped us in developing modes of dealing with less-well-bounded settings. It seemed so natural that these methods could be extended to the complex realms of human issues that we have failed to heed the warnings from those who have most carefully studied approaches to complex issues. For example, in 1974, Russell Ackoff argued that *our rationally planned actions will systematically lead to messes.* He argued that planning can deal only with the major, first-order terms in the processes being planned and must ignore the less central aspects of the starting conditions and less dominant motivations in the model with which we explore consequences. The effects of both the less important terms and the motivations combine to eventually produce results that are radically different than the ones we have intended. Our models of action systematically lead us into *messes* over the long term.

To avoid the limitations of the special rationalities, multidisciplinary teams have been employed in recent decades in the resolution of many issues—homelessness, urban violence, and the failure of U.S. productivity. The attempt is to broaden the variety of initial conditions and motivations that can be considered in the resolution effort. In many cases, and particularly visible in the current confrontation with addictive drugs, the lack of a consistent logic by which to make trade-offs between alternative uses of resources permanently cripples the efforts. Each effort to repair the weakness of the planning model compounds the frustration, reducing our ability to find routes to beneficial outcomes.

To what must we turn, then, to

- explain the success humans have had in dealing with complex issues and
- design for successful encounters with the complex issues that face us now and in the future?

It appears that the answers will not be found in formal arguments, problem-solving models, mathematics, or the use of multidiscipline teams of social scientists. Rather, we may best follow clues that we get from two diverse sources—the study of genetics and narrative logics.

As we unravel the mysteries of genetic reproduction, it becomes clear that the copying of the DNA molecule and the processes by which that molecule induces the growth of the form are *contextual, pattern-following (or morphogenic) processes*. The processes are fulfilling a pattern rather than following a causal sequence of events—though we can so explain the sequences in hindsight. In the biological sphere, the pattern of reproduction is inflexibly followed, barring mutations. I propose that the generation of social product, visible in the stories we call history, myth, and epics, is also the result of following patterns. These patterns are immensely more complex than even the biology of reproduction and consequently have more ways to deviate. Yet, to resolve issues, we may need to know the basic paths of resolution and to consciously use them as templates or, more often, use them to help us consciously guide choices in response to new conditions. The building blocks of the strategies of resolution are the discrete actions we identify as problem-solving modes. The strategies themselves are analogous to the regenerative processes in biology, written in sequences of problem-solving activities that wind around to the right or to the left to conventionalize or differentiate. The form that these strategies take are the *paths of resolution* that are the subject of the next chapter.

IV

Vision Chants

A lone hiker trotted down a ridge in the Sangre de Cristo Mountains north of Taos, New Mexico. He was hungry and began scanning the rocky ridge for a sheltered spot to eat. To his surprise, another man suddenly appeared on the ridge, having emerged from the canyon below. They both stopped, startled at meeting another person, and then were further startled to realize they knew each other.

"RJ!" gasped the second man, out of breath from his climb, "what are you doing here?"

"Just loosening up. I'd have come sooner if I'd known you were hiding out here, Dan!" said RJ. "I haven't seen you in two, three years."

He saw a good resting spot and gestured toward it. "Shall we do lunch?"

They sat down and dug food out of their day packs.

Dan said, "You wouldn't have found me here sooner. This is my first time off in two years."

"Business must be good," said RJ, making it into a question.

Dan reflected a moment. He and RJ had been friends since their teens, had gone to college together, had diverged professionally but remained friends as much as their businesses allowed. Both had become CEOs of major corporations in their early forties. Both were athletic. Both were aggressive, forward-looking leaders. They'd shared tennis games, information, and confidences over the years, but Dan hesitated a moment more before saying, "Well, today's hike is a good metaphor for the past few years." He waved his hand toward the canyon. "I've been down in the depths and didn't know where I was going, but now I'm heading up and out."

AUTHOR'S NOTE: See Donald Sandner (1979) for a further description of the Navajo sand paintings.

"Keep talking," said RJ. "If you're talking business, it sounds like my story. We're going through a major change, too."

"OK. You know I've had a fantastic ride—singing altar boy to my first group to our first label, to a recording company. . . . The Hollywood life . . . aiming at MCA. I was sure I was the best and the brightest in the business. Then some of the bright lights burned out, and our records weren't turning "platinum" any more and we lost our touch for finding new talent. We just argued. I fired half my best people and got nothing but bad advice. The company—leadership and all—fumbled around for months getting deeper and deeper into depression and debt."

"So you were stumbling around in the canyon . . . that's why the metaphor."

"Yeah. I didn't even realize I was lost. I wandered for an hour or so before I came to my senses and looked for a way out. I climbed up the wall of the canyon into a narrow gorge that led up to the ridge. It wasn't easy. Now I see I've been here before, so to speak."

"Here?"

"Just metaphorically. Two years ago in Santa Fe I got interested in sand paintings, particularly one called the *Pollen Path*. They represent creation myths, you know. I guess I was ready for a revelation because, when I read the myth about the Pollen Path, it really struck home. The hero is the son of the Sun God and Changing Woman. He's confused and without direction, yet too proud, stubborn, and afraid to move, just like my company and me. So the youth's spirit guides send him off to climb the Great Corn Plant so he will gain consciousness.

"It's the tale of the conquest of one's own mortality," explained Dan, glancing at his friend to be sure he understood. "I got the message and I went home to start the company along our own pollen path. I called a meeting with everybody either present or on two-way video. Everyone agreed that the company had lost its sense of identity, its boundaries, its purpose, and was in need of deep rethinking. It was scary to share that, to let everyone know that I knew we were in trouble."

"How did you climb the Great Corn Plant?" asked RJ, smiling but with an expression of great interest.

"First I got mixed groups of employees together, to explore our problems, but there were 120 of us, all headed in different directions, all trying to find what business were in. We just got angrier and more confused.

"Then I hired a consultant who brought together a sampling from our organization plus the board members and some outsiders—industry friends, artists, and kids who listen to our records. We talked about the industry, about music, and about what the employees wanted."

"Here, let me draw the Pollen Path for you," said Dan, picking up a stick. He drew a box shape in the dirt. Then he drew a path inside, along the lower end, then made it turn and head up across the figure. He drew a corn stalk and, at its left, a rainbow. Farther up on the right, he drew a lightning bolt. The path continued through the frame and out the top, then turned again and ran alongside.

"We were here," said Dan, pointing at a spot near the rainbow, "like the rainbow, insubstantial and ungrounded. We looked for common goals, expectations, and values and we did some dreaming but didn't get anywhere, just wallowed around. Then we asked what business we wanted to be in and one of the sales clerks said, 'Ya know, we're not here to *record* music; we're here to *sell* music.' Someone else said, 'Our business is *distributing* music; the recording is incidental.'

"That was the lightning bolt!" said Dan, tracing it firmly. "Right here in the middle of the path. It lit my way. From that moment, I saw my business clearly, but a different business, a whole different way of distributing music. That was nearly two years ago. I haven't thought of much else till this week."

He retraced the path thoughtfully and said, "You see, we gained consciousness and conquered our own mortality. The new method of distribution was, for us, a rebirth, just as gaining consciousness is for the hero in the myth."

"Things are going well then, to let you get away?" asked RJ.

"Yes. I decided I could take a few days off when our distributions began to hit the shops by 10 a.m. the morning after the concerts or shows. Business is great and the exciting thing is that we've done it together. It's been cooperation all the way. It would be easy to take control again—my managers get impatient and would jump at the chance—but with everyone involved it's working beautifully. So here I am, walking out my Pollen Path in the mountains and rendezvousing with my old buddy. What have *you* been doing?"

RJ took Dan's stick and pointed to the path in the dirt. "I fit your metaphor. I'm taking the same path, but in the *opposite* direction. Where you are going up, I am coming down." He scratched a second path over Dan's, starting at the top.

"I took a good look at my competition last year. Do you remember that the bottom fell out of the market in 1984? Well, the Japanese must have kept all their workers making crankshafts or something while their R&D developed new machine tools. I didn't. I laid off everyone I could, including my best tool makers. When the market picked up, I hired new people, but none so good as the ones I'd let go. We were at a real disadvantage in the face of the new Japanese designs and production."

"How did *you* turn around?" prompted Dan.

"I took on a consultant too. His name's Kris. He worked with me and my executive team and had us create images of ourselves vanquishing our competition, not just a general idea but really specific details. We made it so real for ourselves that we could see and feel our operations completely revitalized. He assured us that our victory was a certainty, that my team and I were just the instruments of that victory.

"It gave us such confidence that we created a program for quality achievement. The execs worked with staff to produce crisp, vivid graphics and speeches packed with such enthusiasm that all the senior managers came on board. I'm absolutely clear about what needs to be done and am sure that they are in line with my direction."

He scratched emphatically along the lightning bolt. "We're here," he said, pointing to where the lightning met the rainbow. "Does the lightning bolt symbolize clarity? That's how it is for us. The design is fully laid out and the managers know their jobs. Next we just have to get the employees to join us in making quality goods."

Dan took the stick and gestured at the path RJ had taken. "You've done what they call the warrior's work; now it's time for you to get the yield from your efforts."

The two friends, having finished their stories and their lunches, re-packed their day packs and headed off in their respective directions, promising to meet again soon by appointment, not serendipity.

4   Paths of Resolution

What is the set of strategies out of which a person, an organization, a society may achieve major changes? The two executives, Dan and RJ, who shared their paths in Interlude IV, had taken diametrically opposite directions—one learned from an old myth, the other from current practice. How could they know what alternatives there were and how to judge the appropriateness of each for their situations? Or should they, as the planning theorists Lindblom and Braybrooke (1970) and the psychologist Janis (1989) propose, simply "muddle through" the problems and opportunities as they arise?

Most people in most situations are not conscious of any alternative paths to resolution of the issues they encounter. Paths are taken by accident, habit, or ideology. Our culture provides little help, for there is no established guide to the selection of paths, nor any science to alert us that our choices may lead to greater messes than those we seek to resolve. This chapter is an exploration into the existing theories and a presentation of a new catalog of alternative paths, based on the concepts of alternative realities and the problem-solving processes introduced in earlier chapters as well as the roles of myths and stories in finding paths of change.

In this discussion, I intertwine two languages that come from the seemingly opposing cultures of the analytic social sciences and of expressive myth and story. As my understanding about resolving issues and conflicts has grown, I have found that the two cultures are neither opposing nor distinct. I have seen that currently used strategies have their roots in myths of ancient origins. In this view, I agree with Per Berg (1985) that a strategy is a conscious formulation of a myth that can be acted upon. The paths taken by the two business leaders in Interlude IV parallel two great myths of West and East. The parallels are usually not transparent but are easily established. In this chapter, I develop the interpretations of the myths to show how they can provide a foundation for these major paths of resolution and also make the translation into the languages of the social sciences and modern practice. In the final chapter, I return to a further consideration of myths and stories to examine how we choose those that will lead to resolution. As I indicate, the ultimate choice of strategy is a cultural one, and the ultimate wisdom in a culture is carried in its myths spawned in founding events, summit meetings, and executive suites, at sporting events, and in literary creations as well as those brought to us by storytellers of antiquity.

THE LITERATURE OF CHANGE
AND RESOLUTION

A major difficulty in founding a theory of change and resolution in practice is that few of the great leaders and students of change—political, social, or scientific—have written about their strategic processes. When activists such as Thomas Jefferson, Mao Tse-tung, Saul Alinsky (1969), or Lee Iacocca have written of their work, their writings have been focused by their particular biases; moreover, only the more recent of them have described the processes or stages by which they have conducted their revolutions.

A second difficulty is the biased worldviews of social science students who study the processes. The study of approaches to change, like the methods of change themselves, are deeply affected by the worldview of the student. While the creators of social change have come from the whole range of reality beliefs, the literature of change has been organized by reporters, historians, and biographers, political and sociological analysts, psychologists, and philosophers, who, as a group, tend to come from analytic and social worldviews that support observing and evaluating better than they do doing. Such descriptions arise in the worldview of the author and may have little to do with the reality from which those processes arose.

A case in point is the emergence of a standard image of the change process following the work of Kurt Lewin in the early 1940s. Lewin described this formula in his famous epigram, "unfreeze, change, re-freeze." It has appeared in many forms since. Elgin (1977) extends this model of natural transformation by specifying, in a five-step model (steps 2 to 6), some of the aspects of the unfrozen system.

1. decline
2. crisis
3. muddling through and procrastination
4. chaos
5. back to basics
6. transformation and revitalization

In my earlier work on change theory, I created a parallel model that delineates paths by which a system unfreezes—that is, decomposes—before it may reconstitute itself (McWhinney, 1980). This model is one more of the many variations on the Lewinian formula. The pervasiveness of the Lewinian model is further illustrated in Levy and Merry's (1986) presentation of a collection of "second-order change" models chosen from a variety of contexts ranging from physical chemistry to cultural revitalization as summarized in Diagram 4.1.

The mode of thinking behind the formulation is analytic. It is generated by setting up a sequence of processes, motivations, causes, and

Diagram 4.1 "Transformation" in Various Contexts

Cultural Revitalization (Wallace)	Scientific Revolutions (Kuhn)	Dissipative Structures (Prigogine)	Historical Determinism (Marx)	Creative Process (Adams)
Steady state	Normal science	Fluctuations within defined boundaries	Steady state	Preparations
Cultural distortion	Growth of anomalies	Fluctuations past a threshold	Growing dissatisfaction	Incubation
Revitalization	Crisis		Conflicts	Illuminations
Reformulation	Revolution	Crisis	Crisis	
Transformation	Normal science within a new paradigm	Jump to a higher new order	Revolution	Verification
Routinization		Local equilibrium	New order	

SOURCE: Reprinted by permission of Greenwood Publishing Group, Inc., Westport, CT, from *Organizational Transformation* by Amir Levy and Uri Merry. Copyright © by Praeger, a division of Greenwood Publishing Group, Inc., 1986; used by permission.

conditions that appear in each context. In each case, the formulation follows from an essentially deterministic and pluralistic view of change,
whether historical, dialectical, or (social) scientific. It describes the way
things happen out of sensory and/or unitary understanding.

The Newtonian model, like play on the first chess board, confirms
the unitary and sensory beliefs that the world is orderly and, barring
the intervention of God, predetermined. In a parallel fashion,
sociologists' theories of change typically have explained conditions
under which change happens deterministically as opposed to being
caused with intention.[1] Some of the models are developmental, growing from Darwinian evolutionary thinking. Others follow a cycle of
growth, stability, stagnation, and decline, reflecting the natural and,
particularly, anthropomorphic acceptance of birth and death as a pervasive dynamic. Of particular interest are theories of "episodic
change" in which long periods of stability are interrupted by brief periods of revolutionary change (Gersick, 1991). Both gradual and episodic models are framed in the analytic mode in which change is a
sequence of events played out in accordance with precedent conditions and accidents of time.

Students of change following the analytic mode test for evidence that
changes arise from particular sets of prior conditions rather than identifying the decisions that bring about change. See, for example, Crane
Brinton's theory of social disequilibration (1952), Chalmers Johnson's six-
fold typology of mass insurrections (1968), and S. N. Eisenstadt's (1985)
discussions of the cause of revolutions. Reducing the process to a single
path hides the variety of dynamics that are represented within this range
of contexts. They may all be morphological (structural) changes, but gen-
eralizing them as "second-order" changes stretches the notion beyond
usefulness. Even within a useful definition of second-order change, there
are important distinctions. It is clearly a logical error to lump into a single class the two processes that the CEOs described on the New Mexican
mountain. To so collect all these theories into one analytic model is about
as useful as claiming all stories have the same plot because they all have
a beginning, a middle, and an end.

At the base of the problem, the analytic mode does not distinguish
between first- and second-order change, as second-order change is not
a meaningful idea in the sensory or unitary worldview and may even
be suspect by those holding a social worldview. The powerful roles of
symbol and created meaning are almost entirely lost in formal and effective causal modes of discourse. This error of using the writer's culture to describe the actor's reality was typical until well after World
War II when the students of social and organizational behavior more
frequently allowed into their writings the notion that, through

planned change, we intentionally make a difference in the way our societies operate. In doing so, they began to change our image of social
change from a basically passive process, that "other people" did, to
one that held that change comes about, in part, because we choose to
make changes out of a belief that *we can make a difference.*

Other Paradigms of Change

It is difficult, looking back from 1990, to believe that social scientists
and the allied consultants have been so closely tied to classic scientific
thinking until so recently. There are very few works on the choices
one has in creating social change that were written before the mid-
twentieth century. There are some great exceptions, including such
classics such as Machiavelli's *The Prince* (1513) and a number of works
on military and revolutionary strategies. *Resolutionary* thinking has
been mostly the province of those who felt themselves powerful
enough to make changes in the affairs of man—few took the time to
write about them between campaigns. With so little acceptance of
change as a choiceful process, we have been slow to understand large-
scale change strategies in sociopolitical affairs, in business, or in technological settings. As we would expect, the majority of early
contributions were from the "left," calling for revolutionary changes,
both at a local level, such as Saul Alinsky encouraging community
work, and at national political levels, for example, from Latin America
in the work of Che Guevara and Paulo Freire (1972). With the development of social change strategies—particularly the sociotechnical systems
model from the Tavistock Institute in London (Trist, 1981; Van Eijnatten,
1993), training models developed particularly via the National Training
Laboratories, and the emergence of strategic organizational development
in the work of McGregor, Likert, Shepard, Bennis, Argyris, and
Beckhard in corporate management,[2]—intended change has become
useful from a liberal as well as a revolutionary worldview. Working
from the broad strategic view, Bennis, Benne, Chin, and Covey (1976)
and Zaltman and Duncan (1976) classified the various approaches into
four similar classes of change strategies. The first group listed "rational-
empirical," "normative," "reeducative," and "power-coercive"; the
second, "facilitative," "reeducative," "persuasive," and "power."
Proactive strategies from the whole range of reality beliefs are now
visible at every level of affairs and from every political persuasion.
The most visible are those viewed as volitional, arising from social
and mythic realities. Among those strongly dependent on the social
worldview are the facilitative strategies that begin change efforts with

versions of the value systems of the involved culture. For example, the Quality-of-Working-Life (QWL) movement, begun in 1972, created methods for major changes in the work environments that called for redesign based on the values of the employee. The methods in conflict resolution, developed at Harvard also in the early 1970s and popularized in the eminently practical *Getting to Yes* (Fisher & Ury, 1981), work almost entirely from the social reality to resolve conflicts at every level from domestic to international conflicts. From the social view, resolutions are usually obtained by reframing a situation, by reevaluation and creation of new symbols and criteria—working on the fifth- and sixth-level "chess boards." Most of this work proceeds from an increasing awareness of the "paradigm shift" that has led us to recognize that the populations involved in change efforts typically come from radically different worldviews, a point proposed in this study.

A number of major strategies have been articulated that draw on the mythic perception. They derive from the worldview that a person or a group can create the world they wish through deep imaging and commitment. This possibility has been visible in the often dishonored entrepreneurial and charismatic modes of change, but now personal conviction—in the extreme, charisma—is increasingly recognized to play an important role in the outcome of athletic events and community-level efforts. At this level, we are willing to recognize that personal willpower does make a difference and therefore is an aspect of leadership, an important element of a second-order change process. Personal willpower is a central component of the organizational transformation path that has been developing during the decade of the 1980s. Levy and Merry (1986) provide an excellent summary of the use of myths themselves in creating organizational change.[3] Westerners, particularly those of a liberal mind-set, however, are less comfortable with myth and the related charisma leadership, because the presence of such focused energy typically threatens liberal (social) agendas. The models of "rational alternatives" are still more acceptable.

Strategies of Contingency

With an awareness of a greater number of alternatives, it is natural that we should begin to think of how to select among *paths* (which in other places might be referred to as *theories of change* or *strategies*). The concept of contingency—matching the mode of change with the operative variables of the situation—is a critical step in the emergence of a meta-praxis. Calvin Pava (Diagram 4.2) provided one such view of contingent selection among strategies as a function of environmental

Diagram 4.2 Contingencies in Systems Change

	Low Task Complexity (stable, clearly defined problems)	*High Task Complexity* (messes, meta-problems)
Low Conflict	Master Planning: corporate strategic planning operations research Delphi convergence techniques	Normative Systems Redesign: normative planning organizational learning
High Conflict	Incremental Nonplanning: bargaining disjointed incrementalism	Nonsynoptic Systems Change: normative incrementalism theme interventions interest-based planning
	Passive-Responsive	*Active-Adaptative*

SOURCE: Calvin Pava, "New Strategies of Systems Change," in *Human Relations, 39*(7), 615-633 (1986); Plenum Publishing Corporation; used by permission.

conditions. He presented a table demonstrating two dimensions of contingency: the levels of complexity and the levels of conflict in the environment in which the change effort is initiated. The strategic considerations developed in this chapter are built on the idea of contingency, using the *stories* and *worldviews* of the involved populations as the "conditions" on which the strategic choices are based.

Another contingency model, much in the spirit of this meta-praxis, was proposed by Quinn and McGrath (1985) and calls for a fit to the environmental conditions, organizational form, and leadership style. They, as I do, however, find that the contingency model is itself a model of stability, and they shift to a value-free model that identifies but does not prefer congruence. I have taken another route, moving to a theory of change grounded in the multiple realities.

The map of multiple realities and the dialectics of change introduced in Chapter 2 provide a foundation for viewing change strategies as paths based in myths of the broad culture and the micro culture of the organization or community. The map provides a landscape in which to act out these tales and rules of conduct—that is, the problem-solving methods—for achieving resolutions. I propose that the choice of path to follow is a function of meaning given to the situation by the central actors and secondarily of the qualities of leadership, cultural resources, preparation of the involved population or work force, and skills and level of consciousness of the activists. Contrary to most contemporary strategic thinkers, I treat the environment as a function of the culture-forming processes. Elements of the environment become relevant in accordance with the path we follow in searching for a resolution or desired outcome.

In the next sections, I describe two significant classes of paths, expressed via two ancient myths, using these concepts of alternative realities and theory of change to indicate how these myths are metaphors for the processes by which we form plans and resolve issues.

PATHS THAT LEAD TO RESOLUTION

The discussions, so far, of multiple realities, the dialectics of change, and the modes of change provide the basis for the structure of a meta-praxis. Now I turn to the methods of resolution, formulated as "paths." A path is a sequence of steps directed by an overall sense of direction through a space of alternative realities; it is a plot of a story. The idea has an ancient source in the sanskrit word *marga*, meaning the "path" that is followed by people in living their lives. Like the later term *myth*, it refers to an archetypal plot that is "followed" over and over in varying detail. I use the word *path* instead of *myth* because it clearly refers to a process rather than simply a cultural context. The elements of a path are activities diversely defined within the reality in which the actors sense themselves to be. Some activities are explorations, others are interpretations, creations, influences, and so on, paralleling the problem-solving methods described in Chapter 3. The paths are not simply problem-solving activities strung together opportunistically but the elements of a narrative that have a distinct *founding*, a *path*, and a *resolution*. In a very general sense, the resolution of an issue forms the actions required to produce a change in "symmetry breaking," setting direction in an otherwise *undifferentiated* flow of life. Transversing the multiple realities coevolves our worlds and generates tales of the heroic and the ordinary.

It is not of any importance whether Dan and RJ, the executives who met on the mountainside in Interlude IV, were aware that they were "on" the paths of destiny as laid out in the Navajo healing chant or that the Hindu godhead Krishna counseled the young leader Arjuna in a way similar to Kris's advising RJ. To design processes that resolve conflicts and issues, we need paths that recognize the differing worldviews of Dan and RJ and the others who will participate with them in finding resolution. It does not matter whether the participants accept the idea of other realities or even the possibility of a meta-praxis. They simply need to come into step with the narratives through which they have organized their personal and organizational lives. The assumption presented here is that there are paths of great generality, such that most stories of creation and paths of change, at least in Western cultures, can be seen as paralleling one of these paths or fragments of them.

The tales that Dan and RJ tell are not fixed forms that are played out by every entrepreneur or even by everyone who is a party to a founding event. Donald Polkinghorne (1988, p. 73), building on the work of literary critic Northrop Frye, indicates that the link to the past "does not determine what is possible in the present; it merely provides models and plots that can be drawn on to understand and construct the present." A number of students of narrative have proposed that there are but a few such archetypal stories within a culture, perhaps in all cultures. I see this as an overgeneralization at best.[4] However defined, the set of plots is small. In this work, I will focus on just two tales that are related as inverses to each other. They are not the unique paths of resolution—simply important ones in current Western cultures. I suspect they will remain so until a significant portion of the population can effect changes of the third order.

The fundamental bifurcation between two paths is established by the "direction" of change as described in Chapter 2. One set of paths starts in the differentiating direction, the other in conventionalizing, taking opposite directions through the space of the multiple realities. Differentiation leads to resolution by the grand path of *renaissance, a path that leads into and up from despair.* Conventionalization leads to an equally important path of *revitalization, which succeeds by realizing principles.* Both these paths have been recognized and memorialized from ancient times.[5] Dan was aware that his path of rebirth paralleled an Indian creation myth. He could also have seen it as following Jonah into the whale, Buddha into the forest, or, of course, Dante into hell. RJ's attempt to revitalize his firm begins in a path foretold by Arjuna's tale in the sacred Hindu text, the *Bhagavad Gita.* It equally follows Moses down from the holy mountain as well as the paths in a thousand other tales of heroes who have received a direction from a teacher to carry out that which already "was"—what had already come to pass and was simply being played out in secular time.

Neither of these great paths is frequently traversed in its full forms. The living out of either effort makes immense demands on a system, whether of individuals, an organization, or a culture. A person may experience a "little death" and rebirth once or twice in a lifetime; a small corporation might be able to sustain periodic deep change every few years; the massive corporations such at AT&T, GM, or GE may last for decades without either revitalization or rebirth. Cultures may go on for centuries. The Russian society may have had but minor revitalizations in the 700 years prior to the revolution that was begun in the late nineteenth century and has just begun getting back on track after a delay of 70 years.[6] Revitalizations are attempted more frequently than rebirths, in part because they are rational undertakings in contemporary Western cultures. It seems to be a fad in U.S. corporations to attempt to revitalize every time the competition finds a new message and a new guru—Critical Path Planning (PERT) was followed by Zero Defects, Management-by-Exception, Strategic Planning, Quality Circles, "Excellence," Total Quality Management, and, at the moment, reengineering. Each fad experiences a few successful applications, garners scores of advocates, and then fades into disrepute. Few organizations complete a path of revitalization before the majority of members recognize that the new ardor is but another desperate rearguard action for slowing the natural cycle of devolution.

The vast majority of efforts at intentional change and systematic resolution of conflict follow much reduced paths that call for fewer and simpler interventions. In the great majority of situations, such lesser efforts are appropriate strategies. We need not go through the agony of death and rebirth nor shake an existing organization to its foundations every time there is a disturbance in the environment or a failure in the inner workings. Adaptation and slight reframing are sufficient to manage conflict and survivability in the vast majority of situations. But there is a middle range of concern, issues that we recognize as significant—the effectiveness of operation in a company, personal and societal health issues, pollution of the oceans by oil tankers, the quality of inner-city life—that call for deep resolution, but we have not the heart, the courage, to commit ourselves to the totality required for their remedy. Of such a problem, someone said, "We wish to be on the moon, but we are afraid to take our feet off the earth." For such efforts, we will mount a campaign but not go to war.

Often, with such issues, we undertake reduced paths that start off as revitalizations or rebirths but turn back before they are completed. These aborted trips are the familiar stabs at resolution we see in policy planning, legal action, organizational development, riots and rebellions, sociotechnical design, community development, participative planning, social mobilization, trade regulations, and conciliation. As incomplete resolutions, they provide the maintenance and adaptation tools for ongoing workable and orderly societies. There may be little operating distinction between a problem-solving effort and these strategically initiated efforts to resolve an issue or conflict. The distinction is in the considerations that went into choosing the actions. The reduced paths vary from the generative processes that bring new structures to our cultures to those that equilibrate the unending vagaries of that well-designed society. Some are but strings of problem-solving efforts. Others strategically traverse much of a grand path or some combination of elements from the two major paths.

In the next sections, I describe the two grand paths and a selection from among the infinite variety of reduced paths. I make no attempt to provide an exhaustive listing of the reduced paths or a handbook for their use. Space limitations and the reader's patience allow me to present but an overview of the complex mechanisms of resolution. The whole literature of human affairs provides embellishments that cannot be distilled in a written work. In the process of presenting theory, I will continue to use both the literature of change and examples to relate to the readers' own knowledge. The examples are drawn from individual, local, and grand historical instances. I report them via contemporary cases and tales supported by graphics such as the Navajo sand paintings, the directed graphs used by social scientists, and vector diagrams of the sort with which I mapped the alternative realities. The whole discussion of these paths of change is set in the territory of alternative realities and guided by the paradoxical properties of intentional change and action.

THE TWO GREAT PATHS

The great paths of resolution have played great roles in the development of human history and culture. They have appeared from the earliest times in civilizations around the world. They appear alternatively in the great epic tales of achievement and in the tales of death and rebirth. Through their tales and rituals, communities have both vivified their cultures and warned the "travelers" on these paths of the dangers of seeking rebirth. A major portion of all epics, sagas, myths, and fairy tales are descriptions of these two paths, of how they were undertaken, of how and why they failed, and of the rewards of success.[7] These paths have become even more familiar for they are retraced in the histories of many contemporary organizations, communities, and social institutions.

The two great paths are presented in Diagram 4.3 in graphs derived from the Navajo vision chant introduced in Interlude IV. These graphs are a linear form of the circuits of the space of alternative realities that were introduced earlier to describe the differentiating and conventionalizing directions. While the linear and circular representations are interchangeable, I use the chant version here to introduce a number of aspects of the strategies less visible in the directional models.

The descriptions provided here are pointers to the grand traditions and complexities of these routes to intended change. The two paths

Diagram 4.3 The Two Grand Paths

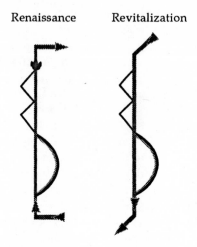

represent diametrically opposite approaches to achieving deep changes in a system. While they are most often used together in practice in an unconscious way, I discuss them separately first to show the differences in the pure forms and to aid the user to see how one can systematically follow one path or the other separately. In the subsequent paragraphs, I identify some of the ways in which the paths are intertwined in the service of producing intended changes.

The initial separation of the paths may lead the reader to view them as simplistic models. The paths, even the reduced paths, are archetypes, intentionally stripped of the complications of actual practice. Indicating that they are typically used in combinations is a first step in exploring their practicality. In Chapter 5, I discuss the ways the selection of the paths of resolution depends on the dynamics of the culture, with a particular focus on the qualities of the leadership and followers. No theoretical discussion can capture the specificity of practice, but working back and forth between examples and analyzing the elements in relative isolation raises our ability to see the operation of a meta-praxis in the complexity of the natural setting.

I continue the disclaimer that I introduced earlier that limits this study of meta-praxis to Western cultures. I strongly suspect that radically different cultures of the Orient and the southern hemisphere will have mythic traditions and customs that lead to quite different strategies of change. I reserve the exploration of these paths for a later volume.

 REVITALIZATION

Western Democratic Revolutions,
Organizational Transformation, and Crusades

> Managing corporate identity means preserving the roots and
> fostering the growth of the tree. In other words, we cannot
> violate corporate identity. On the contrary, we must try to find
> out what is fundamental in this identity and on what roots the
> tree will be able to grow.[8]

Revitalization provides images and direction to an organization, society, or individual that point to how it expresses its ideal; how a government should become democratic; how all mortals should follow
religious truth; how there is one aesthetic; and so on. The path of revitalization may begin with an assumption of a belief or accepted theory
that establishes the desired outcome and the means of achieving it. By
assuming the path, the members acquire energy and focus through the
leadership of a charismatic individual or movement. The mythic charismatic image provides a comprehensive vision for working the issues
toward a desired future. Once the vision and particular goals are established, revitalization proceeds by conventionalization of members
or citizens who adapt, propagate, and eventually carry the results into
operation in the social and sensory realities.

Revitalization is basically a top-down strategy. Revitalization may
build from so simple a principle as "no taxation without representation" that led many to join the American Revolution against England.
More frequently, it grows from a broad set of principles that form a
political philosophy, a religious dogma, a humanistic vision, or all
three. This route to defining the way the world is to become has been
increasingly followed by U.S. industrial organizations trying to
achieve "excellence," following the lead of a few corporations that
took significant steps in the 1970s to improve productivity through effective management of people and thus other resources. The industrial
campaign of the 1990s to achieve "quality" is intended to revitalize the
U.S. economy by making work be done as it should be, that is, in a
way that conforms to the standards and ideals of the owners and executives. These efforts typify the way this path is used to revitalize a society

or organization through clarifying and repropagating the principles on which it was built.[9]

The path begins in the revival of belief in the courage, thus single-mindedness, to demand that the foundational beliefs of the organization be lived. It may begin with an effort to recover the radical, core belief or with insisting on an expanded interpretation of the maintained truths. The majority of the Protestant revivals began with the first approach, more or less as returns to fundamental beliefs. The American Revolution, following the second route, was a demand that the foundations of British law be applied to the colonies. The path is often considered by its followers to have a spiritual base, sometimes patriotic or religious. It is always patrilogical, following from first principles.

The ideal form of this path begins with the awareness of the principles to be established, raised by a sense that something is wrong. Once the "error" is located, the problem is embodied by a champion who will lead the crusade. So George Washington did not initiate the American Revolution, nor did the recent drive for high productivity in the United States come from the captains of industry or government. Washington, Martin Luther King, and Bill Hewlitt and David Packard all inherited their missions from a political constituency or other leaders currently in the field. Here the charismatic leader is the instrument of propagation, not of invention. The leader's task is to mobilize efforts to introduce change. In some cases, the leader will assume a prophetic role and appeal to the true believers. In other, more liberal developments, the leader's work will exemplify the principle, as was done with the good worker Shakhanov, whom Stalin made into the hero of Russian industrialization prior to World War II.

The leader's work begins with an organization having a vision of a desired future. Assuring that there is a vision is the first responsibility of the leader. Once it is clearly articulated, the second responsibility is to gain commitment to the core idea from the members or citizens. This is essentially an indoctrination process through which the articulated principles are passed down through the organization. The leader must be a role model and embody, or at least appear to embody, the desired attitudes and behaviors. Indoctrination is a conservative task—setting boundaries and direction. Typically, it is directed by a group of executives acting as disciples, magnifying the image of their charismatic leader. An important role is cleansing the organization of dissonant ideas and activities that have accumulated, in some cases, from contact with alien cultures, in others, from prior leaders and activities. Some of the dissonant material is reinterpreted and some is simply rejected, resulting in a more orderly structure.

The embodiment of the refined structure is celebrated by the adoption of new symbols, titles, and organizational forms. These new symbols contribute to the acceptance of the revitalized image. In some organizations, acceptance is gained through a charismatic presentation, in others, by being propagated down through the authority structure. The next, and often concurrent, step is implementation. The people—citizens, labor, members—participate in realizing the clarified mission by taking on assigned work, allocating resources, solving problems, adapting designs, and evaluating results. By this means, the community's culture is revitalized and cleared of old practices and beliefs—demythologized in the service of acting clearly. Wallace (1966, p. 160) suggests "the basis of [revitalization's] appeal is the attractiveness of identification with a more highly organized system, with all that this implies in the way of self-respect." This top-down path that the executive RJ was following is illustrated in Diagram 4.4 as an inversion of the spirit path depicted in the Navajo sand painting.

The diagram indicates the entry onto the path in the confrontation of some perception indicating a deviance from the principles of the entity. The perceptions may be as simple as "our quality is poor compared with that of the Japanese" or "there is discrimination in hiring" or "our economy is threatened by the Iraqi takeover of Kuwait." The mission is identified as a confrontation with a current policy that threatens the system and must be taken up by an individual, or by a group, or by the defenders of the establishment. This confrontation is the occasion for change or, as seen from the perspective of leadership, an occasion for correction of the behavior of the system back toward its principles. So far, this is a monistic path, conserving the established truths. It is a path to the right of center[10] and one I identify with a patrilogical, masculine mode of operation. The leadership for the first portion of the path is usually masculine, usually people in the executive ranks who are strongly identified with the organization or government. I present this as a definition of the revitalization; it appears as well to be the typical behavior in U.S. political and commercial organizations.

The second half of the path is gaining acceptance and concrete procedures for the new "corrections" in the way things are to be done. Acceptability is achieved in the social reality and subsequently develops a yield in the practical world of products and services. "Yield" is a key notion. The desired outcomes of revitalization, both overt and covert, are encompassed in the range of meanings of *yield*: the product in goods or services; a repayment for having provided resources; a surrender, "handing over" and "devoting" oneself to someone; and, finally, giving away under force or stress and therefore "losing."

Diagram 4.4 The Path of Revitalization

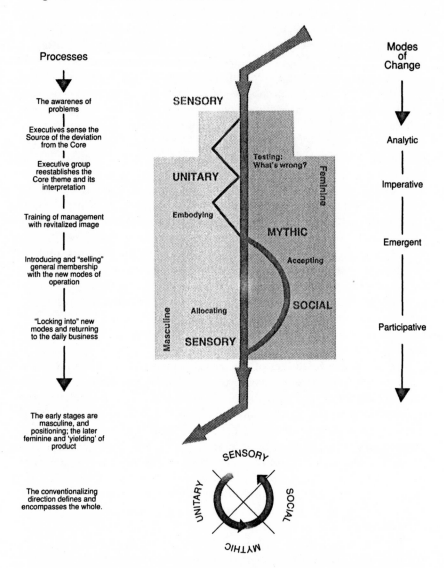

Implementation takes place in a pluralistic environment representing the variety of values and situations to which the principled design must accommodate. The Navajo depicted this pluralistic portion with the multiple strands of a *rainbow* to convey a sense of the diversity. In this revitalization path, the rainbow portion symbolizes acceptance and the distribution of resources. With acceptance by the people involved, the process continues on the path toward implementation and testing, completing realization of the orthodox interpretation into the sensory world. This stage is the more earthy, responsive, and feminine aspect of the path. It is often introduced by the human resources elements of a corporate or agency staff or, in the peasant village, by the women. The last stage is managed by the supervisors, the overseers of the laboring force, who are caught in the middle and held responsible for the realization.

This was clearly the path taken by the new American Republic as it settled with the new orthodoxy of Jacksonian democracy. It is the common path for the high-energy change efforts in U.S. industrial management practices that have been occurring during the last decade as discussed in Peters and Waterman's *In Search of Excellence* (1982). David Hurst (1986) described the path in rich detail in his article "Why Strategic Management Is Bankrupt." It is now frequently labeled "organizational transformation" (OT) as in John Adams's *Transforming Work* (1984) and Levy and Merry's (1986) survey of OT.

This OT is portrayed in dozens of books on planning. Peter Harris's handbook for senior managers presents a typical listing of the stages:[11]

1. changing the corporate philosophy, ideals, and ideas that the organization lives by;
2. transforming organizational identity;
3. changing purposes and standards, values, and norms;
4. revolutionizing corporate processes and activities;
5. changing career development patterns;
6. transforming organizational relationships through team participation, trust, openness, and authenticity; and
7. transforming recognition and reward, care for health and ego needs of workers, actualizing employee potential.

The first three stages are monistic, beginning with the exploration of principles. This exploration typically is fundamentally conservative, returning to the roots of the organization. These stages may appear to clear (purify) the path from that root or may produce a more mythic resymbolization of the organization's principles. In either case, the process reestablishes boundaries and, in particular, separates itself from those who have "contaminated" its image or who have been associated with the old images that are now rejected. Revitalization is established by such resetting of the organization's identity.[12]

The last four stages are pluralistic, designed to enhance the yield of the organization. They are accomplished by constructing a fit between the policies derived from the organization's principles and the needs of managers and of workers. The result is that the workers are able to carry out the design of the organization more effectively than they would have when the image and purpose were less clearly articulated and symbolized.[13]

The path is not always coolly pursued. Revitalization may impose revolutionary changes, as in the expansionary socialist takeovers that ripped apart the Third World in midcentury, as in the apparently quite different case of the liberation theology movement whose change efforts for social justice were also based in doctrine. In that case, the Christian beliefs called for liberation of the person, particularly women and the poor. Liberation theology strongly exemplifies the revitalization path—beginning in Christian doctrine, led as a charismatic movement (in both the political and the religious senses), and expressed through the person and the community. Whereas the typical use of this path in U.S. industry emphasizes the masculine aspect of the path that embodies the policy, the liberation theology emphasizes empowering the people to correct errors in the allocation of social goods—a distributive function more associated with the feminine. Nevertheless, both efforts exemplify revitalizing transformations carried out to increase *yield* in one or more senses of that word.

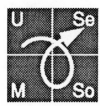 RENAISSANCE

Lewinian Change, Open Systems Planning

A journey along the renaissance path may be initiated when a person, organization, or society senses that its efforts are without meaning, that the criteria for choosing one outcome versus another are inadequate, that not enough energy can be marshalled to go forward in the resolution of an issue, and that the forces that hold a membership together have drained away. So the American society began to fall apart in 1930 and 1931. On a daily basis, so do marriages, corporate entities, and communities lose their meaning. Whole communities such as the South Bronx, Brooklyn, and Newark signify the loss of spirit of their minority populations as they trash the space that denies their dignity. Most often, systems simply decay, as a marriage does when the children have left, as a city does after its sources of wealth collapse, or as NASA did when its high mission succumbed to political squabbling. The path begins with "a little death," an awareness that the organizing energy has failed. Often it continues along this decline until all the spirit has left the system and the little death becomes terminal. In other cases, the members awake, encouraged by a possibility of rebirth.

This path of death and rebirth (Diagram 4.5) has been chronicled since earliest mythic times. While it appears opposite to revitalization, it is not simply a "change from the bottom up." It is Jonah's journey through the belly of the Whale and Ulysses' epic voyage after the destruction of Troy. It is Jesus' return to Jerusalem for crucifixion and redemption. It is a private path taken by many at midlife, beginning then for Dante, who found

> *Midway in our life's journey, I went astray from the straight road and awoke to find myself alone in a dark wood. How shall I say*
> *What a wood that was! I never saw so drear, so rank, so arduous a wilderness! Its very memory gives a shape to fear.*[14]

Less frequently but no more dramatically, the path is embarked upon by corporate giants such as Chrysler and AT&T. It is the path taken in the redevelopment of communities such as the city of Newark and once or twice in a millennium by a major power such as France 200 years ago and the Soviet Union and Eastern Europe today.[15]

The change begins when a person or people in the system can no longer hold together the structure of its current existence. Without principles appropriate to live by, the sensory world becomes a hell of indirection. Kurt Lewin called this first step, simply and undramatically, "unfreezing." That is, the letting go of now-meaningless structure signals the death of the system as a purposeful entity. Letting go is a political act that denies that the old principles can guide the entity. It obliterates the criteria that define problems and allows the boundaries of one's system to be breached in preparation for the return for a better start.

This more or less choiceful descent begins the "dark night of the soul" the Greeks called *nekyia*, in which the bonds of community and corporate existence dissolve in order for people to find a level of association, of organization, at which there is enough integrity to regroup and begin a new collective search for meaning. The trip may call for a metaphorical

Diagram 4.5 The Path of Renaissance

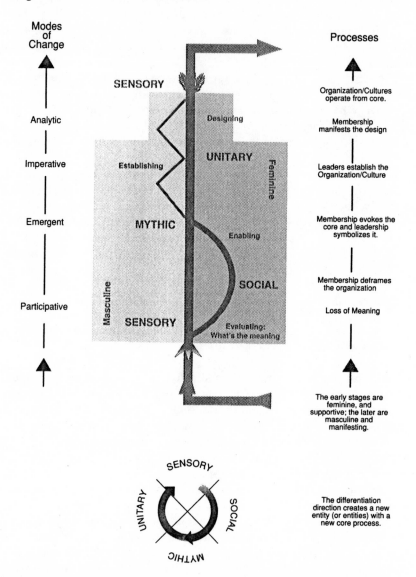

"forty days in the desert," or be a five years' journey a man takes to recover from the depression he encounters at midlife, or the decade it took the United States to come out of the mindless orgy of the 1920s. The degree of dissolution can vary from letting go of some unattainable goal, through dissolving a government, to giving up a way of life such as occurred with the end of state socialism in Eastern Europe. A couple may have decided on a divorce, a person may have let go of a subpersonality, a company may have merged with another, or a community may have given up some tattered image of itself. In a variety of cultures, this portion of the change process is one of disintegration into fragments (as was the case with AT&T and, in an amusing parallel, the Egyptian demigod Osiris). There is no guarantee that a system will come out of the hell it has entered. If rebirth is guaranteed, then the path is not one of rebirth.

Regression leaves the person or social system without meaning, boundaries, or authority, without a clear version of its history or a vision of where it might go. There seems to be no way out. It appears to be a sinkhole but it serves as a space in which to entertain possible futures. The regression provides a "quiet before the storm"—a time for exploring, political positioning, floating trial balloons. Its occurrence was visible in the decades before the French and Russian revolutions turned violent. Regression also appears frequently in the corporate world during this era of mergers and takeovers. This is the period the Navajo identified with "living with the rainbow"—scattered like the light, diverse, ungrounded, and unapproachable. It may be hard to recognize such a period in the operations of a firm that is failing or in the mayhem of an inner city in self-destruction. Yet such a loss of meaning underlies bureaucratic obstructions, logjams in the legislatures, a company's repeated failure to bring new products to market as well as the gray years of a midlife depression.

There are a series of processes that carry a system through the crises of meaning. The first is deframing, getting rid of structures that had to do with the definition of the prior entity. In the corporate setting, this includes formal acts of divestiture, selling off noncentral business activities, reviewing market assumptions, and sloughing off principles of organization inherited from early stages of the organization's history. The second is mourning the passing of the old to make way for new configurations. Following ancient practice, a number of change professionals help individuals and organizations to let go of emotional attachment to the ways to which they have become accustomed. The third consists of exploring the values of those who are involved in a rebirth. An instrument of such exploration is a "search conference," so named by Fred and Merrelyn Emery (1996). These are community events, collections of people who, to the best of the organizer's information, represent those concerned with the presumed issues that are facing the failed/failing system. Although for overtly different purposes, such a collection would be invited by the Navajo singer to participate in the chant or to resolve a family issue.

The outcome of such events is a shared awareness of the values of those concerned. Occasionally, it may induce reframing, which itself may produce a resolution; such happy shortcuts are discussed below in the discussion of the dialectic path. More commonly, gaining shared values simply prepares the ground and identifies the potential members of a reemergent organization.

These processes are conducted within a setting of the social reality. The actors have given up mechanisms for allocation, for action in the practical world. The deframing has rejected the structures of the unitary mentality, and the energy has not yet collected for the mythic act of conception of a new core of ideation and activity.

There comes a time to collect the available energy and move on. The paleontologist and mystic Teilhard de Chardin (1960, p. 48) noted of his personal journey,

> At each step of the descent a new person was disclosed within me of whose name I was no longer sure, and who no longer obeyed me. And when I had to stop my exploration because the path faded from beneath my steps, I found a bottomless abyss at my feet, and out of it came—arising I know not from where—the current which I dare call my life.

While the preparation is often a hellish experience—uncovering that which has been hidden, removing scabs on old negligences and misdeeds, exposing prejudices—Teilhard de Chardin suggests that the rebirth can be indescribably enlivening. The reborn person or organization chooses a program of action, returns to daylight, and goes on to build the structure that will allow it to affect the sensory world. The renewed organization is thus founded, and Lewin's refreezing begins. This is a mythic occasion, creative and evolutionary, and, in general, unpredictable from prior conditions.

A fine example of discarding baggage initiated the development of the microelectronics technology that underpins all our current computer and communication machinery. There is a tale, perhaps apocryphal, from the 1950s about designing a vastly miniaturized computer to be used in fighter planes. Two groups of engineers were assigned to redo the physical design of computers. One team "deframed" the image of a computer by rejecting the impression that its electronic functions need to be separate from its structure. The team members asked, for example, why an induction coil had to be wound around a form; could not the wires be self-supporting by winding them in glue and could not condensers and resistors form the frame that supported the vacuum tubes? By eliminating the separate material support, the engineers were able to save half the weight of a computer. The second group "deframed" all the way down to the basic level of electronic phenomena, asking the question: "How many electrons are needed to carry messages reliably?" The answer was many orders of magnitude less than had been assumed in the old habits of thinking derived from working on electrical machines. This destructuring idea led to the recognition that so little current is needed that the wire could be replaced by a thin film of metal painted on a sheet of plastic. Realization of this new core idea allowed the engineers to reduce the size and weight by 10 times. This insight provided the first step toward the incredibly compact printed circuits that now make up computing devices hundreds of thousands of times lighter than in the designs of the 1950s.

From such an initiating core idea, an organization is generated to realize the product in the physical reality. The processes of design explore among alternative forms for those that give the greatest comparative advantage. Ideally, this is done by creating and proposing various comparative (and frequently competitive) scenarios that have the potential to realize the ideal scenario. Each is tested against assumptions about the future environments within which the new organization would grow. This design process is done with a unitary worldview, one responsive to the needs for power and authority.

In the rebirth, a new self-concept is formed; a community gains an identity, a core process[16] is created that drives it. The core process is the essential "doing" of a created entity, a construction arising out of a mythic reality. It is pure action, generative, such as the idea of *painting wires*. Mission and goal statements are dualistic inasmuch as they presume a separation of the current and future states. The core statement is an image around which an ideal scenario is evolved. The core could lead to a new organization, the resolution of a major issue, or a normative plan that sets the expectations of a community for its rebirth. It also could be a technological idea around which a total effort is organized.

Whereas a revitalization is conventionalizing, the renaissance process is differentiating. Even in a pure form, it calls for paradoxical thinking. It does not provide participation as used in patrilogical organizations. Ideally, a group creates the design through all its stages to implementation. There is no need to transfer the design out of the hands of the originators, usually a staff group or top managers, to those who would be "participatively" involved; they already "own" it. We do not have a common language to differentiate between the two modes of involvement—the one in which members participate in the design created by others and that in which they manifest their own collective work. The two processes share many common elements as they both move through all the realities. But there is a radical difference in the power relations that arise because of the inverse relations between what is accepted and what is controlled in the two modes. Revitalization yields a product or, in personal terms, the members yield their product to the monistic leadership; renaissance manifests a product or the members express their joint pluralistic power. No better examples of such expression could be found than the emergence of the free governments in Czechoslovakia and Hungary in the fall of 1989.

The two paths that flow from the differentiating and conventionalizing strategies are infrequently experienced in a near pure form within organizations or in the community at large. To illustrate the great differences in the processes, I provide a detailed example of a differentiating process in a rather simple community development issue.

Open Systems Planning:
The Site Selection Issue

Open Systems Planning (OSP) was developed in the early 1970s to facilitate the creation of high-performing manufacturing plants and, secondarily, for community development.[17] The ideas emerged, initially, out of the ways in which groups of workers evolved the organization of their own jobs. In a seminal case, the ideas emerged from the way a group of warehousemen brought on and trained new "buddies." The emergence of such organizing ideas in a number of manufacturing sites and community projects paralleled the process I here identify as the path of renaissance.[18] What had begun as a local invention in response to the failures of the managers grew to be modern examples of this ancient pattern.

I introduce a simple example of OSP in a community to illustrate the differentiating process, focusing on the emergence and acceptance of the core process as the instrument through which resolution was achieved. The three phases illustrated in this case are

1. descent (individuating to shed the contrivances of the conflict)
2. re-creation of a core meaning
3. transcendence of conflict and articulation of the design

The presenting issue on this occasion was the need to resolve a long-standing racial and community conflict regarding the location of a new community college in Los Angeles. The conflict had prevented progress in establishing the campus for more than 10 years. The intensity of the conflict arose from the presence of three ethnic groups who would be served by the college for each of whom it would fill quite different practical and symbolic functions. The Black population had been the major force in getting the city to authorize a new college in the district, but the geography of the areas suggested that the school be located in the Mexican American neighborhood. The Black and Mexican American groups saw the college as facilitating their first two years of education prior to entering a university. The Anglo population, on the other hand, wanted it to offer continuing education for older adults to resume degree programs interrupted years earlier. Their need supported placing the campus away from the town center. The entire community shared only a need for a symbolic gesture of respect from the county education officials. The struggle among the community leaders in prior years had left bitterness both within the community and toward the Education Department. Those responsible for coping with the bitterness and resolving the issue were the administrators of this college that had been growing in storefronts and office buildings scattered around the town center. I was working with a small consulting group that provided the guidance through this issue-resolving retreat.

Phase I: Descent. The work began with an overview of the process to identify the requisite set of participants for this event. The prime consideration in selecting the participants was political, both to resolve the issue and to communicate the outcome to the various stakeholders—in the terms used here, to gain authorization to destructure the issue. The college administrators identified a set of people who would cover the range of the politically involved as well as most of the functional groups of students, teachers, grounds men, and so on. Because this was a public issue, media representatives had to be invited to present the event live on TV and report it in the newspapers. An assumption of the retreat is that, with deep enough preparation, any one person could speak for the community. A broad representation had to be formed, however, both to avoid any impression of favoritism or bias and to provide the participative mass through which to gain acceptance of the resolution. Representation did not have to be balanced as none of the processes required voting. In this case, the major power figures, such as the members of the board of education, were not invited so as to make it easier to release the constraints on working with alternatives. The initial list of participants called for about 60 people, larger than optimal for the process, but we expected that many of the volunteers would not stay through the entire process. This group, labeled "the core group," was to form the heart (*cœur*) of the process.

The first phase took place over a two-and-a-half-day weekend in a site isolated from interruptions and open to the natural outdoors. The participants stayed together Friday evening, from early morning until late evening on Saturday, and through the whole of Sunday. The work the first evening was training and preparatory. It raised awareness of the immediate situation of each individual in relation to his or her environment and the tenor of relations with each organization in it. The participants each presented their worldviews to a group of the others, talking from large sheets of paper on which they had graphically presented their images.

This experience was "of the rainbow" of individual values. The exercise was evoked by having them all search for personal *peak experiences* (in Maslow's sense of the term) in their encounters with education and then identify the values that were in those experiences. Then they strengthened their appreciation of those values by developing an ideal scenario of some future experience in which those values were accentuated. With this base, they created images of themselves as moving toward their ideal educational worlds. The exercise concluded with each person sharing his or her self-image on the path toward the ideal. Phase I was a preparation for the mythic, enabling processes that would lead to formulation of a sense of their collective core processes as they applied to personal development and education. It was an individuating experience, encouraging them to focus away from the traditional values of their community and on their own emergent ones.

The first evening then served a double purpose along the overall path to resolution. It trained the group to identify core values and processes, and it "destructured" the community as present in the room. This is shown in Diagram 4.6 by the larger movement from the sensory into the social reality. The individuation process re-creates an image of self at a level below the community to allow the community to be reformed around a common objective—in this case, the community college. By exposing the participants to the mythic work on them-

Diagram 4.6 Site Selection: Phase I

selves, as shown by the miniature of the total path in the diagram, we anticipated the work of the second phase.

Phase II: Re-creation. The second phase, accomplished over two weekends, focused directly first on creating a core process for the community college and secondarily on finding the location that best suited that process.

When the search for the core process began, the group was as divided on the college's mission as it was on the location. The professionals and school board authorities had thoroughly argued the question, as well as the location issue, without achieving agreement on a specific mission or site. In the opening step of this search, the participants made a vast graphic collage of the siting of the nascent college, which disclosed

1. the intermingling of students with shoppers, workers, and street people
2. the confusion, noise, and liveliness
3. the lack of identity of programs and of the college itself
4. the lack of focus on studies and energy for new learning among the students

In the second step of Phase II, the group extracted critical events in the schools and the community's history and identified the values implicitly expressed in these events. Some saw the school rising out of the community college traditions, some out of the early agricultural foundings of the region, some out of the ethnic histories, and still others could not go back beyond the issues current at the time of their own enrollment. A particular awareness was that the college related more to the older citizen than to either the younger adults or the academic professionals.

The third step was designed to bring out stereotypes of what the ideal campus should be: a new Cambridge or Ivy League school, a vocational school of the 1920s, or a continuing "Chautauqua." The participants' commitment to the traditional models illustrated the normal regression to the familiar when one is under stress. To again destructure their thinking, we projected the group into the future to envision the events of a day on the new campus. They manifested these images in a series of playlets of campus life in such settings as a parking lot, a classroom, a coffeehouse, the admissions office, a faculty office, on a path early in the morning and returning again in the dark evening. From these embodiments, the group identified a variety of needs: personal safety, hospitality, privacy for and access to the faculty,

Diagram 4.7 Clustering Confluence

definitions of the curriculum, and involvements specific to the various age groups that would make up the student body.

From these disparate graphic images emerged a common sensing of the ways people wanted to feel on the campus. These were uncovered by asking the groups to talk of their feelings as they imaged functioning in the various settings. The dominant image was one of both confluence and differentiation representing, as in Diagram 4.7, a core process, labeled a "clustering confluence"—the image itself was more impactful for the group than any verbal label. While the image was recognized as close to that of a "cluster college" that had been widely recognized by the professionals, it arose out of the group's sense of their own emotional, physical, and educational needs. One critical feature of this image was that it differentiated on dimensions central to educational processes—access to information, privacy, freedom to cluster—rather than on age or racial background.

The group had settled on this core image of confluence. At the following break, a large poster of the image was drawn and hung in front of the hall. This was the symbolic rebirth of the college/community interface—a mythic event. With a core focus established, we turned to the issue of site.

Three sites were in contest: (a) A compact site located in the midst of an older part of the community needing renewal was highly accessible to all potential students but was in a racially segregated area. (b) The current temporary site commingled with the shops and offices of the city was an advantageous and enlivening setting for all the various age groups but was not integrating well with the needs of the merchants. It would be inexpensive but least able to provide the distinctive "college" environment. (c) A hilltop site above the shopping district, distant from the older residential areas, would require considerable reorganization of public transportation and utilities but, in the end, would be a "proper," stereotypical location for a campus.

Each site had advantages and disadvantages for each community group. The racial segments, planners, politicians, and academics were at odds on every aspect of the project. The decision provided a classic example of selection among alternatives where none was accepted as dominant on the most important criteria. The failure to resolve the issues had held up building for several years already, and evidence of the rancor appeared in a variety of minor protests, demands, and staged "walk-outs" during the session. To form the newly accepted core image of the campus, however, old priorities had been set aside and the rational processes that had supported the argumentative modes had been replaced by a search for a unifying image. The participants' ideas of the physical plant were as varied as had been the image of the educational processes, ranging from storefront to imitation Gothic. The various advocates were not conscious of the source of these images and thus could not argue for them. A second destructuring process was initiated to bring awareness of the sources and thus free the participants of their unconscious control. The two emerging designs are shown in Diagram 4.8 in the two arrows emerging from the mythic into the unitary.

We raised awareness of the sources of particular images of the campus through a series of four exercises with toys selected to show how individuals' preferences were based in their dominant realities. We organized small groups that wandered from one set of "toys" to another, sharing the ideas and feelings that were evoked. For example, the traditional worldview was evoked by having the participants play with sets of children's fine oak blocks. The play evoked towers, castles, grand gates— all manner of majestic structures that were clearly related to high regard for European origins of the university tradition and a wish to keep the intellectual experience elevated above daily commerce. Cutting and forming large piles of styrofoam scraps evoked mythic fantastical images, and bits of fabrics, leaves, sticks, rocks and other natural objects evoked sensory

Diagram 4.8 Site Selection: Phase II

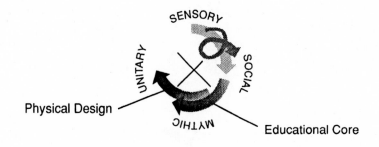

and social images. Sharing these expressions freed the participants of their (unconscious) attachments, allowing them to create designs in line with the desired educational process. So prepared, groups were then organized by their academic interests—arts, sciences, humanities, and administrative studies—which again indicated that there was an unrecognized parallel between their academic and architectural preferences and their dominant worldviews.

With their "clustering" preferences acknowledged, the final design exercise dealt with "confluent" aspects such as welcoming, directing, finding sustenance, transportation, solitude, and congregation. This was done by laying out a great "map" covering the whole floor and walking through it to gain an embodied feeling of the relation among the functions. With little further discussion, the need for an easy flow between functions made it clear that the site in the center of the city, interwoven with commerce, was unworkable. It disappeared from consideration.

The educational plan could be realized on either of the two remaining sites. But the very act of planning the meetings destructured the political situation that had locked in the conflict. First, the media coverage of the event led the board of education to express greater interest in the new campus and, in the intervening week, the board acknowledged there was sufficient money available to make the hilltop campus feasible. Then, perhaps because of the openness of the process, the supporters of the original site in the Black neighborhood admitted that issues of zoning and land title seriously clouded its availability. With that admission, the charge of racial bias in the site selection just simply disappeared from the conversation. There was a natural reframing and thus resolution of the issue.

Phase III: Transcendence (of the issue). With the disappearance of the unworkable racial issues, the transition to the selection and planning phase happened smoothly. As is typical in a transformative process, there was nothing left on which to focus conflict. Support for two of the alternatives had disappeared, so the group's energy focused on designing the new site in a manner appropriate to the education model. Those who had originally advocated the urban renewal site formed a task group to separately create a light industrial park with a trades-oriented high school annex, building on images arising in the earlier education discussions. Those interested in the commercial in-town site found involvement in the designing of the traffic flows between the hilltop site and the center. By the end of the second weekend of work, the group had established a unified policy for both the school board and the architects who would make the formal educational and physical designs. The two thrusts of core mission and site came together as is illustrated in the converging arrows that indicate that the process is being manifested in the sensory reality, as shown in Diagram 4.9.

The planning organization that emerged was a combination of the county community college board with community representatives, many of whom were registered in the college's programs. Its job was to carry forward the image created in the planning event. That is, it was to reify the mythic idea. Though financial obstructions continued to slow the progress, the core committee sustained the chosen themes all during the planning and construction phases.

This example is a rather straightforward exercise in resolution of a conflict through a renaissance path; the contrast with the ideal revitalization process is obvious. While the preceding description gives the sense of a smooth flow, the event was spiced with political infighting, public "uproars," and withdrawal of participation. There were reversals: hardening of positions that set back progress toward resolution and countermoves in conventionalizing directions, such as calling up legalistic issues. Power plays—changing the rules of the game—and proselytizing were common. Apparently, the strength of integration of the group process with the "core process" image sustained a resolution.

Mixing of modes of change appropriate to the two grand paths is itself a strategic alternative of great importance. I discuss the practices of interweaving the two paths in the course of a resolution before discussing the reduced paths.

Diagram 4.9 Site Selection: Phase III

INTERWEAVING OF PATHS

The two grand paths are fully experienced only in heroic times, in the revitalization or rebirth of a society. The normal behavior of a culture is to interweave the directions of change, differentiating and conventionalizing, that produce daily changes beginning with the most trivial levels. We infrequently experience enduring efforts in either direction. This is another way of saying our lives are seldom organized to achieve grand purpose. We will see intention expressed in the planning of a day, in laying out a new work process, in setting students their lessons, or, conversely, in stepping away from our routines to examine the habits and values that normally drive them without conscious choice. Somewhere in our lives, there will be efforts to clarify and revitalize an activity and, in another place, there will be efforts to break old perceptions and establish new meanings, but for the most part the directions of movement are mixed indiscriminately. This mixing of behaviors holds our life in place with an ongoing balancing. Roy Wagner (1975, pp. 52-53) identifies the balancing process as a dialectic,[19] commenting that

> differentiation and convention stand in a dialectical relationship to one another, a relationship of simultaneous interdependence and contradiction. This dialectic is the core of all human (and very likely all animal) cultures. As a way of thinking, a dialectic operates by exploiting contradictions against a common ground of similarity, rather than by appealing to consistency against a common ground of differences, after a fashion of rationalistic or "linear" logic. It follows that cultures that conventionally differentiate approach things with a dialectic "logic," whereas those that conventionally collectivize (like our own rationalistic tradition) invoke a linear causality.
>
> This dialectic has its own continuity built into it; whichever aspect an actor chooses as the control on his actions, whether he collectivizes or differentiates, he will counter-invent and "set up" the other aspect. Convention, which integrates an act into the collectivity, serves the purpose of drawing collective distinctions between the [given world] and the realm of human action. Invention, which has the effect of continually differentiating the conventional, continually puts together ("metaphorizes") and integrates disparate contexts.

This is the balance that maintains a culture in place. The balance tends to prevent either changes in structure or carrying new schemes into action. An accidental or systematic (heroic) imbalance in the interweaving is required to sustain a change program. There need to be substantial periods that are dominated by one or the other direction followed by a reversal for a change program to accumulate its results. This is evident in the growth of a child as well as in the development of a community. Both are sustained by a web of resolved conflicts.

Parenting and the Development of Community

The effect of the periodically interwoven path is nowhere better displayed than in the processes of bringing a child from infanthood to maturity. That path shows a daily shift from conventionalizing pressures to individuating opportunities. The changes the child undergoes cannot lead to maturity if both pressures are unremitting. The one forms structure on which the other builds an increasing self-sense. The alternations must be slow enough for work done moving in each direction to produce a distinct gain. Conventionalizing produces skills, language, sensory and social coordinations; differentiation produces powers of sensory and social discrimination, activation, confidence, and self-image. The one produces a social animal, the other an initiator. Turner (1974, p. 298) comments: "Man is both a structural and an anti-structural entity, who grows through anti-structure and conserves through structure." Too rapid alternation interferes with growth, effectively keeping the learning (change) at the first level, that is, on the first board. Too slow an alternation ends up producing its own dialectic; the child moves to the countering strategy. This timing is critical to growth as is illustrated in the difficulty in coming of age—coming through adolescence—during a period of high social change. And, of course, the rate of alternation must vary with the child's worldview.

The same balancing process is needed for social as well as individual development. A community, whether a remote village or a face-to-face work group, requires a similar balancing to grow—a period of growth followed by a consolidation. The more openly switches are made from one path to the other, the less will be the uncontrolled counterinvention. Uncontrolled counterinvention tends to send development into an eddy just as counterdependence in the child blocks the path to maturity.

The interweaving in these two settings illustrates the use of the two directions in a particular setting. A conventional structure provides the "vessel" for the differentiating process through which change occurs. Just as parents provide the vessel for the child, the governance process and traditions provide the vessel for the growth of new elements of community life. The roles of the conventionalizer are distinct from those of the differentiator. The sequential dominance of one or the other leads to change. The balanced interweaving supports the existing culture. One of the most pervasive and clearly established joint uses is in initiation rites through which organizations gain members.

Initiation Rites

The phrase *initiation rite* carries within itself the internal dialectic of interweaving. The term *rite* (which is akin to *rhyme*) carries a unitary, conventionalizing sense of the established way, the traditional rhythm of dance, processions, and marches; *initiation* implies a new beginning, differentiating a person from his or her past to create a new relation. It is a specific form of interweaving in which the two great paths are entered, as it were, at opposite ends simultaneously with the "processions" coming to meet in the center for consummation. It is an archetypal form of change in which the establishment stays the same, except for the moment of taking in "foreign matter." It is a critical process for maintaining a community or organization, though one that has fallen into disuse in most Western institutions. I use it to illustrate the systematic intertwining of the grand paths, particularly as an example of the joint process of revitalization and rebirth (Diagram 4.10).

Traditionally, initiations have been used to bring children into the adult community, new members into religious orders, men into military organizations, couples into marriage. All of these rites include the same three stages: separation, transition, and commitment.

The prototypical initiation begins with the organization preparing to accept new members. The community members begin secret preparations, the priest reaffirms the *Credo*, the military force parades in its finery, and, concurrently, the initiates are undergoing separation trials from their former roles and being indoctrinated with the traditions of the institutions they are about to join. During this period, they leave their familiar settings to reside in an antistructural, usually informal, egalitarian *communitas*. This is the beginning of the deframing of the renaissance cycle. To enable the initiate to throw off the protective covering of old habits and roles, an encompassing vessel is created by the initiating organization. This haven is provided by a strict hierarchical boundary between the new members and the facilitators, who control the process and safeguard those being initiated. Oddly, the task at this time is not to learn to conform, as it often appears in the popular literature, but to individuate. The initiate must be an individ-

Diagram 4.10 Initiation

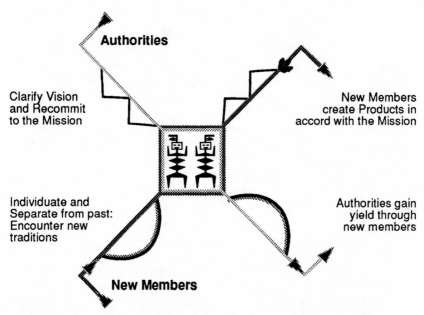

Initiation begins with the dual process of the authorities renewing commitment and the potential members separating out from their other world roles and individuating to allow them to "join" the organization as individuals. In the mystical initiation, the new members become one with the organization and produce "out-of-themselves" to provide the organization with its yield. This is the ideal "issue" of an initiation—each makes gains from the joining of the new members.

ual, with a sense of his or her own power to be able to "join." This is the reason for the various tests of manhood, whether killing a lion or passing comprehensive examinations. Thus the initiation process begins with simultaneous entry into the two grand paths: revitalization by the institution and renaissance by the new members-to-be.

The second stage of the joint journey is the merger; the contract is formed by taking oaths, signing agreements. The incorporation into the organization is a mythic generative event that transforms the individual. Its importance is recognized in the exchange of tokens (including blood), in the taking of new names, and in the formation of new organizational entities as occurs in the marriage ceremony. The initiates commit their new individuality to a belief system, and the institution takes the somewhat dangerous act of opening its boundaries to new members, that is, contracting with outsiders. At this point, the two paths entwine but continue on in their original directions as illustrated in the right side of Diagram 4.10.

The third stage is an enactment of the new roles within the authority of the institution, the consummation of the marriage, carrying out a "duty," producing "goods." When this is carried out properly, the institution has gained sustenance for its belief system and the individual has gained "meaning" as well as access to the resources of the organization.

This form of change is periodic, repeated at intervals more or less related to a sacred calendar, allowing the institutions to remain the same while the individual is changed—revitalization through an act of merging with the reborn. The process is carried out in a far less ritualistic manner in employing new people in a corporation or other social institution. We can get a better image of the employment process by comparing it with the initiation rite.

Coming into Employment

On most occasions, we hire a person to work in a organization, or admit a student to a school or a person to membership in an association, with little ceremony. A few rituals are carried out such as the affixing of signatures as required by the state. Financial obligations are assured, introductions to comembers are made, and the individual is given perfunctory explanations of the organization's goals and purposes. It is assumed that people know what is necessary for them to forward the mission of the organization. In the worst cases, one only needs to know simply to "do what you are told to do." But in organizations that are trying to change the relation of the employee to the work, to engage them in participating in its management, there is a far greater emphasis on the rites of passage into employment. The new employee both has to know what the company expects and has to be trained or indoctrinated into the requisite mode of work. In developing this deeper relation, both the company and the new employees go through rituals of revitalization and rebirth, sometimes at a trivial level, sometimes with deeply transformative effects. There needs to be some degree of individuation of the new employees. Without it, they lose their sense of individuality and thus their independence and ability to contribute to the company as a total human being.

The stages of initiation were well laid out in a program for adding new cohorts of employees to a small high-performing division of a large Canadian company.[20] There were a series of stages that clearly were revitalizing to the company and a path that had the ability to transform—rebirth—the new employees. The stages converge on the mutual accep-

Diagram 4.11 Rites of Employment

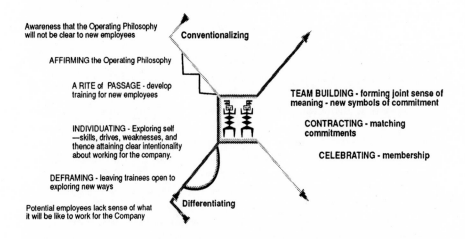

Awareness that the Operating Philosophy will not be clear to new employees

Conventionalizing

AFFIRMING the Operating Philosophy

A RITE of PASSAGE - develop training for new employees

TEAM BUILDING - forming joint sense of meaning - new symbols of commitment

INDIVIDUATING - Exploring self —skills, drives, weaknesses, and thence attaining clear intentionality about working for the company.

CONTRACTING - matching commitments

CELEBRATING - membership

DEFRAMING - leaving trainees open to exploring new ways

Potential employees lack sense of what it will be like to work for the Company

Differentiating

tance of worker and employment just as they do in the traditional initiation rite described in Diagram 4.10. Both management and the potential employees start with a sensory awareness of a problem; the company knows the workers will not be able to anticipate the demands of the cooperative teamwork, and the workers are often threatened by casual information they have received about new responsibilities they must take on. But beyond this common start in confusion, the two groups take diverging paths: the one conventionalizing, the other differentiating. They follow portions of the two great paths until they met in the contracting, the mythic founding step that allows work, that is, reification, growth, and generation of wealth. Diagram 4.11 presents these stages graphically as a rite of employment, a path exactly analogous to the initiation rite shown in Diagram 4.10. It, similarly, is a joining of the two grand paths. Following the joining of the paths—at the mythic point of conception—the new employees and related members of the organization establish the team as a "communitas," complete the work contract, and, ideally, celebrate.

The stages on the left are essentially separate. That is, the management of the company separately affirms its visions and organizes the training rituals. The new, or potential, employees must do their own individuating work separately, even though it is done within a "vessel" provided by the employer. The stages on the right side of Diagram 4.11 are the "coming together" that sanctions contributions to the product of the organization. In most situations, a management, usually the founding group, takes in the first group of employees with such a celebration but neglects to participate in further initiations. It is the wisdom of the great fraternal organizations, whether religious, spiritual, military, or craft based, to continue to reaffirm themselves and the individuality of the member with each new induction.

Failure in the Employment Process

This setting of the initiation rite points to a difficulty in using it as an employment process and to a more serious failing in our employment process programs in general. They both arise from failing to recognize the differing worldviews of the individual employees and mismatching the path of the training processes to the flow of the initiation rite.

The first issue, that of the differences in various qualities of the new employees, has long been recognized in the selection of people, but the importance of their worldview has become particularly significant since the first high-performing organizations began calling for employees who could work with a new "paradigm" variously labeled "open systems," "system thinking," or "team based." These modes of work relation call for a generally volitional mind-set, using both mythic and social realities. The workers are expected to take initiative, work with and respect others in their teams, and understand that they are responsible for what happens in their immediate environments. Without an understanding of the characteristics of the alternative realities, it is easy to confuse these values with the holistic values of the unitary reality. The outcome is unfortunate, for people of the unitary mind-set do not thrive in an open system environment, becoming disoriented by the frequent need to adjust. They eventually focus on getting tighter boundaries on their work conditions. Because management will not provide such boundaries, say, in the form of supervision, employees often resort to a third party, the labor union, to provide that structure.

The second danger arises from the design and execution of the employment process. If it is treated basically as a training process, it will produce a conventionalizing change, from the employee's initial lack of understanding to a definitive and habituated image of the work. Initially, the training appears to support the worker as a member of a team, but it fails to support the volitional aspect. It is thus an indoctrination into a belief system, not a rite of passage. Such work units rapidly deteriorate because they have neither the form of a unitary operation nor the volitional worldview. Unfortunately, this is a common outcome because the training profession and personnel functions tend to support conventionalizing changes.

While this misapplication of the conventionalizing approach causes particularly difficult mismatches during a period of great cultural change, it is a dysfunctional aspect of any structuring process. The very act of creating and diffusing new processes eventually counterinvents the need to bring in disciples and followers who will conform to the founder's ideals. Only by re-creating the organization with every new member is it possible to avoid the decay of conventionalization. The initiation rite was created to avoid the horns of the dilemma of chaos versus decadence, to reaffirm the existing and to give birth to the new simultaneously. It is a grand compromise. There are lesser compromises in which a clear differentiating or conventionalizing path is pursued, but incompletely. These, which I call *reduced paths*, are the topic of the next section.

Before going on to reduced paths, I mention one other joint use of the two paths that is commonly embarked on as a compromise or a "pressure release valve." In a large ongoing organization or society, it typically appears wholly infeasible to risk destruction of the whole in the deframing retreat that is central to the renaissance path. In such cases, the leader, an executive group, or the board of directors will undertake such a retreat within the "vesseling" of an outsider whom they trust to contain the regression. The grand path is completed, at least in summary form in the executive group, and a revitalizing message is brought back to the full organization to be inaugurated by a conventionalizing indoctrination. This is a rebalancing process used to manage an ongoing organization or society. It is one of the many devices for managing conflict by periodic renewals or inversions, such as saturnalias, in which the lower levels of the organization are briefly allowed the privileges of the senior levels. In saturnalias, such as the original Mardi Gras, the poor blame the rich for the day, make the laws, and repress the upper classes—and all is forgotten the next morning. In today's "saturnalia," the workers are given carefully restricted discretions over matters once decided by managers to provide the workers a sense of power in exchange for being controlled in the rest of matters of common concern. I return to discuss these processes in greater detail in Chapter 5 in the section on culture-forming processes.

These paired uses, under the best circumstances, achieve a rebirth within the existing structure. Moses' trip onto Mount Sinai is an example of the leader's retreat followed by his return to revitalize his people. The attempt to use such mixed strategies also points to the difficulty of their use in corporate America. The executives may create a powerful new image "on retreat" but have great difficulty selling it "back home." This path is often taken by OD professionals who see it as a safe way to achieve large-scale changes.

REDUCED PATHS

The grand paths of resolution form the ground of intentional change strategies. But the vast majority of the change efforts undertaken by organizations and community leaders is done along the reduced paths that involve some but not all of the stages of a grand path. Between the grand paths and the variety of reduced paths, I think we will find almost all the processes of resolution used in Western cultures. We have labels for many of these processes, although a general classification scheme has not been devised. Case examples abound in our records of sociopolitical history, community and organizational studies, and tales of family life. I don't catalog the variety here, but I illustrate the way in which all these schemes can be understood as reduced versions of the great paths described above.

In developing this work, I classified popular schemes of change into four groups. Two basic reduced forms, *systems analysis* and *pluralistic development,* include the majority of approaches used today in rationalistic and democratic societies. Two others I consider extreme forms. One is the *dialectic,* which is extreme in the sense that it recognizes only the social and unitary realities, thus excluding any creations or changes that involve the physical world. The dialectic paths are ideological paths central to sociopolitical issues that are avoided in most U.S. political and corporate efforts. The other extreme form is the *creative.* It is an extreme in that it is not properly a path of resolution. It is better treated as a setting of conditions out of which new ideas arise and work in the appropriate reality. This organization leaves out a few forms of importance such as demagogical changes that are imposed in a dictatorial manner and, very likely, a number that I have overlooked or that I have not yet identified as distinct paths.

I have chosen to describe the four groups briefly. Originally, I had planned to make these descriptions the major part of this work, but I increasingly realized that there was no way to stop short of a vast catalog of paths and the involved methods. Other writers have already done this task well. I decided it was better to give the space to the theory of intentional change and resolution.

 CREATIVE

Entrepreneurialism

Creative paths originate on the fifth board. We see the "destinations" as new meanings, new structures and rules, new techniques of play. We don't see the creative act. We see symbols that close the seams between dissonant cultures; we see new organizations that focus efforts on a task; and we see machines and programs that transform resources. So creative paths lead to all manner of resolutions. What makes them special is the originality of the responses, the ability to find a solution where there was nothing before that would have resolved the issues. But a creative response to an issue of conflict must be more than an idea. It must be established in the ongoing system without creating counterinventions, in spite of the fact that the very birth of the idea requires instability, and then, in turn, the idea further destabilizes the environment in which it was nurtured.

A creative endeavor can work from either direction. Typically, we think of an invention as a differentiating act, something coming from nothing, pushing its way into consciousness, but much ingenuity appears as "repackaging," as an object is transformed into *found art* by the act of noticing and labeling it. The conception typically appears within a mythic context, but it can be manifested in any other reality. An idea may gain its first impact through persuasion, by gaining a following; it may appear as an physical object that "works" in a sensory world; or it may engage others in a process of codevelopment. So, regardless of the direction by which the idea is born, the critical process is how an idea gets accepted within the reality of those involved in the issue at hand. This is the critical question for a meta-praxis, but first let me briefly discuss the creative process itself.

Preparation and Incubation

There must be preconditioning before one sets out on a creative path, activities that prepare the individual to play with ideas. By definition, the sources of these ideas cannot be specified in advance. No

research has found any optimal sources of ideas or any degree of association between the areas of study, the problem area, or the degree of
immersion, but studies do indicate that most creative geniuses have
been deeply knowledgeable both about their immediate issues and
about many other apparently unrelated topics. After the fact, we can
see that the unrelated topics often provide knowledge of structures
that are analogous to the solutions at which the creative person often
arrives through totally unexpected associations. A perfect example in
this context is the tale of Einstein doing his armchair experiment of riding on a light wave to imagine what we would see traveling at "the
speed of light." In addition to being deeply trained in physics, he had
retained memories of his boyhood delight with swinging and riding. I
don't include the acquisition of knowledge in the path of resolution
because it is simply the whole of one's past (and it seems unnecessary
to identify it as part of the resolution effort).

The beginning of the path is best identified as the point of taking on
the problem or feeling the conflict, as illustrated in the inception of
both the great paths. Following recognition of the issues, the creator
typically continues to prepare, including making efforts to "find" a solution. The focus on the outcome, however, is likely to be interrupted
by counterinvention, by intrusions into the work that prematurely test
the ideas or allow other irrelevant fears to block the problem solving
(as experienced before the entry into either grand path). At some
point, a person recognizes that he or she will not find the solution
within the reality within which he or she is working and moves into
the "asylum" of mythic reality.

The mythic work takes place within an asylum, a vessel that protects the effort from intrusion by messages from other worldviews.
The asylum can be a literal hideout from the world's activity or it may
be the vessel composed of irrelevant activities—the proverbial
"shower bath" wherein some of the contents of this book first appeared to me or "a walk in the park." The structuring of the asylum
allows the creator to play freely across all the visions of reality, to create hypothetically in each reality to form the image that will resolve
the issue when exported back to its proper domain. Some of this work
may be "vesseled" within the unconscious to protect it from our internal judges—such as Freud's superego. Maxine Junge's study of writers and painters (1991) provides evidence that some artists create their
own asylums, shells of worldviews that provide a balance of
worldviews surrounding an intense and private monistic world. The
mythic activity may also be vesseled by shifting to a metaphorical
realm where the known constraints of the problem are inoperative,
thus giving free reign to the imagination. Einstein did this in his "arm-

chair experiments." We all play metaphorically to a degree when we think "as if . . ." Also, we build models of the issue to allow us to systematically introduce the outside world at a pace that we can manage without losing our sense of mythic freedom. We even work the problem of understanding the creative path by modeling it.

Prigogine's theory of the *emergence of self-organizing systems in environments far from the equilibrium* is an idea I can use both as an example of metaphor as well as to explore what is going on in the mythic world used as the first step of the creative path. The equilibrium system of worldviews is one in which there is a random mixture between the conventionalizing and differentiating forces. Neither one nor the other is allowed to be pursued long enough to establish a trend or stable change in the environment. For a new organization or idea to emerge, there needs to be freedom from interruption while the new idea emerges and "sets." Erecting an asylum provides a protective conventional "umbrella" over the differentiating thrust. The umbrella provides a space and time during which the creators can play in metaphorical spaces, proposing solutions, detailing future scenarios, even surreptitiously testing them in other realities. Philip Slater (1974, p. 166) comments: "Insulation allows independent evolution so that when exposure does come what is exposed has meaning and impact." A grand example of such an umbrella was that erected over Kelly Johnson's "Skunk Works," the secret design shop at Lockheed from which came so many of the design ideas for military aircraft in the 1940s and 1950s. The secrecy gave Kelly and his team the freedom to design new aircraft without all the "yes, buts . . ." that normally block development in situations of "near equilibrium" of which government bureaucracies are prime examples. This umbrella plays a role here similar to the vessel that envelopes new initiates as they individuate.

Creating Belief

The need for an umbrella is dual. It is not just to protect the fragile, fledgling concept but also to protect the environment of the issue from the disruption of novelty. Issues are not solved by new ideas but by their acceptance into the context of the issue. It is unusual that an important idea will enter a conflictful environment without further disturbing the situation. Even those that come "uncalled for," such as the automobile, the electronic computer, or HDTV, disrupt the fabric of the society. Others, such as Marx's version of socialism or an innovative tax in a depressed economy, which respond to identified issues, are likely to be disruptive because such extreme ideas seldom have acquired a sufficient (conventionalizing) umbrella to protect either the new solution or the portions of the population that will feel most attacked by its introduction. There seems to be a "you can't get there from here" situation that renders the best ideas unusable when they are introduced at the time they are most needed. This was our feeling in the mid-1970s when the new open systems of organization met so much resistance.

The strategic problem is creating belief without producing undue counterinvention. An invention, technical or social, has the potential of "tilting the playing field" as it can change the rules of game. As in the introduction of an innovation such as HDTV, there are impacts in every part of the society, and those of each reality respond at different rates and with different motivations.

Creative ideas that affect unitary systems encounter the fear that the idea is original—meaning, outside of the established principles—so resistance is to be expected. There is also the "Galileo problem" in which the authority system's leaders already understand the invention—in his case, discovery of Jupiter's moons—but cannot admit the new knowledge until they find a way to introduce it without exposing any essential principle to doubt. For those in the economic (sensory) systems, the reaction and delays come while they reevaluate alternatives and search for advantage in the new situation. And for the social, there will be uncertainty about how relationships will be affected. Any significant creation has to be integrated into institutions spanning the whole range of realities and certainly at a slower pace than the mythic creators can abide. The history of innovation from the Garden of Eden on is mostly one of shock and countershock, repeating in diminishing cycles until the diverse impacts have been sensed and accommodations made.

We must take into account that invention is an insult to many of the systems of belief. The insult is felt not only by adherents to traditional rituals and customs but by the holders of established scientific theories and valued relations. When the established forces are particularly dominant, innovation is most likely to be accepted through one of the great paths as a program of the establishment or an instrument of a rebirth. In times of less certainty, innovative forces polarize and upset establishments to gain acceptance through revolutionary victories and suffer the consequences of counterinvention. This is the pattern of most great political innovation, as seen in the cycles of violent reform and counterreform of the French Revolution or in the way the "Russian Revolution" continues to play out the innovative thrusts of Marxist socialism.

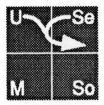

SYSTEMS ANALYSIS

Organizational Design, Urban Design,
Corporate and Public (Strategic) Planning, and
Sociotechnical Systems Analysis

Systems analysis has its foundation in the grand image of planning. It arises from the deep conviction that a science of planning can lead to effective social change and has been developed for various different applications such as strategic planning, urban and organizational design, and sociotechnical systems design. This approach to change and resolution of issues maintains that a desired outcome emerges if the proper initial conditions are established, and, given those conditions, the person, organization, or society will move along the desired path toward a preestablished goal.

Systems analysts are latter-day utopians, free of romanticism (or perhaps the most romantic of us all) and armed with the natural and social sciences. Their path of resolution arises from a faith in the possibility of rational control of human affairs. The approach is straightforward: Develop a full understanding of the situation, apply scientific methods, and a plan will emerge that necessarily results in the desired goal—with fewer or more adjustments along the road to account for omission, errors, and unforeseen aspects. By this assertion, neither I nor one holding to this worldview would imply that it is easy to come up with a full understanding or to get the data with required accuracy and currency, only that this is the way to go about resolving issues. A systems analyst may combine processes of adjustment to correct errors in the data (or theory) as identified by feedback on deviations from the intended outputs. Stafford Beer (1985) has developed a full cybernetic of social activity that so corrects the error of design at a number of levels closely matching the first four "boards of play."

The Path

Systems analysis works by designing from an accepted theory of social and technical planned change—systems analysts don't recognize

Diagram 4.12 Systems Analysis

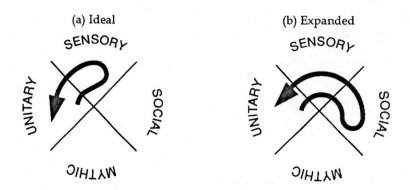

conflict, only poor planning and execution. This approach to resolution of issues assumes that, if the theories are sufficiently inclusive,
and if there are accurate measures of the empirical situation, the resulting plan will be accepted and will work. The planners don't have
to "do" anything once the initial conditions are established. Change
occurs just as rain falls and organisms are born and die. It's "all in the
cards"; one simply has to "stack the deck," then "start the machine"
appropriately. The path can be undertaken at two levels of awareness
as illustrated in Diagram 4.12. The *ideal* model is deterministic; only
the sensory and unitary realities need to be involved. Yet, many practitioners have expanded their awareness to at least recognize that
there are local variations arising from the specific situations and the
involved people's abilities and motivations. They have seen that the
individuals could "absorb" the local variance if properly motivated,
but to incorporate such motivations in the design required analysts to
use methods of the social reality. More paradoxically, the very design
process requires that the designers display intentionality, which is
outside their deterministic worldview. Thus, in practice, systems analysts *expand* their view to include social reality, accepting a degree of
free will and innovativeness as part of their design. This aspect is further elaborated in the examples provided below.

History

Systems analysis has a long history. While examples might have been
found in ancient times, in irrigation and city planning, in the storage of
food supplies, and in setting military campaigns throughout the Mediter-

ranean and the Far East, the current forms probably follow from the tradition that Leonardo da Vinci and Machiavelli enhanced at the founding of the Age of Rationality. The brilliant minds of the day, such as these two, were commissioned to design the physical and political structures of their respective city-states as well as being involved in the implementation of related changes. Both Machiavelli and da Vinci were involved in planning for organizations, in particular, governments, urban and regional systems, and strategies of action, military and political. The notion that changes and resolution of disputes should be done from a centralized and analytic worldview continued even into the romantic, revolutionary nineteenth century. Socialists and Syndicalists equally supported the planful direction of change from the "top" either of the government or of the opposition.

These activities form what is still the focus of systems analytic work, though it has been extended into the private and industrial sectors in all Western economies (Lilienfeld, 1978). With the repeated failure of such schemes as scientific management, urban master planning, and socialist state planning that had emerged in the first half of the century, we might expect that the methods would no longer be popular. It is, however, the natural style of that significant portion of the population I label "designers," so we should expect that the analytic strategies will continue to be used and further developed to incorporate new techniques emerging from science and mathematics, so long as the sensory-unitary worldview is in vogue.

The systems analytic approaches have been extended by the recognition of the social reality and of the individual person as contributing more than would be expected of an element in a complex machine. Prior to 1950, those of the analytic view considered individualized needs and contributions to be aberrations, seldom of a useful nature, to be reduced wherever possible. A dramatic reversal in this approach was achieved in simply honoring those differences, noticing that workers could and do come up with schemes that are effective and by which they gain meaning in guiding their own operations. In the coal mining studies conducted by the Tavistock Institute (London) around 1950, Eric Trist and Ken Bamforth (1951) noticed the miners had made changes in the operations that "jointly optimized" the social and technical aspects of their jobs. Trist and others noted that the workers continually adapted their work, expressing values and using skills that were not in the designs created by the engineer or manager. They improved on the designs based on feelings and ideas of the social reality, thus extending the models to include issues of feelings, values, intentionality, and meaning. From this work emerged the general approach to organization design labeled "sociotechnical systems" that explicitly operates with three of the four realities.

Ideal Forms

The ideal form of the systems analytic path is a deterministic path, as illustrated in Diagram 4.12. The path to a resolution begins with the assumption that a solution can be developed from principle. The domain of the problem is identified and a solution process is selected via one of the problem identification methods. When the process is viewed as a problem-solving exercise, the next step is to collect data about the problem setting and to work back and forth between the principles and the data to find the optimal solution. When analysis is used as a strategy of resolution, a more complex path is followed, though along an obscured route.

The strategic form takes a conventionalizing route, beginning with the principles and moving quickly to assert—"hypothesize," if one is speaking carefully—that a particular proposition will lead to a solution in the current case. This proposition may appear to follow from the logic (unitary) of the situation, but the act of asserting it is mythic. Having formed a solution in the abstract, the designer can move directly to use data to determine parameters and resolve questions posed with the assumed hypothesis.[21]

The assumption of the hypothesis, and of the theory of which it is a derivation, is a political choice, in the sense that it is based on expectations that the choice will be accepted as the appropriate vessel for the ordering of the "facts." The resolution follows from a particular form of law, scientific proof, architectural style, or other principle that has been adopted by the society or individual designer. This is the only choice made at the strategic level. The setting (and perhaps defense of the choice) is the strategic act; the particular solution follows from measuring and interpreting data. Once the design is accepted as satisfying the design criteria, the remaining work is viewed as a mechanical calculation with adjustments to deal with omissions and measurement errors. I do not believe the path is this simple, but to introduce any suggestion that the designer intends to resolve the issue implies a willfulness, value, and meaning that are not part of the reality of the systems analyst.[22]

The systems analyst has a second, less alien approach to dealing with intentionality that provides a second important variation on the system analytic path. The analyst can reformulate a problem or conflict as a "game." The initial act along the path is setting rules, a second board activity, and then making "plays" on the first board. Here the systems analysts assume that there are opposing interests with two or more "players" holding opposing criteria. This assumption expands the approach to include economic analyses and explicit conflict situations, as in military confrontations, athletics, and even domestic settings. This approach was extensively developed via game theory, particularly by the mathematical psychologist Anatol Rapoport (1970). The theory provides a very general way of dealing with conflict, either with explicit opponents or as games against nature.

There is considerable power in the game theoretic approach if the intentionality of the opponents can be captured in statements of their criteria for success. With such established criteria, we can resolve conflicts either by finding a successful set of moves, that is, a route of play, or by changing the rules so that the players will themselves choose a path to the solution. These approaches to resolution are used not only by the engineer-designer but also by psychotherapists. Whereas designers aim to model the "players" and thus find optimal solutions, therapists empower their patients by letting them find their own solutions in an appropriately designed space of alternatives.

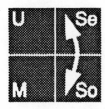

PLURALISTIC DEVELOPMENT

Incrementalism, Organization Development,
Community Development and Search Conferencing, and
Social Mobilization

Pluralistic development arose in the late 1950s as an awareness of the contrast between two opposing factors in the Western world. One, in the United States, was that of the backlash of the two wars: The moral convergence that brought victory in war did not hold to resolve the issues of a peacetime economy. President Eisenhower briefly conserved a rather saccharin society, blanketing its problems with middle-class prosperity; under that was a growing humanistic awareness calling for a recognition of individual values and dignity. By the early 1960s, the cold war and hot urban summers destroyed the facade of the well-structured society. The other factor was the growing awareness that the actively planned, social democratic economies of Europe were not able to make their plans work. Without the focalizing threat of external enemies, pluralism has grown to replace the planning state as the major force for progress. Whether because of social awareness or the failure of state planning, pluralism has become a major path for social change.

The first and broadest response to the incipient chaos of the late 1960s was a retreat from planned change to incrementalism, that is, responding to issues whenever there was a felt need for change rather than working from a design that involved a systematic engagement with the entire issue (Pava, 1986). Incrementalism, as first described by Lindblom, is a method of carrying out the expectations of the governing authorities under conditions that made programmatic execution unworkable. As a method of resolving issues, it recognized that there was too great a diversity of goals, of personal and public needs, to be all taken care of in a monolithic master plan. At best, one could find targets of opportunity along a generally accepted direction of development. Incrementalism was and is an attempt to deal with the plurality of society from a position of authority (Pava, 1986). The issues of the 1960s, however, were as much as anything an expression of volition in all sectors of society as they were a call for particular social and economic gains. Populations at all levels of society wanted a say in the management of their families, their workplaces, and their governments. It became obvious that resolution of major issues would depend on the participation of those who were concerned with the outcomes. So there developed new paths of resolution based in participation rather than in any particular personal, social, and political principles or programs.

Resolution of complex issues without accounting for a social reality is an unlikely event in this intermillennial era. Any method designed to resolve major issues must recognize that the parties to the conflict have differing concerns and differently value those things of common concern. From the assumption of this pluralism, I have re-created a new family of paths all characterized by the processes by which consensus on values is developed among the involved parties. The ideal form of this family of paths is illustrated by the left side of Diagram 4.13. One such path has evolved to work within the boundaries of existing organizations; it is generally identified as organizational development. A second variation works with the development of communities, which could range from the size of a city block to a group of nation-states. A third variation is the development of a population transcending current definitions of social units. This is the social mobilization approach that is associated

Diagram 4.13 Pluralistic Development

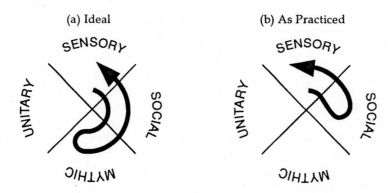

with the work of the revolutionary Brazilian educator Paulo Freire, the Highlander's Institute in Tennessee that played a critical role in both the development of union strategies in the 1930s and civil rights in the 1960s, and various groups that have emerged to support Third World, postcolonial societies. These *resolutionary* processes are fundamentally democratic in that they do not recognize an independent authority or principled constraint—they return to the democratic consensus and re- ification without "passing through" the authorizing stage. Ideally, the pluralistic path will include a founding journey into mythic reconcep- tualization (Diagram 4.13), but, most often and particularly in organi- zational development, the existing core or its residue remains the vessel in which the resolution is formulated.

The essential commonality among these variations is the respect for and development of individual as well as collective responsibility to ensure that the population is capable of sustaining its development. The development is usually framed in terms of education, access to economic opportunities, and equality under law. The path of resolu- tion is a spiral of participation in data collection and creation of mean- ing, that is, a construction of a social reality in the context of an objectively defined world. On the right side of Diagram 4.13, the path appears as a simple looping between the sensory and social realities. The essence of this path is not in the route (the structure), however, but in the processes that generate it.

The most defined, perhaps most confined, pluralistic path is in *or- ganizational development*. Its target is improving conditions of work and effectiveness for a specific set of employees of an organization. Its basic goal is to improve the work conditions of the employees, that is, to make a social gain, without reducing the economic effectiveness of the organization or its ability to deliver its services and products. Its best uses have led to economic gains for corporations and improved quality of working life for employees. It notably avoids dealing with power issues; that is, it avoids play on the second board.

The goal of community development is the resolution of issues facing some elements of a society in ways that do not reduce the quality of life for others. A community may consist of many different populations: rich/poor, educated/less educated, landowners/renters, families with children/isolated individuals. Making any change in a city's or rural region's facilities is certain to induce displeasure and conflict among the various constituencies. Whereas the incremental approach is to deal with problems as they arise, the community development strategy is to build a consensus framework within which individual problems are worked out. Community development projects focus on developing resources within a community to enable it to solve its own problems. Two key resources are leadership skills and the ability of the community members to convene for focused action. In this role, the community developer is not a problem solver but works to create a more powerful "social field" in the community.

The path of community development may begin with a conference that invites all the recognizable interest groups to work collectively to discover, or create, routes to progress that will be satisfactory to almost every interest group. In some instances, the outcome is the development of community agencies to deal with issues that have become locked in political skirmishes (Campbell, 1989); in others, it leads to the formation of new governing bodies and new organizational forms. Beginning with a "search conference" (Merrelyn Emery, (1996) creates a unifying process in a community that transcends the mission provided by common employment and the corporate purpose. In the smallest instance, a search conference might be used to pull together a neighborhood; on the largest scale, the conference path has mobilized interest groups across a nation to change its social consciousness, as did SNCC (originated as the Student Non-Violent Coordinating Committee) in the 1960s.

The overall process is described in an example of the search conference approach used for mental health planning in Rhode Island beginning in 1986.[23] The Governor's Council on Mental Health took on the responsibility for creating a new plan, after "testing the waters, to make sure that political, fiscal, and advocacy support was ready for a state plan that would promote systems change." The Rhode Island planners (Romeo, Mauch, & Morrison, 1990, pp. 1254-1255) wrote:

The goal for managers in planning is to turn potential obstacles into opportunities for fostering among politicians and others a sense of ownership in the planning process. Managers can best accomplish this goal by ensuring that every possible constituency is represented among the planners. . . . In addition to consumers—who were on virtually every committee of the planning project—groups represented included family members, other advocates, elected officials, insurers, providers and related state human service agencies, members of refugee and ethnic minority groups, and interested citizens.

The integration of all these constituencies into the planning process allowed the incorporation of their valuable and divergent views of the mental health system. . . . Often neglected sources of input are the mental health plans of predecessors, whose wisdom is incorporated into current planning, avoiding the temptation to jettison all prior work because of personal pride.

Given the rapid turnover among state commissioners, it is particularly essential that community leaders commit themselves to a state plan rather than simply to an individual commissioner who may be serving a different state by the time the plan is implemented. And if the elected officials . . . feel their views make a difference, they will be more likely to commit their resources to implementing the final plan.

The state planning project used a fully participatory process over an 18-month period to improve the health system. The participants assessed the needs according to a sound and value-based methodology, expressing their prevalence and scope explicitly and in accordance with a set of intrinsic values for community health care. The planners based their recommended services both on research findings and on the individual needs of the clients. . . .

Maintaining and broadening the coalitions that implement these initiatives requires consistent work by state leadership inasmuch as environmental factors exert constantly changing pressures on the system. . . . [I]t is extremely important that planners build considerable flexibility into their scheme for implementing the state plan. . . . Successful planning requires both elements from the empirical model and an attention to political concerns. . . . It can be a major challenge for managers to entrust some control of the system to the coalition, but managers who do so are usually rewarded by lasting system change that reflects the diverse needs of the mental health community and of citizens at large.

The article makes no mention of a mythic, creative phase in which new models were created; neither does it mention an overt confrontation of political establishments. The shared presentation of values reshapes the politicians' playing field, however, enabling or disabling their ploys. The Rhode Island search conference was an effective development of an implementable "renewed vision" that ensured that the participants' values were incorporated into a fair and feasible plan that was passed by the legislature.

The apparent strength of pluralistic development is the creation of an articulate and cohesive value system among the constituencies. While there may be efforts to change values in the system relevant to the problem, pluralistic developers do not expect to challenge the assumptions of the society or organization within which the issues have arisen. With an acceptance of the overall sociopolitical framework, the pluralistic planner's method focuses on goal setting and problem solving, ranging from the step-by-step skeptical minimalism of the incrementalist to the more radical mobilization of the citizenry for legislative reform via value shifts. These are pragmatic paths as illustrated on the right side of Diagram 4.13, dealing with current issues arising from current concerns, attitudes, and analyses of the relevant situations.

The various minimalist forms of change exemplified in incrementalism (Hirschman & Lindblom, 1962; Pava, 1986) accept society to be basically autoregulating. Consequently, one does not expect to make changes in its base through programmatic efforts. These strategies take advantage of opportunities, working with openings to improve the society according to dominant though not pervasive values.

The search conference and related value explorations expect change to come from a mutual understanding of values in a community. That is, the best paths to change can be located if we know the needs and preferences of all those involved in an issue. Recognition of the social reality may be more to gain information than to direct the planner's efforts.

The most active form of pluralistic development, social mobilization—as illustrated by the racial struggles of the last three decades— creates changes by returning to the core principles of the society or organization to ensure the population that the state or other authority operates as intended. Again, this is not so much a path of change as it is a method for enforcing the overt principles of the society.

This rather innocuous image of participative planners may be misleading. The methods in working within the agenda of the establishment are themselves the source of new values and organizing principles. The workers or rural poor who are involved in a participative research project and the community leaders who take part in a search conference are being introduced to a new vision of society that transcends the political ideologies that have dominated both public and private models of organization and conflict resolution. The new vision is contained in the processes of work rather than the ideology of the system present or desired. That is, the method of pluralistic development leads to a radically different society than would result if issues were resolved along systems analytic and other revitalizing paths. Clear examples of this effect are found in educationally based revolutions produced by the pedagogical methods of Paulo Freire, in the methods used to train activists for nonviolent action in the civil rights movements of the 1960s, and, increasingly, in the work of organizational consultants, change agents eager to "transform organizations."

DIALECTICAL PATHS

Adjudication, Polarization and Synthesis, Ideological Revolutions, and Reframing

The dialectical approaches are as ancient as the grand paths. The label has been attached to a great variety of approaches to resolution. The word *dialectic* has the same root as *dialogue*, but it implies disputive and critical aspects of conversation. In ancient and modern times (Toulmin, 1972; Locke, 1996), the dialectic has been used as the method of proof of the truth of one position over some alternative by the logical use of evidence in argument. It has been the method of the law courts and arbitration. In that sense of the word, it was used to describe the relation between the disputants interpreting a unitary truth. In recent centuries, the term *dialectic* has been expanded to deal with issues of value and fairness arising from a social worldview often in counterpose to a unitary position. The dialectic does not work with sensory phenomena, nor has it any use for the willful assertions of the mythic's inventions. The Hegelian (and so the Marxian) dialectics recognize a general process of evolution from one truth system to another over time—over the course of an argument or over centuries of cultural evolution. My definition includes both, the argument set within the unitary worldview and played out as games of logic and power—that is, play on the first and second boards—and the speculative dialectic that evolves from the established thesis to antitheses and, if successful, to a resolving synthesis. The synthesis can be viewed as a solution or merely a resolving stage in an unending cycle of dialectical evolution.

For all the mystery surrounding it, the dialectic is the form of conversation by which we solve problems on a daily basis, by which we answer: "Who's right?" It is used in many forms of personal and family therapies (Reigal, 1976) and is the basis for methods of arbitration and mediation that are belatedly developing to remove civil disputes from the tyranny of the (unitary) law courts.

What distinguishes the dialectic path is that it assumes a conflict between two defined positions—two people, two belief systems, two territories, two cultural trends. A dialectic is undertaken to settle a dispute. It is not used to remove angst or resolve a social issue or invent a solution to environmental decay, although, at the grand level, the dispute may be joined between great contradictions of socialism and capitalism, of religion and state, or men and women. Certainly, one of the great ongoing dialectics in the West is the gender issue, which is, at times, defined as a dispute between the sexes.

The most general classes of dialectic resolutions are those that *redefine the boundaries around conventionalized positions.* At the simplest level, as discussed in Chapter 3 in the section on the influential mode, a problem is solved dialectically by eliminating the alternative. *Adjudication* is an example—a judgment is made from an official "chair" that separates acceptable from unacceptable. An entirely different approach is resolution by *reframing,* that is, by changing the apparent "rules of the game" in such a way that both (all) contending positions are included within the accepted whole. But I am defining the paths of a dialectic resolution as the entire resolving process.

Logics of the Dialectic

Fundamental to the dialectic is the concept of rightness, that there is a set of principles that are true and, in relevant settings, are discoverable or revealed. The monistic worldview calls on one to be right or to search for the right. This is a perfectly acceptable notion in mathematics. It is expected within religious traditions that one accept "the right," that which has been revealed and decreed. Such rightness also underlies the concept of a lawful society, and thereby it rules out conflict.

From the outside, the dialectic appears quite different. An observer would say a dialectic approach resolves issues by setting the rules of a "game." Once they are set, no player, by definition, is in conflict. To violate the rules means to be in conflict and denies that one is a player or, more generally, denies one the status of being a "member." A member could be thought of as an instance in statutory law or mathematics—"137" is a member of the class of rational numbers—or as a person associated with a religious community or social organization. Thus an issue is resolved dialectically by establishing rules that hold for a significant set of members. From this view, there is no path of change in the dialectic. Rather, resolution is achieved by gaining adherents to the solution that exists or has been discovered and by rejecting disbelievers.

The dialectic path begins with the awareness of a potential split, a denial of the established convention. Those upholding the unity may feel the tensions of dissatisfaction, pain, or alienation but have not formulated the condition as arising from a contradiction. They don't acknowledge that the definition of the situation itself is in question, whether the issue is as routine as the child coming into maturity and becoming independent of the family or a grand conceptual model such as the economy or science or the primacy of nation-states. For example, the established view in the United States does not see a contradiction between notions of wealth and welfare. Some part of the society, however, will have recognized the idea of an alternative, that there could be an opposite, as simple as "you are not me," that a slave is a human being, or that a good society may not have to have everyone earning a wage.

Contradiction drives a person or a community from the first awareness of negation to a resetting on a new truth. Few people have been comfortable living without some mode of establishing what is true, right, better, or more beautiful. Yet progress comes by letting go of one truth to explore another. This exploration is the heart of the dialectic. The contradiction may come from recognizing exclusive alternatives. Some are logical alternatives, such as odd and even, true and false, unity and plurality. More commonly, we sense contradiction between concepts that appear as extremes along some dimension: rich and poor, near and far, masculine and feminine, or such complex ideas as liberal and conservative.

Mao Tse-tung, one of the deepest of dialectical practitioners, created a list of the deep contradictions that separated the Chinese society from his ideal in the 1950s. I sample from his list in Diagram 4.14. The list provides the reader with one of the difficulties of understanding a dialectic process, for what were issues of great moment 40 years ago now and far from China seem neutral, certainly not the issues over which to evoke a great revolution. But, at the time he wrote of them, each contradiction pointed to new possibilities, new opportunities, for Chinese peoples. This contrast between seeming neutral to me and revolutionary to those involved is characteristic of processes of deep change. For those inside, at an early stage, the alternatives are initially unthinkable and therefore of no moment. With time and commitment, the unthinkable alternative becomes possible and threatening and attracts advocates. It is hard to sense the energy arising in the confrontation of such "contradictions" without experiencing them presenting new possibilities. To get a feeling for how impactful is the appearance of "opposites," you might sense your own feeling toward the idea of living in a world without

Diagram 4.14 Contradictions of the Great Leap Forward

A	B

I. Economic Contradictions (The Dialectic of the Economy)
  Contradictions of sectors:

A	B
modern	traditional
coast	inland
industry	agriculture
heavy industry	light industry

  Contradictions of goals:

A	B
select development	simultaneous development
long term	short term

  Contradictions of scale:

A	B
large-scale industry	medium and small-scale industry

  Contradictions of function:

A	B
production	consumption
production	accumulation
accumulation	consumption

  Contradictions of operation:

A	B
capital intensive	labor intensive

II. Political Contradictions (The Dialectic of the State)
  Contradictions of conception:

A	B
centralism	democracy
"from the top down"	"from the bottom up"

  Contradictions of administration:

A	B
center	region
centralization	decentralization
vertical rule	dual rule
branch principle (vertical)	committee principle (horizontal)

III. Social Contradictions (The Dialectic of Society)
  Contradictions of social stratification:

A	B
workers	peasants
intellectuals	worker-peasant toilers

  Contradictions of political stratification:

A	B
bureaucrats	masses
bureaucrats	cadres
cadres	masses

  Contradictions of values:

A	B
expert	red

  Contradictions of social cohesion:

A	B
individual	collectivity
"organic" solidarity	"mechanical" solidarity

  Contradictions of role:

A	B
specialists	generalists

  Contradictions of motivations:

A	B
material incentive	ideology
individual rewards	collective rewards
wages	distributions

NOTE: The first column (A) contains elements stressed during the First Five-Year Plan Period, referred to as the period of "one-sided development." Those in the second column (B) were no longer seen "in relation to the A elements but in contradiction" (Mao, 1960).

"scarcity" or one in which "time" and "place" have disappeared, being replaced with "patterns of harmony."

The first stage of the dialectic is the *negation of the absolute*, the recognition that there is another way. In negating an absolute, ideas that were subordinate concepts, held "in relation to" some encompassing whole, are transformed to stand "in contradiction to" that whole and thereby become distinct. In the pure case, the dialectic resolution begins with an argument between two parties that, in their essences, do not recognize each other's existence in the matter in dispute. The holder of the society's or profession's thesis declares the opposition to be nonmembers. The opposition, whatever their own reality, find the thesis empty and thus its holders void. There can be neither argument nor resolution between the parties, as each calls on different and incompatible logics of resolution. This extreme is visible in the views of the medieval church and in current orthodoxies of Judaism and Islam. The nonbeliever, or an intentional violator of the law, is judged to be outside the membership and thus beyond recognition, beyond existence. If the opponent is also of a monistic worldview, either unitary or mythic, this denies the truth of the establishment, holding its members to be living "in sin," and thus the opponent cannot recognize their existence. If the opposition is of a pluralistic mind, the paradox is softened because the opposition at least recognizes the establishment's existence, but it still cannot work with its mode of argumentation. Thus even the "rational" paths are lost when the parties have gone beyond polarization to deny the other's position. The pain of such impasse is visible in the abortion debates, in the Jewish-Palestinian conflict, and in the daily engagements of social service administrators and their clients.

In the second stage, as the split develops, the protagonists of the established and opposing positions *polarize* their formulations. The focus narrows and issues are prioritized to make clear what conceptual boundaries are under question. The differences are exaggerated while they are narrowed. Typically, polarizing is accompanied by struggles within the adversarial forces—minor parties struggling to form coalitions, claimants in a legal suit trying to make their dispute central to the case, and legislators shifting the priorities to bring the uncommitted onto their side. The dialectic become a crucible in which the characteristics of the combatants and their issues are refined. Polarizing is a necessary step in a dialectic—failure to polarize drains energy from the cause, postponing any confrontation of the issue—although it makes it more difficult to find solutions by other methods. Once on a path of opposition, it is difficult to backtrack.

The next stages of dialectic differ radically according to whether the contradiction is to be approached *conventionally* or *differentiatedly* as determined by the relative power of the parties to the conflict. In the conventionalizing direction, the settlement is arrived at within the established logic of the unitary worldview. When both parties are working from a unitary view, the argument can be settled—by clarification in an adjudication or by a violent overthrow of a government as in the unending rebellions in the South American and Middle Eastern countries—because the parties are playing by the same rules, or the argument could be solved by systematically working for compromise, as in labor-management contracting. An issue might be "settled" by going back to the original situation, as in a failed rebellion. It is common in the period following the settling of a polarized conflict that the policies of the "winner" will gradually drift toward the position of the loser, as the welfare programs of the Democratic party that were originally rejected by the Republicans have been absorbed into the Republican programs as that party came to power (see the left side of Diagram 4.15). When one of the parties to a dialectic is of a strong social orientation, a conventionalizing path of change leads to standoffs, as there are no grounds for compromise. This was the fate, for example, of the women's movement all during the nineteenth century. It was not until the suffrage movement succeeded in the early twentieth that the movement had the power to demand that the issues be confronted on grounds more appropriate to the issue. With this success, it became a differentiating effort, a crusade rather than a pleading for a hearing.

The differentiating effort follows a different path to its outcomes because no solutions will satisfy both parties *within the terms of the overt conflict*. Resolution between the social and the unitary requires a new logic, a redefinition of the issue, a change in values by which decisions are made. Though this stage of the process appears to be a polarizing fight between parties on the opposite ends of a log, in the differentializing situation, the parties are using different logics and different forms of criteria for a solution—the fight is not conducted along one dimension. There is no playing field with a goal at opposite ends or monetary value to distribute between contestants. This is the polarization, for example, between a work force wishing dignity and self-respect confronting a businessman who is bargaining over overtime rates. When there is a successful resolution, it forms a new synthesis that more or less rapidly makes the prior positions seem inadequate or dated. For example, out of the intense effort of a joint labor-management committee, a new sense of mission may displace the competitive "bidding chips" that had provided political clout in the prior unitary constructions of "reality." Or, in postcommunist Central Europe, a new economy may be emerging that will arise out of the examination of capitalism by a socialist critique to produce not a new socialism—which

Diagram 4.15 The Dialectic Follows Alternative Paths

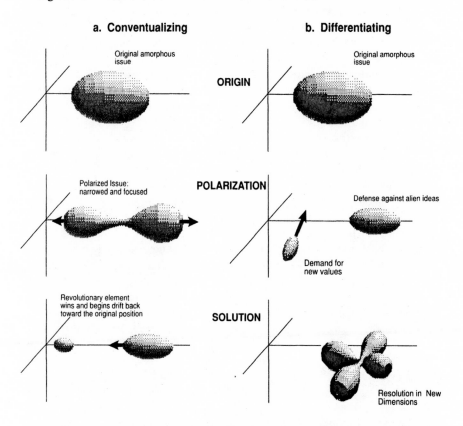

a. Conventualizing

b. Differentiating

Original amorphous issue

ORIGIN

Original amorphous issue

Polarized Issue: narrowed and focused

POLARIZATION

Defense against alien ideas

Demand for new values

Revolutionary element wins and begins drift back toward the original position

SOLUTION

Resolution in New Dimensions

would be a collapse onto one of the alternatives—but new institutions outside of either the private profit or the state management designs.

This dialectic is a third board game, a fight to establish new rules when the old rules of relations have been lost. The issue becomes an even deeper dialectic if the values by which the old games were guided are also in question. It thus becomes a compound of third and fourth board games—a situation without stability of criteria or expectations of conduct; that is, it produces life without culture.

Solutions that lie mostly within the territory of either party are not easy to come by, as we can see in the long fight to get a new "crime bill" through the U.S. Congress. There are certainly few dimensions shared between those believing that punishment is part of the judicial system and those that hold that the issues can only be resolved in terms of social and personal change. It is unlikely that any crime bill formulated in the linear, conventionalizing logic could ever resolve this dialectic (see the right side of Diagram 4.15).

There are also great differences in the ways in which the dialectic process itself fails when the parties "collude" to avoid a return to the prior absolute or to move to a new position. Attempts to resolve conflicts in conventionalizing directions depend on the logic natural to the dimension of the conflict. The failure of such attempts, when neither party has the courage or drive to push through to a solution, results in a running standoff that I call an *operational dialectic*. The "cold war" of the Soviet Union against the Western nations is a perfect example of this standoff. We run much of our lives as operational dialectics. Certainly, family life, now and in the past, has seldom been better than that, in spite of the idealizations of the family. Sometimes the operation is a constructive and well-managed effort at compromise and problem solving, but that is not a resolution of the issues, nor is it likely to be stable. It may collapse back to a denial of the issue as in a divorce or a denial of relationship as in the Israeli-Palestinian controversy. In some cases, the parties may grow intolerant of wasting their lives and move to a resolution, as did the Soviets in ending the cold war. But, more often, with persevering management, the energy of the conflict will gradually decay, and the involved system, the culture, will die, "not with a bang, but a whimper." Such an entropic decay results in the dropping of the system to a lower level of organization, to a new dark age, a going-out-of-business, or such great alienation that a couple cannot even manage a divorce.

Alternatively, a "failure" in a culture that resolves issues by differentiating may produce a *ritualized society* in which the failures are managed by periodic *reversals of the acceptable*. Such occasions include Halloween, the Mardi Gras celebrations, and rites of transitions, such as graduation events. Examples on a broader level include the organization of Italian society to accommodate the Mafia or, in the Japanese Society, the "Black squads." These devices do not resolve the issues, but they create a stable society, continually regenerated by the ritualized status reversals that allow expressions of the repressed emotions, angers, jealousies, and other, typically disowned emotions. These institutions of inversion have declined in U.S. society as the conventionalizing rationality increasingly eradicated the traditional cultures that arrived with many of the immigrant cultures.

The Paradoxical Resolution of a Dialectic

While this investigation of processes of change has encountered paradox in every path, none is so tightly wound in paradox as dialectical resolution. The first of these paradoxes, or maybe just an oddity of the dialectic, is that the most elegant resolution involves the least change, calling only on operations within the unitary reality and following no distinguishable path to attain the resolution. This direct resolution is *reframing* that simply changes the boundaries of the issues, thereby dis-solving it. Watzlawick (1974, p. 95) says that to reframe is "to change the conceptual and/or emotional setting or viewpoint in relation to which a situation is experienced and to place it in another frame that fits the 'facts' of the same concrete situation equally well or even better, and thereby changes its entire meaning." Reframing does *nothing* except destroy the logics of opposition of the disputants. Reframing destroys the polarization by creating a new dimension, a new space, within which the disputants can communicate (see the right side of Diagram 4.15). A simple case illustrates this process.

A labor-management committee was sharply polarized over management's desire to put into effect stringent penalties for absenteeism among the primarily female work force of a canning factory. The management argued that even a few absent employees forced the shutdown of the production lines. The union argued that the women had to have time to deal with family emergencies and other personal business that single parents had to take care of during work hours. The contract blocked the imposition of penalties, but management applied pressure by demanding that workers put in overtime—permissible under the contract—which put even more stress on the families. In this conflict, the logics were incompatible, with the management trying to force the union to accept its economic argument without regard for family values, and the union similarly demanding the reverse. The whole issue collapsed when management was asked what it needed out of the work force. The answer was not "attendance" but "predictability." Out of habit, they had equated the two. So, when the issue was rephrased as one of getting a predictable work force, the ill-formed boundary between the two positions vanished. It was agreed that, if the supervisors had 36 hours' notice, they could recruit part-time labor to fill in for almost all of the (low-skilled) positions. The usual arguments against the costs of part-time employees evaporated when it was calculated that the program would be less expensive than any other alternative. The reframed situation was free of conflict, so, with a bit of joint problem solving, the issue disappeared. *The issue itself was not solved*; rather, it was avoided by reframing the situation on the dimension of predictability.

Resolution by reframing usually begins with entertaining contradictory or absurd alternatives. The above absentee issue was dissolved by pressing those involved to think about what would happen if the absenteeism grossly increased. At first, the concern was with discipline, which was clearly a hidden dimension of the conflict. But, as the group was pushed to consider extreme levels of absences, the mangers protested that they could "never plan anything with such unpredictability." That phrase broke the boundary that had maintained the polarized issue.

The paradoxical approach builds on the fundamental principle of dialectic thinking, that every position implies it opposite. Here the extreme of absence was total attendance, that is, perfect predictability. The principle appears everywhere: If I adopt the principle of life, I must confront it with dying or transcending, or, if I adopt the criterion that one should grow up independent, I must deal with becoming interdependent. If I take pluralism as my assumption, then I must discuss it with the tools of holism such as comparing (which assumes that things coexist) and boundary setting. Conversely, if I take a holistic premise, it is only with the tools of pluralism that I can articulate its arguments. So determinism is meaningful only in the context of free will, and choice is discussable only in referring to limitations. When one is hooked on one horn of a dilemma, then the other horn becomes the probe with which to investigate the situation.

The internal inconsistencies of the dialectic are also evident in approaches that have traditionally been used to resolve the issue—that is, to step out of the issue, to deny it, to move the resolution effort into another domain. The effort is thus translated into games of power that can be played out in any of the realities but that almost certainly fail to resolve the issues. A brief consideration of the other approaches will indicate why such reoccurrence seems likely. A polarity can be suppressed by any of the following three dynamics.

Force (sensory reality). When the Inquisition determined heretics to be unrepentant, they were "turned out" to the civil authority to be dealt with in the sensory reality, where they were exiled, stripped of name and property, jailed, or executed. Conversely, when a heathen force won, the leaders of the old faith were similarly disposed of. The threat of being so treated by the civil authorities clearly can be sufficient to "resolve" the conflict in many situations.

Persuasion (social reality). All the methods of the influential mode of problem solving can be brought to bear to convince the nonbeliever to "atone" (to become at-one with the belief) or to be recruited to the new belief system. The advantage in this game is with those with a social reality for it is of their nature to care about the other. This advantage is obvious in the adoption of a social caring approach by the true believer to induce a "confidence." But, like the route of force, it is a ploy, a ploy that often backfires by counterinventing a divergent unitary belief via the extreme focusing on a particular item of social thinking. This is a common outcome exemplified by the Franciscan brothers, who came to be the champions of the Indians they were sent to convert. So with the prison guards who take on their prisoner's faith. There is another unintended outcome of the persuasion in which the social activists counterinvent themselves as unitary true believers—the reformers become as dogmatic as the old regime, as we saw in the excesses of the antiwar movement in the 1970s.

Charisma (mythic reality). The charismatic gains the confidence of others by the immediacy of his or her[24] presence. Whether representing the thesis or the antithesis, the immediate effect of being created by a charismatic person who is presenting the case may transcend the habits of belief. Preachers, demagogues, healers, and artistic performers all bring into the "fold." The charismatic may be a member and true believer or a hired mountebank selling influence. We may question the beliefs espoused by the Hollywood stars campaigning for a political candidate or an issue, even when we are being influenced by the opportunity to be identified with them.

These three are widely used in attempts to resolve disputes, but, in their efforts to bring about change, each counterinvents the opposing force, assuring that the issue will reappear in another guise.

The Dialectic as a Tool for Problem Solving

Just as all the modes of resolution can be used to suppress a dialectical dispute—that is, a polarized dispute between parties, ideologies, or claims—issues of all sorts can be reformulated as dialectical confrontations. For example, a strategic issue for an organization can be approached by identifying a potential solution and then creating a polar position. If advocates of these opposing ideas can be identified, the issue is suitable for a dialectical engagement. This is the basic mode used in designing formal debates. The path has been developed for use in the corporate setting by Ichak Adizes (1978) and by Mason and Mitroff (1981).

The method is designed to establish the conditions for making a judgment between parties, then converting the current issue to a dispute form. The enabling condition is establishing the authority of a superior power. Typically, the power is represented by an executive whose responsibility encompasses all the issues in dispute; it may also be represented by a mediator or a respected consultant, that is, a wise and neutral person who can provide a psychological "vessel" within which the dispute is contained. Setting up the vessel, in effect, establishes a common membership so that the conflict is redefined to be between polarized parts, not distinct enemies. With such a vessel enclosing the conflict, those involved can establish criteria to choose between contending proposals and then use an appropriate method to find a correct or best solution. With containment by statuary or psychological protection, the actors in this "courtroom" dialogue can move into the reality of the argument. Frequently, both positions will be within a unitary, or sensory-unitary, worldview, allowing the solutions to be analytically judged. The more difficult and risky encounters are designed to differentiate, with the intent to attain a synthesis that will move the whole issue into a new "space." The synthesis is valuable for itself but it also means that there are no losers. When those involved cannot produce a synthesis, the situation may easily be played out as a highly polarized debate producing an unintended enmity between the actors in the artificial dispute.

The important contribution of this mode of resolution is to help us see that any issue or conflict can be *designed in ways that are suitable to the resources at hand*. But, we can also see in the process of polarizing, whether naturally or by design as Adizes does, that any issue can be reformulated as a dispute *by the processes of resolution themselves*.

CONCLUSION: THE SCALE OF CHANGE

Hammering and sawing make changes. These intentional acts solve problems occurring along the path of building a house. This chapter has provided a discussion of those paths that organize the hammering and sawing and contemplating and surveying and painting and landscaping necessary to complete a residence. In this chapter, I have written about grand paths and lesser ones that our society has used to resolve issues, issues so slight as building a home or so significant as an international crisis. The grand paths may be equally required to reconstruct the self-respect of a battered woman or to preserve an Amazon village from the onslaught of modern commerce. Conversely, a rather simple, reduced path may land an astronaut on the moon. Changes required to make U.S. industry vital may also follow a rather simple path, but the massiveness of the requisite reeducation makes the issue seem intractable. The complexity of the path required to resolve an issue is not a function of the numbers of people, of the miles to be traveled, or the resources that are threatened but of the degree of restructuring that we perceive must be done to ensure the stable reconfiguring of organization or community. This is equivalent to saying it is a function of the plot of the story to guide the path of change.

The required scale of a change effort is, in part, a function of loss (or change) of culture that makes visible the fundamental, ontological gaps that separate those involved. When grand anomalies surface, paths of a grand scale are required to resolve them. For example, recognizing the anomaly that the "correction" system has no logical, much less moral, connection to the judicial system calls for so great a change that we have offered up our society's bounty to avoid seeing what changes are required to produce a harmonious society. In part, we may avoid dealing with anomalies of such magnitude because we do not understand what it would take to resolve them. The existing structure provides a facade for the meaninglessness that lies hidden behind it. Without an image of the path to resolution, it may be easier to stay within the hell with which we are familiar than to work openly with the anomaly. Having a theory of paths makes it easier to image the course, but we also need to know what resources and what courage we need to take a particular "trip."

If we follow the models of problem solving and strategic response, the resources required to follow a path are defined by our environments. That is, according to current conventions, we need to identify the political, technological, cultural (structural), and legal constraints and opportunities in our environments. In the approach I take in this meta-praxis, however, these elements are but constructions of particular realities. Therefore, they are "encountered" only when the paths of resolution take us into the reality in which they are defined. In this theory, the choice of a path of change is not determined by the characteristics of the environment that are defined within particular realities as is done in contemporary planning models. It is more nearly the inverse—the relevance of any factor is determined by the choice of path. The choice is not dependent on the political climate or the stages of technology or the form of the government. The choice of approach to resolution is nearly context-free, for it is not embedded in the realities in which the issue is formulated. Rather, it is founded in a "logical space" of alternative realities and realized in the particular distributions of beliefs of the involved populations. The primary "reality" is the meta-reality within which the stories of the culture are written. The choices are thus made in terms of the stories that are relevant to the populations involved in the conflicts. The role of the facilitators of change, whether outside advisers or central actors, is to select a journey and *encourage* those involved to pursue it fully.

To discuss this process of selection of the stories, I need ground from which to build, arbitrary as it is.[25] I choose to build on the ground of the *processes by which cultures are formed* in a space of alternative realities and the qualities of the active agents, that is, *the leaders and followers*, who will affect the changes. These are the topics of the next chapter.

5 Leaders, Followers, and Cultures

In the last chapter, I described the paths of change that lead to resolution of complex issues. The paths describe the *processes of change*. The changes occur within the territory of the alternative realities and are manifested in the behavior of the actors—the *leaders and followers*. The *cultures* in turn are characterized by their dominant realities and the history of their evolution. The way in which these three factors contribute to resolution is the topic of this chapter.

Meta-praxis is a situational theory of intentional action. It indicates that the way change is brought about is a function of the situation and that the outcomes depend greatly on how well the path is matched to the issues and the realities in which it is embedded. In this chapter, I deal with three aspects of the realities as they are manifested in the environment.

Leadership style: what types of leaders are appropriate, even necessary, to traverse a particular path

Worldviews of the population, the followers: the impact on the selection of the paths of various distributions of worldviews among the involved people

Culture: the qualities of the culture relevant to resolving the conflict, viewed from the processes through which cultures are formed

In most approaches to the resolution of conflict, the environment of a conflict situation is described via factors such as the economic conditions, technological development, legal and political constraints and opportunities, and human and natural ecologies. When I began this investigation, I too assumed that these were significant elements of the "situation." I, and most others in Western societies, are habituated to viewing the world in these terms. But, as I developed the work and experienced it in practice, I recognized in what I myself had been writing that these are but aspects of a particular reality. They are the environment of the solutions, not of the issues. They are aspects of a constructed reality within which we choose to operate to achieve a resolution. It is difficult for me to keep away from these familiar constructions as I think and write about meta-praxis. Even at this stage of my thinking, I still want to hold on to some of the characterizing qualities of the sensory world. In this chapter, I write in terms of the existing distributions of beliefs among the relevant populations. But, for the most part, I limit my dependence on the situation to aspects of the believers that particularly bear on our choice of paths and the ways in which each aspect aids or inhibits the progress toward resolution.

LEADERSHIP

Leadership is the most important single factor in achieving resolution. For all the designing, all the goodwill, and all the insights we bring to bear on resolving a major issue, without adequate and appropriate leadership, our efforts will be for naught. But to say that is meaningless without a clear idea of what is meant by *leadership*. The claim of importance is safe to assert if leadership covers all the aspects that contribute to a person or group being able to direct an effort. It is a more useful and testable assertion if the definition of leadership is limited to the *style* (approach) and the skill that are used by a person or group to guide an effort.

I define *style* to be the normal behaviors that follow from the worldview that one maintains. For example, a person taking on leadership from a unitary worldview behaves quite differently than one who operates from a social view. The former sees leadership as exercising authority; the latter, as facilitating participation in an agreed upon project. My definition has nothing to do with an individual's *ability* to lead, only with how the leading is understood.

Identification of style provides the basis of a theory of leadership but it is not itself such a theory. Many of the theories that have been developed during the past century can be fit into the map of realities and seem to follow from the assumptions of their placement. I assert that this is because the proposers of the theories see leadership and leaders from their own worldviews. So one who develops an exchange, environmental, or contingency theory is likely to be coming from a sensory mind-set, augmented by unitary or social assumptions. A pure trait theory arises from a unitary worldview, and a "great man" theory from a follower of the mythic. Each of these theories applies to situations defined by the appropriate worldview, but each is no more general than is the worldview on which it is based. The current work transcends that limitation, at least to the extent of the range of worldviews held in Western cultures. So, while it is not a theory of leadership, it incorporates leadership as an element in a theory of intentional change. In this function, it does indicate, however, that the existing theories of intentional change are all bound to be inadequate for they do not deal with the issues of change that are central to any significant theory of the way in which people are *led*.

Fully recognizing that my own worldview produces this preference, I am inclined to agree with Burns (1978) that the term *leader* ought to be applied exclusively to those who effect great purpose. I see these leaders, in most cases, to be charismatic, thus operating out of a mythic worldview. I am aware of occasions, however, when those of other worldviews do "lead" populations to the resolution of issues, so I will continue to use the popular designation of "leader" for the whole range of influencers and change makers and explain the different ways in which they affect a population.

The Leadership Topology

An exploration of the "topology" of realities suggests we should find a dozen or more distinct *styles of leadership*. Again, these styles are not indicative of skills or effectiveness. The skills are a complex matter of heritage and training; the effectiveness is a question of match to a situation. In Diagram 5.1, I present the 10 different styles of leadership that are based in a single or pair of worldviews.[1] Many of these styles are familiar. Some will be new to those readers who have primarily been concerned with U.S. corporate management. There are a variety of classification schemes already in the literature; some, such as those of Michael Maccoby (1988), span much of the topology of this scheme. I introduced this scheme (McWhinney, 1985) as an application of the multiple worldviews and include it here to show the role that each style has in supporting one or another of the paths of resolution.

The styles can be grouped into three sets selected so as to clarify the way in which a leader with a particular style contributes to the resolution path, as follows:

Diagram 5.1 Leadership Styles

SOURCE: Adapted from McWhinney (1985).

Authoritative: authoritarian, task, and expert
Pluralistic: integrative, participative, and consultative
Charismatic: prophetic, entrepreneurial, and facilitative

Leaders in each of these styles have a base in a *given* reality *from which* they lead. Their choices of actions and their impact on the world are *controlled* by criteria found in a second reality. I am not entirely clear on identifying the role of the two realities. In the descriptions of the leadership styles, I characterize them according to which reality is most often the given reality, but there are interesting examples of alternative assignments. For example, a facilitative leader could accept the individuality of people as primary but guide by capturing the followers' energy in new ideas, stories, or symbols. I think it more common that the facilitator accepts his or her own primacy as given and works with a belief in values of individuality.[2] So there are two possible forms of facilitative leadership. In the extreme form of authoritarian, expert, and integrative leadership, the "leadership" is within the same reality. In this theory, this should produce a null case of leading. We see examples, however, of leaders who seem to be so singularly defined that it is worth noting their characteristics.

And, making the picture even more complicated, there is evidence, in my studies and in Burns's (1978) and Bennis and Nanus's (1985), that leaders who show strong use of three realities are likely to be more effective than those using but one or two. Here I treat the "superleaders" of whom Bennis and others write as leaders skillful in the combining of two or three *styles* in their work. With these combinations, we can describe three more styles. That there are further distinctions is more significant than giving them particular names or categories.

The description in the following sections focuses on characteristics that are relevant to matching the style with the requirements of a path of resolution. The majority of space is given to exploration of the charismatic styles as they are involved in all deep changes and are less understood than the others. The other leadership styles play lesser roles in change processes though they do have essential roles in the reduced paths.

Charismatic Leadership

> *All people dream: but not equally.*
> *Those who dream by night*
> *in the dusty recesses of their minds*
> *wake in the day to find that it was vanity.*
> *But the dreamers of the day*
> *are dangerous people,*
> *for they may act their dream with open eyes*
> *to make it possible.*
>
> —T. E. Lawrence

In the half century since Chester Barnard successfully initiated the study of the rational executive with his *The Function of the Executive* (1938), American students of organization and public administration created an image of leadership as a logical process that draws upon the rational tools of decision making as well as personal and interpersonal influence. Beginning with the emergence of the humanistic psychologies and of the personal psychologies of spiritual leaders such as Norman Vincent Peale, we again recognized that leadership depends significantly on the special qualities of vision, self-assertion, and charisma. We came to recognize the volitional component of leadership, that "the dreamers of the day" create the worlds we live in to a far greater degree than the rational deterministic theories had allowed. Gradually in the 1960s, the post-Hitler taboo about studying the charismatic diminished sufficiently that serious political scientists and sociologists picked up where Max Weber had left off with his seminal 1947 work. It was not until the mid-1970s that organizational theorists moved their attention to the commercial and industrial entrepreneur as an exemplar of charismatic and transformational leadership.[3] The renewed interest in charismatic studies parallels the emergence of a general theory of change. Now we can see that the study of the charismatic is critical if we are to understand the processes of social change and conflict resolution.

Charisma is a quality of a person who operates from a dominant mythic reality. It originally meant a *gift of divine grace,* often with a power of healing or prophesy. Its meaning has been broadened to include the *power to captivate and energize a following.* "Scientific discovery, ethic promulgation, artistic creativity, political and organizational authority, and in fact all forms of genius, in the original sense of the word as permeation by the 'spirit,' are as much instances of the category of charismatic things as is religious prophecy" (Shils, 1965, p. 201). In a systems framework, charisma is the ability to entrain, to bring others into step with, to create a flow of energy between systems. The force of charisma available to one of a mythic worldview can vary from none—a quiet poet living his life out as a typist—to a totally dominating influence we associate with the great leaders of good and evil—a Buddha or an Adolf Hitler.

The mythic grounding of the charismatic is the ultimate differentiating act. It is born within the "rainbow" portion of the path of rebirth. To bring the mythic image into the community or to a physical realization, the leader must conventionalize, moving it from "soul to power," transforming the inner formative struggles into a confrontation of one's idiosyncratic vision with a public. The move from soul to power is the transition from the diffuse "rainbow" to the focused, directing "lightning bolt." It is with the "lightning bolt" that the charismatic leader "subordinates the self-balancing tendencies of society to the will and desires of a 'power.' "[4] This is the essence of *courage.*

The central role of the charismatic leader in a change process is to create meaning, symbols from which the society derives "substance," things that "matter," the "stuff" of life. In the extreme, we sense that the charismatic *creates the followers.* The absolute construction of reality by the mythic act is stated succinctly by Albert Camus (1956, p. 22): "I rebel, therefore *we* exist." In a revitalizing path, the charismatic gives body to "the truth." The prime example is the messiah, but many other heroes fill this role, even an Elvis Presley, or a Lee Iacocca as the leader of U.S. industry in the battle against Japanese industry. In a renaissance path, the leader stands for the people. He literally gives personhood to each follower as Camus decreed.

The mythic's acts of leadership are necessarily ones through which he creates himself. They arise out of the identity of the individual mythic person. When that identity matches with the community's needs, the leadership is accepted; if there is a mismatch, the acts and leaders are rejected as irrelevant. We cannot independently test the match of the community image with a mythic idea, but one indication that a leader will be socially validated is the degree of association with founding myths of the society or organization. For example, if the leader's being calls to mind ancient stories that are recorded as myths and embodied in ritual or in the histories of persons, families, and whole peoples, they are likely to be seen as in tune with the community's direction and will be accepted. So Martin Luther King was a leader calling his people out of ancient strengths to achieve a dream of the future. This calling was for a revitalization rather than a renaissance.

Charismatic leadership has always been difficult for the culture into which it irrupts. By definition, a society has no rational means by which to judge the appropriateness of a great "program." Compare the public's responses to Roosevelt's, Hitler's, and Lenin's sociopolitical programs following World War I; each seemed to be a savior in his society in the early years. But their quality differs greatly in ways that relate to the degree of access each had to his own unconscious "dark side." The difficulty with a charismatic is that a dark genius arising from a "possession" will create a more energetic engagement with his society than will a stalwart supporter of community values.[5] We can so compare Hitler with Roosevelt. The vitality coming from a leader acting without grounding in a "reality principle"—Freud's characterization of a strong mythic—will attract people of similarly highly focused energy in the community and thus lead to lopsided agendas and eventually a social mania.

Charismatic leadership takes hold of a population in situations of uncertainty. The uncertainty may arise from explicit danger, rapid environmental change, or significant creative breakthroughs and the opportunities the breakthroughs create. The leadership that appears at such times creates order, gives guidance to the population, and establishes a source of meaning, protocols for action, and criteria for selection among alternative courses. The leader of ideas, the steadfastly courageous, is the one who creates great devotion, brings hope to the hopeless, and sees beyond current dilemmas by drawing on a mythic worldview. The mythic character is, in the extreme, Churchill saying "I am Britain" and Napoleon declaring "I am Charlemagne." These leaders do not stand for, or imitate, but are the larger images. The leaders may find this image in the archetypal tales they grew up with, in reading histories and biographies, or in following the advice found in parables and proverbs. Tales of the lives of the great religious prophets have provided guidance to innumerable leaders, even to the degree that they may take on the persona of the prophet.

Taking on the *persona* of the fabled or historical hero is a common though paradoxical aspect of the charismatic leader, an admission that one is not the creator of oneself but that one is a manifestation of the heroic or of the founding myth of the culture. This fantasy turns out to be an important one for the selection among paths under the conditions of greatest uncertainty. I will return to this issue in last chapter of the book.

When mythic leaders fail, whether at Waterloo or in Nixon's Oval Office, the mythics' behavior may turn solipsistic—they isolate themselves from disconfirming evidence, going into asylum often created by their disciples, as was certainly the case with President Nixon—a mythic personality if not charismatic. One of the consequences of the mythic's failure, or simple departure, is that charismatic leadership is followed by a "leadership by disciples," an authoritarian leadership that inhibits any change that diminishes the image of the fallen or dead hero. This has been repeatedly observed in political history; it is equally to be seen with the death of entrepreneurs such as David Sarnoff of RCA or Walt Disney. Their death or failure produces a radical shift to an authoritarian style that holds on to power in proportion to its lack of vitality.

For all the generative power that flows from the great charismatics and their sensory expressions, the mythic leader is not easy to follow. For Americans accustomed to having everyone whose job it is to influence their subordinates being called a leader, it seems paradoxical that these men have been the greatest of all leaders. Their freedom from the constraints of the sensory reality, from the moral concerns of the social, and from the canons of the unitary leads them to violate everyone's sensibilities. It is not possible for charismatic leaders to give credit to other people for their ideas. The mythics will unconsciously accept ideas—absorb them into their monistic egos—and moments later issue them forth as their own creations. A strong charismatic may take ownership of ideas, stories, or whole schemes moments after they are communicated to him with no recognition of the sources. Similarly, the leader may change his mind frequently, leaving followers out of step, working on "the wrong track", thus destroying work already accomplished. What was said yesterday does not matter for the past is re-created as part of the charismatic's future. There is no "truth" but the leader's. Of one such leader, it was said, "And thus, in his considered view, what did not suit, could not be true." Yet, there is no greater leadership than that which creates meaning in the lives of the followers. The irrational that arises from the charismatic's leadership eventually becomes the rational by which a society is led.[6]

Three Forms of Charisma

I identify three forms of charisma that I distinguish by the *reality from which the control is exercised in any change effort* (see Diagram 5.1). The charismatic leader creates images within the mythic but must reify (take control of) them in a second domain. For example, the demagogue exerts influence by preaching his word in a unitary frame (the prophetic form) and great teachers evoke from their students ideas and self-respect, thus controlling from the social reality (the facilitative form). Pure charisma is pure creativity—ideation lacking substance. It is only in the expression through another controlling domain of reality that we recognize the presence of leadership. The pairing of the control reality with the given mythic reality gives the three forms that cover a rich and provocative range of leadership.

Prophetic. This style of leader manifests a truth system that is defined by a unitary dogma, often in the form of a "received" text, a symbol that captures a culture's essence or defines its territory (as a surrogate for a cultural definition). He believes he has a transcendent message or understanding that is to be transmitted to a following. In some cases, he clearly believes he is the creator, but the more common experience is that the mythic is the carrier of a message. Churchill and Ronald Reagan saw themselves as reflectors of tradition rather than creators of it. The religious prophetic typically speaks as a *channeler*, bringing messages of the Absolute from a spiritual source. Moses is the archetype; Mary Baker Eddy, founder of Christian Science, is a more recent exemplar. There are lesser prophetics who hardly merit the title but who are important in the theory of change. One type, the preacher-charlatan-hypnotist-promoter, includes individuals ranging from TV evangelists who may sincerely believe they are channelers of a true faith to effective promoters selling a product or service with spiritual, patriotic, or tradition-maintaining absoluteness. Even a Michael Eisner, chairman of the Walt Disney Company, plays the prophetic in his promotion of the Disney tradition in successful combination with his entrepreneurial role.

The prophetic leader is a major factor in a change process, both in differentiating and in conventionalizing paths. For the "true believers," the prophetic leader conventionalizes symbols, carrying the message of salvation, of certitude. The conveyed message reaffirms the truth, perhaps set in new symbols and images. In this role, he is separate from the people, a demigod dressed in clerical gown, a fighter-pilot's uniform, or a rock and roller's costume. General Robert E. Lee is the epitome—a soldier standing tall in the saddle, in the service of principle. I don't have enough data yet to know whether the prophetic leader takes his own mythic world as the given reality and uses the unitary image that he channels as the control, or the reverse. The claim must, of course, be the latter—that the truth is absolute and the leader is but the messenger. Viewed from a pluralistic reality, I am inclined to think the former is more often the case. That is, it is easy to view the prophetic personality as ego based.

In a differentiation path, the prophetic's role is clearer. He is the personification of the collective myth or the explicit purpose. He is the symbol of the belief that the community or organization can control the forces of history and achieve its transcendent objectives. He is one with them, not separate. He is Shakespeare's Henry V at the battle of Agincourt. There is a familiar problem with successful prophets—they have feet of clay. That is, the mythic leaders all have strong egos, so one who has begun as a banner carrier for a community may lose a sense of integrity with that community and choose to impose his own path. Lech Walesa of the Polish Solidarity movement typified the leader moving forward his people's needs, but, as he comes into the presidency, the inherent self-centeredness of the mythic becomes more apparent.

Entrepreneurs. The entrepreneur, impresario, innovator, producer, developer all take the day's dream into the possible, realizing the idea in the physical reality as an object, an organization, or a production. In some cases, they create from "nothing"; in others, they reformulate an existing idea. A charismatic's entrepreneurial impact on the sensory world, initiated as a hunch or informal hypothesis, may become a scientific proposition or a technology. David Sarnoff, the entrepreneur of RCA, transformed his fantasy of a color television into a fact of the world by organizing a staff of technologists. Sarnoff was the "possibilizer." His articulate image and demand for its realization made it possible for the staff to accomplish that which they, not being mythics, did not, and perhaps could not, imagine happening. So it was with lunar and space exploration, which Philip Slater (1974, p. 167) says "represents the extreme form of agency, of limitless narcissistic striving."

I have pictured entrepreneurs as working from the mythic base into the physical world. It is more often the case that they are creative "designers," using their imaging power to drive their (unitary-sensory) design work. That is, their mythic ideas are structured by the logic of the "sciences" within which the design is realized. This follows a differentiating path, which could begin anew or, more commonly, is generated by some need or image the entrepreneur found in his environment. Entrepreneurs do not make contributions to a conventionalizing path.

Facilitators. The name itself indicates that there is ambiguity in the role the facilitator plays in creating change. It calls for a mythic person to facilitate for others when *by definition* there is no plurality. The facilitation works between the social and mythic realities to enable the emergence of new symbols, entities that have meaning—"substance that matters." When the leader takes as given his mythic reality, the facilitation gains acceptance in the community for the new symbol. The leader "charms" the members into the feeling of co-ownership in the symbol's creation and propagation. This is the genius of a coach or teacher who builds the self-confidence of an individual or group by gaining their participation in a creative work. The great football coach of Alabama, Bear Bryant, exemplifies the form. This form of facilitation works in the conventionalizing direction.

A facilitative leader can play an opposite role as well, enabling the group to create a new unifying symbol or image that they form and make real by their pluralistic involvement. This is a fundamental differentiating act of *founding*, of initiating a group by the members' involvement in cocreation.

As with the prophetic leader, it is hard to tell even from the inside of the process which process is going on; one needs independent knowledge of the leader's style. The best effort at gaining acceptance will look very much like enabling.

A leader with a combination of charismatic styles may use elements of three, even four, realities, thereby gaining greater flexibility and power. The ideal American executive is one who shows the qualities of both the entrepreneur and the facilitator—mythic plus social and sensory. The television ministries have shown aptitude both as prophetics and as entrepreneurs—mythic plus sensory and unitary. Like an artist, a leader can gain power by "vesseling" a pure mythic persona within a more balanced personality comfortable with all the realities. His executive skills vessel the mythic creativity and guide the realization of the ideas in accordance with the demands of the environment.

Leadership Is Irrational

The view of charismatic leaders presented here is strikingly at odds with leadership theories, at least those developed prior to the recent extensive interest in transformational leaders (e.g., Burns, 1978). Any purely mythic act of leadership is *irrational*, in any of the usual senses of the concept, because the leader's reality is outside the established rationalities of the society. U.S. military planners were convinced, for example, that Churchill could not outlast Hitler's onslaught on the British

Isles in the early 1940s. He was considered no more believable than Don Quixote. With the same cautious skepticism, bank officials resist providing entrepreneurs with capital for new ventures, and new religious leaders are attacked as heretics. The leaders do not make rational decisions; rather, they provide guidance out of integral expressions of themselves.

In a quiet time during which a culture holds to a settled and accepted paradigm, the course of a person's or a community's life will be decided, more or less effectively, by an accepted *rationality* based in a unitary truth, a sensory evaluation of data, or a consensus of values politically attained. At such time, the leader's sense may be in tune with the culture's. But, in crisis or with the failure of the prevailing paradigm and the accompanying loss of dominance by one or another reality system, leaders must find another source of wisdom that precedes rationality, to create anew or refound their society's course in archetypal images.[7] Using such a source is a reversion not to irrationality but to the collective unconscious, to the mythic font of the society. Thus the British population became the yeoman citizenry that Churchill conjured; the Indians stood with Gandhi; and the Red Army followed Mao on the Long March.

Authoritative Styles

Authoritative styles of leadership stem from a deterministic worldview—they make no provision for intentional change. Authoritative leadership serves to articulate and establish positions. Ideally, the deterministic world is a vast algorithm for articulating designs, rules, facts, and programs. Leaders (and everyone else) simply turn the crank. Of course, it is hard to imagine a purely deterministic world without a degree of intentional action, but we can get a clearer picture of the anomalies of change if I stick close to the ideal form in describing the styles. Also in a world that is otherwise full of change, deterministic positions appear to be regressing, not keeping current. The regression, or simply the resistance, makes it particularly important for those who are attempting intentional change to understand the worldview of the authoritative styles. That a significant portion of the population of Western societies as well as its leadership is of a strongly deterministic worldview gives further reason for making this exposition.

The authoritative is the world of science and technology, law, religion, accounts and property rights, and social custom. Within the deterministic worldviews, there is no justification for conflict. There is the "right" position; others are excluded, whether from the rules of a science, a religion, or an administrative structure. But, as has been often observed, in the denial of conflict is the greatest source of violence—the more we repress the causes, the more likely the eventual eruption will be violent.

Again I identify three styles: the pure authoritarian, which is particularly interesting because it is so rarely discussed in the social change literature; the task leader, which, conversely, is a style that has been thoroughly discussed; and the role of the pure expert, which is also rarely encountered but is an interesting contrast to the mythic. All merit a revisit.

Authoritarian. The defining qualities of a unitary leadership are certainty, clear direction, access to information, and just treatment. As in other aspects of unitary thinking, it changes nothing and thus does not participate in a second reality. In practice, it provides comfort and guidance and, in many cases, elegance and harmony. So it seems from within. Its ideal exemplars are the Catholic and Orthodox popes, but there are ordinary examples in teachers, military officers, priests, supervisors, and parents. In the contemporary folklore of organizations, this style is held to be an ineffective form of leadership. Mostly this damning image comes from people who are themselves of a pluralistic worldview, so they see imposition of unchanging order and harsh restraint, not loving support. Of all the styles, the authoritarian is least supportive of change, as it denies that human interventions have any meaning. But, as in most human affairs, it counterinvents that which it most denies, an opposition, the antileader.

The style of the antileader comes from the *dialectic* process and is carried by the person who leads from opposition to the established authority. The basic style is the same as the authoritarian described above but it is aimed at producing ideological revolution. Initially, the dialectical position provides a freedom to set to one's course in almost any direction, a freedom that is experienced briefly in the "free-float" after a revolution. As the forces of revolution replace those of the establishment, the dialectic system increasingly mirrors the one it is replacing, and leaders emerge who again are of the authoritarian style. Most revolutions don't proceed with such perfect symmetry; other forces enter, and the initial dialect may be replaced either by renaissance forces that dismantle the given system or, more commonly, by a revitalization that establishes a refined version of the one replaced.

Task. Locating the controlling reality in the sensory produces a more familiar, if less dramatic, style that is personified in the *task leader* (Tannenbaum & Schmidt, 1973). This is the traditional style of the supervisory role. One leads in this style by presenting a task, particularly as a series of steps or processes, and assuming it will be accomplished. The skill is in the proper formulation of the processes—that is, the technology—in relation to the sensory reality of the task. If the tasks are skillfully performed, the functions of leadership are unnecessary. If not skillfully done, the system, that is, the members and supervisors, are simply separated from that task responsibility. The deterministic worldviews have no model for adaptation, so failure can only lead to separation. The reason that hierarchical organizations promote the skilled technician is that the task leaders have no place for participative or charismatic leadership.[8]

Expert. An alternative name for this style is *authoritative*. It is the simplest of all guiding processes, just providing knowledge of "what is" in the sensory reality. One may wish to contest this basis for knowledge, but, in practical affairs, there is great value in simply knowing of what one speaks—knowing about a city, a subculture, the plants in a forest, the financial records of an industry, the member of the board, the history of an organization. In many cases, the test of the knowledge is immediate, as when the librarian finds the obscure reference. In other cases, for example, the historical fact is trusted because it is part of a web of facts on which the expert has given good testimony in the past. As with the pure authoritarian leadership, there are no processes of change, thus no second reality is involved.

This leadership style is strangely linked to the mythic style. Both charismatic and expert present their world as simply, unarguably existent. Both hypnotize their followers with that simplicity and often complement each other powerfully. Perhaps common simplicity is the basis for the effective collaboration of Thomas Edison or Walt Disney with their technical staffs.

Pluralistic Styles

The dominant quality of the pluralistic leadership styles is recognizing other people and valuing their opinions and data. The skills integrate these values and data into coherent arguments for action and adapting people and resources to their intended functions.

The typical social leadership form is *integrative*. It is other centered, emphasizing the development of the other—the followers—to accomplish the system's goals. While the integrative style is often associated with indecisiveness, its strength lies in raising value issues, exploring opportunities, balancing (allocating) interpersonal needs, and resolving conflict. Integrative leaders are likely to be confronting, encouraging, and open in emotional as well as intellectual task directions. It is now a well-understood form, described as the subordinate-centered end of the scale created by Tannenbaum and Schmidt (1973).[9]

Integrative. The subordinate-centered leadership style arises in the social reality and is primarily concerned with maintaining *fairness* in an environment seen as continually changing. It is a stabilizing force in an organization—"homeostatic" in system theoretic terms. This style is not a sufficient basis for initiating an effort or leading an organization, though a leader who is primarily an integrator may come to the top to facilitate the implementation of preestablished direction. Dwight Eisenhower, both as general and as president, used an integrative style to pull together disparate forces in the armies he commanded and the political situations he inherited. In a change process, the style has the most relevance under "the rainbow" segment of the grand paths.

In a differentiating path, the integrative style is supportive, providing the "vesseling" that protects the system while it is undergoing radical change. In a conventionalizing path, the integrative processes provide the adaptive environment in which individual differences are accommodated in the drive toward productive efficiency.

Participative. While pure integrative leadership is still a rare form in the West, the combination of integrative with expert leadership (from the sensory worldview) has been a major development in the United States during the past decades. The combination produces a managerial style in which the central focus is the managing of *valued things.* Here I use the term *management* rather than *leadership* because, in this combination, the behavior is more accurately an allocative function than the typical motivating, inciting, directing, or exemplifying processes we associate with the role of leader. During the past three decades, the U.S. business community has used this notion of leadership as the central image for development of managers and, unfortunately, for senior leaders as well.

For all the appearance of its progressiveness, the participative style does not have a role in either of the grand paths of resolution. It has no place in a differentiating path because questions of allocation are rendered irrelevant by the loss of direction and meaning within the organization or community. A conventionalizing path tolerates "participation" in the final stages to adapt its principles, at the margin, to the pluralistic environment. This is done with disdain, just as the church keeps a distance from secular matters; the participative style is appropriate for the *procurator* of a religious institution, a necessary function but one without substance. (For me, here is a clue about the failure of U.S. management. It might be that, by insisting on confronting the authoritarian models with the participative, we have, unknowingly, blocked the kind of change that is seen in the Japanese society and perhaps the German. It may be a particularly inappropriate combination in high-performing systems, a fact that has been implicitly recognized by those managers who have shown no enthusiasm for the open-system type of organization that is popular with OD professionals.)

Consultative. There is what might be viewed as a transitional style between the monistic and pluralistic styles that was frequently used in the movement from a *Theory X* to a *Theory Y*. In the past, I frequently worked with leaders who "listened with a participative ear" but made decisions from a unitary position of authority. This produces what was experienced as *consultative leadership.* The typical exchange with subordinates began with a consultation to obtain their opinions and data followed by an indication that the leader had the information he or she needed to make a decision and, sooner or later, would make a pronouncement of the decision. The leader could have been making the decisions on social or sensory criteria, but it has been my experience that the decision was an "interpretation" of the authority vested in the "superior" decision maker. Because of the apparent similarity of the social and unitary concern for colleagues, that is, members of the community, it is often difficult for the sensory or social subordinate to know from which reality the superior is operating. The social phase of a discussion calls for informing, questioning, and formulating ideas, and the unitary phase, for acceptance, support, and filling out details of implementation.

If subordinates continue to operate out of a social reality after the superior has shifted to the unitary mind-set, it appears that they are being "insubordinate." Such ill-timed behavior is sensed as a threat by the superior and is so punished, a classic example of a double-bind situation. The long-term result is that the subordinates learn it is better to be silent than to risk punishment, and the leader ends up frustrated because he or she gets less and less advice. This style, at its best, is adaptive, but it can contribute to an organization only by increasing the discipline of the subordinates. Based on a small sample, I find this style is used by a person of a unitary worldview that includes the belief that one should listen to others; the "participative" behavior is thus consistent with a unitary assumption.[10]

The effectiveness of a leader is in part a function of his or her followers. That is well understood. What is less well understood is that not all "followers" are alike in their response to leadership and to the cultures in which they operate. So, to understand the ways in which the leader should act, we must know something of the composition of the "followers."

FOLLOWERS COME IN SEVERAL FORMS

"Can't we have a supervisor?"

This was a query, more a plea, from a woman who had worked for a couple of years in a new high-performing manufacturing plant under conditions that were among the best of any place in the United States: good pay and work conditions, respect, involvement, opportunity to learn and progress, even control over the amount of variability in her work. But she missed the freedom from responsibility and making choices. She had come to work hoping to find a friendly place and expecting she would be told what to do. Now she was tired of making choices and hoped someone would improve the quality of *her* working life. This woman wanted to be a *follower*. Being a follower is compatible with her unitary worldview. Being a part of a group in which she did not have to make decisions would free her from unending conflict within herself and with the group and her husband. She is like a few million other Americans, men as well as women. In our efforts to improve the QWL to revive U.S. industry, there are still a lot of unexamined factors.

One *style* of being a member of an organization fits with the reality of the woman in the above example; people of other belief systems work best with other styles of "following." Followership styles have received little attention to date, yet the styles of subordinates and community members are as significant in conflict resolution as are the styles of managers and leaders. The development of differentiating tools such as the alternative realities (or the Jungian Myers-Briggs or Kolb learning style typologies) provides a way to understand *followers, colleagues, independents*, and other styles as we have come to understand leaders. In this section, we take a brief look at this property of a population to understand the terrain that a path of change must traverse.[11]

The Manner of Response to Leadership

The focus of the question "why work" has always been viewed in isolation from the context in general, but, in particular, from the leadership for which the work is being done. The meanings of the "stuff" that makes a person work is a function not only of the reality from which a person works but also of the setting in which the work is done. During the past century, the factors contributing to the diversity of meaning and response to leadership may have been of relatively little importance. It has been a male work force, with male leadership dominated by a deterministic worldview, and with little threat of significant sociopolitical change. As I point out later in this section, the predominance of that mind-set allowed investigators to limit their attention to very simple models of response. It is obvious that we will have to go into the question of the manners of response more deeply to confront new issues in organizations and local and international communities. My first look at the leadership/followership patterns discussed in our literatures indicates that those we have been using are now of limited application and one that will diminish even further in coming decades. The renewed interest in leadership during the 1980s may be the defense of a dying issue as our cultures shift away from the strong bias toward the deterministic worldviews.

The various relations between those who are in positions of leadership—"power" might be a better overall characteristic—and those who are dependent on them are not clearly identified in the literature of organizations. The dominant images of this relation have come from economists and sociologists with strong deterministic worldviews. They ignore additional relationships that are obvious to a depth psychologist or a political scientist, including relationships that arise from historical conditions, either in the person's life or in the society, and the special forms of followership that occur in the resolution of issues. But, before discussing these relationships, I wish to describe the forms of followership that occur in formal work organizations (see Diagram 5.2).

Using the framework of the four realities, I see four categories that account for a significant portion of the different roles, as follows.

Followers. The classic name for the subordinate role represents the relation that held for the majority of the population as recently as the early twentieth century. A clue to the importance of the relation is that the word *follow* in the original Teutonic language meant to *serve, attend, minister to,* even before it was used to indicate a relation in time or space.

Subordinates. This is the relation between craftspeople, experts, technicians, or professionals in which the superior is an expert in the same field as the subordinate. The relation is based in part on respect for skills but, more important, on exchange. The subordinates are followers only in the deference they give to the leader, who has superior, relevant skills. People stay in such a relation because it provides a better life than other alternatives.[12] I derive from Michael Maccoby's study (1988) of workers in Information Age industries and government that this coworking relation is by far the most common form of follower-ship in large industrial and bureaucratic organizations.

Team members. I choose this label to represent the feeling tone of fol-lowers where the leader is viewed as a helper, friend, guide. The subordinate's productive skills may be entirely different than the superior's. The workers, or members, expect support, guidance, and protection from the leader, often to allow them to "do their work" without interference from the organization or community at large. In this relation, the followers work/live in relatively unstructured teams, in which a prime value is mutual respect.[13]

Independents. This role is the least involving form of followership, more typical of contract workers and consultants (and, at one time, mercenaries) than employees or members. Independents relate to the supervisor contractually and are paid for work done with little expec-tation of tangential values in the work engagement. This role has al-ways been a part of a commercial society—necessary, if not fully respected. The great Japanese film *The Seven Samurai* shows the samu-rai as the epitome of it; we also see it in professional athletes, actors, and highly specialized crafts people.

These four discriminate well among most of the types of subordi-nate relations that are commonly visible in stable organizations. But there are many distinctions that appear in considering the relation of particular forms of leadership and conditions of change. To illustrate the interdependence of follower and leader styles, I constructed a ma-trix of relations between subordinates and leaders as defined by the four alternative realities (Diagram 5.2). The cells suggest a number of relations that appear to be nonconstructive, pointing to failures in leadership that are familiar to anyone working in present-day organi-zations. Examples are the counterproductive relation between people of social and unitary worldviews and the pervasive disconnection be-tween those of a mythic persuasion and their supervisors.

In the familiar *conventionalizing change*, there is a clear distinction between the role of the *leaders* and the *followers*. The leadership carries responsibility for mission or story and the followers support them, not interfering or attempting to redefine them. In the ideal *differentiating change*, all those who are present at the rebirth or enter into the storied space are best viewed as *members*. Some will be viewed as more senior than others either because they appear to have a better grasp of the path or because they have ownership of the organization's resources,

Diagram 5.2 Leaders and Followers

Follower's Reality	Leader's Given Reality			
	Unitary	Sensory	Social	Mythic
Unitary	*Follower:* provides certitude to each other; follower can also see leader as anti-Christ and thus strongly oppose	Nil: little respect for leader, ignores and passively blocks any change efforts	Nil: disrespect unless they share normative position; feels threatened by social values	*Follower:* strongly supportive if leader is charismatic, equally opposing if leader calls for unacceptable changes
Sensory	Acquiescent: accepts power and rules, so long as they work	*Subordinates:* authority given to expertise rather than the person	*Independent:* low regard for leader, ignores ideas and value considerations	*Independent:* unbelieving, but will use the opportunities provided
Social	Reactive: usually counters leadership—reactive, negative	Unwilling follower: low regard, in current cultures, often has to "go along with" while attempting to expand worldview of leader	*Team Member:* trust, cooperation, good communication	Involved: Usually counters, unless the leader is strongly facilitative, then a strong supporter
Mythic	User: uses the leader, even when in a subordinate role, as a (channel) source or as a front for follower's operations	*Independent:* uses resources to accomplish own aim; the purer the sensory, the more likely to have the mythic's respect	Nil: will use leader to "vessel" own development	Learner: will not follow, but learns from leader often in a strong love/hate dilemma

NOTE: This diagram indicates the behavior of pure types; the actual behavior of subordinates will be some mixture of the archetypical behaviors, depending on the balance among the beliefs of both leader and follower. Entries in italic print are strictly positive forms of *following*. The "independents" are in an exchange relation; they follow orders in exchange for personal value but make no commitment to organizational values. The social's "involved" response would typically be negative or reactive to mythic leadership except in the facilitative form under which the social subordinate can be an enthusiastic supporter. The mythic follower as a utilizer of the leader may be very supportive of his program but only because it serves the subordinate's needs.

a difference generated by rules of the surrounding economy or political structure. The stronger the differentiation, the more likely the members will identify with the leaders and in so doing move easily from their familiar realities and worldviews to join with the path of resolution. This is a central phenomenon of crusades—religious, political, or social—and is considered a desirable condition in the new "high-performing" and "transformative" organizations. Thus, in newly formed organizations, there is little systematic separation of followers with differing worldviews. As the organization settles, however, the personal and professional habits of the members lead then to clustering according to the reality demanded by their job and supported by their comfort with associating with people of like worldview. The tendency to differentially cluster leads to the emergence of subcultures, thus greatly increasing the complexity required of the paths of resolution.

Clustering is but one form of culture-forming processes that will be encountered in resolving issues. In each process, leaders and followers play different roles and respond differently to efforts to introduce changes. In detail, every culture will differ, but the basic processes of culturing are related to the realities of the involved populations—as well as their histories. In the next section, I look at how the different culturing processes establish the context for any change effort.

CULTURING WITHIN THE FOUR REALITIES

Thinking about the environment of a change process requires us to go beyond the logics of consistency that have been the domain of theorists, academics, and planners. I believe it requires us to go beyond even the counterintuitive and paradoxical thinking to which Quinn and McGrath (1985) refer in their exploration of what is necessary to change an organization's culture. An act of leadership determines what must be taken as real just as is required to initiate the change itself, because whatever facts we take as given will determine the success of the effort. The normal inclination in resolving issues is to take the culture as defined by our social sciences as the environment—it is, after all, describable in objective, factual terms, and the cultural language is close to that of the leaders and the professional "change agents." This choice assumes, however, the separation of the environment from that which is to be changed. An approach more in tune with the resolution effort is to define the environment in terms of the processes by which cultures are formed. This course removes one level of anomaly, a source of absurdity in attempting change, by working with "what is going on" rather than "what is in place." That is, it is easier to resolve issues when the environmental conditions surrounding the issues are viewed as changing rather than fixed. I have followed this path in the above discussion of leaders and followers as evidence of ways in which leaders and followers relate to ideas and to other people. Here, I continue this mode of discourse, weaving the choice of paths of change with the dynamics of culture formation.

I begin by describing two culturing processes that evolve in the monistic realities and then the two that devolve from these two with the assertion of pluralistic thinking. The monistic processes are *storying*, which arises from a mythic reality, and *clustering*, which arises in the unitary. The logical foundations for these two are so utterly different that it is misleading to systematically compare them. I can "rationally" compare them, and we do it every day in discussions of organizational life, but the effect is reductionistic. The most useful way to give a feeling for their differences is to present graphic images of the two as done in Diagram 5.3. A scanning of the diagram should inhibit the reader's natural tendency to immediately construct parallel descriptive categories.[14] There are two pluralistic culturing processes—*materializing* and *democratizing*—that emerge from the monistic cultures. I describe these in the following paragraphs and introduce some thoughts about the role these four culturing processes have in the composition of Western organizations compared with the organizations created by Japanese culturing processes.

Storying

Every culture begins in the winter of another, in antipathy to the crystallized essence of the old culture. We date the beginning from the symbolizing acts of the charisma that gives life to the story, usually in a renaissance but also as a revitalization of a faltering organization or community. There is some founding event or, more commonly, a set of neighboring events that are woven into the myth of origin of the culture.

The culturing process is one of bringing stories and members into a path, that is, creating a stream of *belief*, a web of stories that are believed by a population. In the most common form, a micro culture is formed around a familiar tale of birth, life, and death, of the love that founds a family, or the courage that founds a city that maintains the culture's basic forms. The great cultures are created by beliefs, by epics, of great complexity. Occasionally, these are originated by a particular charismatic leader, but more often they are webs of tales devel-

Diagram 5.3 Two Forms of Cultures: Storied and Clustered

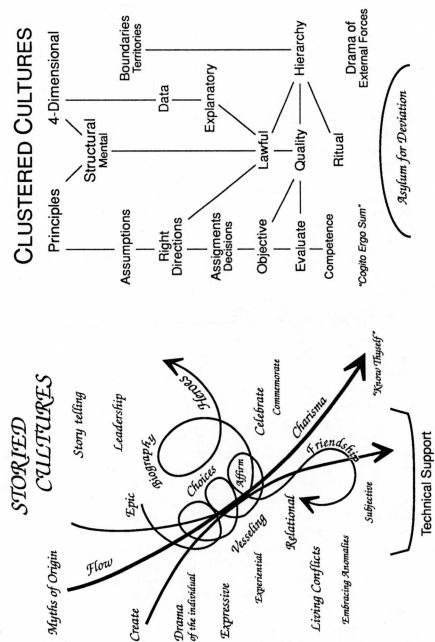

oped by a committed innovative group. The stories range from cyclical tales of everyday life to archetypal stories that have formed the great religions and secular empires. The Navajo tale of the Pollen Twins is the myth of every man expressed as a myth of origin, of death and rebirth. Arjuna's (RJ's) tale would celebrate a migration, a military victory that founded a dynasty, survival of a natural disaster, a crusade, a political revolution, or a scientific/artistic "paradigm shift." The stories that are founded in such events create a culture. Whatever the time span, the storied processes exist in time, with a beginning, a middle, and an end, *as do the cultures they create.*

A storied culture is a "project organization." It progresses toward some image, a goal or ultimate ideal state. It is creating—not simply transforming—resources, expressing greater concern with the unfolding story than the product. The pervasive drive to accomplish entrains the members, with each carrying the whole myth.[15] Work is focused around *nonrepeating tasks*—even building a process or mass production operation. The enculturation to a set of myths, and thus values, creates a strong common direction. Membership is a commitment to shared action that leads to the feeling one is "chosen" for a privileged membership, such as the members of the Mayflower group that arrived at Plymouth. This feeling denies diversity and is antipathetic to measurements that indicate differences in quality or achievement. The culture is developmental, evolving, dynamic, "Dionysian" but ultimately *self-destroying.* Its leadership is charismatic, but the followers, by definition, operate out of other realities. They convert the "dreams made real" of the leaders into programs that they understand according to their own realities and thus create the diversity from which other cultural forms emerge. New England's founding exemplifies the cultural "project organization."

The creating of belief is a self-terminating process. The process creates the storied culture and simultaneously sets the condition for its replacement with another form. It fails or decays for two reasons. First, in its birth, it has set a path toward a goal. Either the goal's achievement or the awareness that it is unachievable will take meaning out of the culture, causing it to decay. Second, the process of creating the new symbols and having them accepted by a membership creates a legacy of beliefs. Over time, the message will change, if for no other reason than that the leader or founding group will initiate different and often conflicting beliefs that will be adopted by successive followers. The followers will have come to use different codes, different interpretations of the founding message. We have seen this in the arguments over the interpretation of the U.S. Constitution, in the textual arguments over the true meaning of holy scriptures, and in the everyday reading of a body of work, such as Beethoven's or Sigmund Freud's. The need to resolve conflicts over orthodoxy leads to the forming of an authority and the emergence of a unitary hierarchy. The best documented conversion is the routinization of the charismatic leadership into authoritative rule, that is, in the founding of a religious movement or a political regime. Weber (1947/1968, p. 369) observed this conversion as one that would reduce charismatic governance to habit: "The process of routinization of the charismatic group tends to develop into one of the forms of everyday authority." This is the familiar path but, as I will describe later, with the maintenance of symbols and the sense of story in a dominantly social (reality) environment, the charismatically initiated culture may move into a democratic form.

Clustering

The organizing power of the story carried charismatically to a broader population initially is a source of hope, of a unified image by which a population may conduct its affairs. But, over time, the story decays into disjoint rules, habits, and rituals. It becomes a source of difference, of dated truths and diverse constituencies, and, ultimately, of conflict. Those who support a given view tend to cluster together to clarify their views, support each other, and distance themselves from discordant views. Clusters of followers collect around early and late versions, around the interpretations of one or another disciple, and around the styles of interpretations that arise from the follower's own worldviews. In this process, they eliminate the temporal character of the founding myth, replacing the narrative logic of episodes, the *dialectic,* with an analytic logic of classification. Symbols become names, and names are used to contrast and collect. The celebrations of victories become the rituals of conformity, and the dramas of the individual become the practice of every man. This has been the fate of most U.S. historical rituals such as the "celebration" of President's Day, Memorial Day, and the singing of the national anthem.

In a mature society, clustering arises not only from the diverse response to a recent story but from the diversities that have already led to the formation of local custom and occupational and professional groupings. We expect to find, and demonstrably do find, sharp differentiation in worldviews between groups of, for example, production engineers, social workers, and financial accountants. Clustering serves a number of uses such as supporting the development of skills, reducing the energy required to deal with novelty, and protecting our beliefs from

conflicting alternatives. These purposes can be summarized by proposing that clustering manages conflict. To further explain the processes of conflict resolution, I offer that *cultures arise to manage conflict.*
Clustering is a powerful way to organize people to stay out of each
other's "way" while living in proximity. The apparatus of clustering provides labels, language, customs, social orderings, and so on that reduce
the occasions on which peoples of different realities will have to act together. The clustering process manages conflict by exporting it beyond
daily activity, establishing authorities that have the power to eject that
which persists as inconsistent with the core principles.

The clustering process creates a culture based in consistency, ideally
derived from a single principle or teaching (as would come out of a
story). In its pure "Apollonian" form, it is an internally holistic, time-
less entity. Its ability to remain so, paradoxically, comes from its
advocates' ability to establish differences—to know who is one of us
and who is not. This ability is expressed in the workplace in performance skills and concerns with evaluability, quality, and correctness.
In theory, that should lead to a deep sense of unity; in practice, it
leads to sharp differentiation and gradations in membership. In society, this drive leads to a class structure; in the workplace, to a variety
of job titles and levels through which people are classified. The particular horror of the authoritarian society, as dramatized in Franz
Kafka's novels, is to be denied an identity in the eyes of the officials of
the society. The need to classify, however, to distinguish among those
who are "the same"—some are more the same than others—eventually
produces differentiation. Different reality beliefs, histories, and myriad other factors partition the consistency into subgroups and social
classes. What had began as a unitary expression of authority becomes
an articulated hierarchy, the *differentiated form* that follows the attempt
to maintain the *conventionalizing thrust.* The "simple" truth becomes
articulated in a nesting of progressive deductions, of departmentaliza-
tion of an organization, of a science, of the aspects of daily living,
until the fragmentation of the whole matches the (sensory) perception
of the parts. An elegant unity that was typified by the classic Greek
aesthetic is fragmented not only by the evolving concepts of truths of
the mythic origin but also by the diversity of concepts of reality held
by its members.

To illustrate this growing fragmentation, I describe a simple example of clustering in an organization, a process that is replicated in
many social settings as well.

Clustering Within an Organization

Clustering begins when new employees are selected into an organization, either on the basis of some rudimentary qualification—say, to do manual labor—or because they have special talents or training. In the latter case, there is a good likelihood that they have worldviews similar to those of members of the group into which they are inducted as mechanics, social workers, financial analysts, mathematicians, or animal trainers. We don't need a fancy theory of caste formation to justify such natural selection. New employees having similar worldviews to those of the existing employees are less likely to induce conflicts than ones who have different worldviews. Also, it is likely that the employees of like worldview will stay with their occupational group. Gradually, all those who do stay in the group will tend to have similar reality assumptions due to the combined effects of migration and adaptation to the central mode of thinking. Those who maintain difference will *tend* to leave the group, even the profession, as they feel the continuing conflict between themselves and the occupational group. This is the progressive differentiation of a society that produces alienated subgroups and classes, each with a narrow range of worldviews.

Over time, the professional units of an organization progress to become internally homogeneous and strongly differentiated among themselves. This convergence will happen at a slower rate in portions of the organization that do not have strong disciplinary bases. A labor pool to which people have been recruited randomly and that may have a higher rate of turnover is likely to begin less homogeneously, but selection based on interpersonal forces will eventually narrow the range of realities represented in any work group. I compare the evolution of a work group to a distillation process in which the people with different worldviews leave at different rates going along different routes. So, in a relatively stable environment, an organization might come to be made up primarily of homogeneous units, separated from each other not only by their tasks but also by their dominant worldviews. Diagram 5.4 shows a hypothetical distribution over a typical organizational hierarchy.[16] It could just as well describe a traditional society, such as in Spain and Portugal, or the increasing mixture of traditions found in Israel as hundreds of thousands of highly skilled and "cultured" Jews emigrate from the Soviet Union.

The distribution of clusters in Diagram 5.4 shows a characteristic pattern. At the top of most organizations is a leader with a degree of entrepreneurial style, sometimes enforced with a principled belief and sometimes supported by a concern for the human values of his or her

Diagram 5.4 Hypothetical Locations

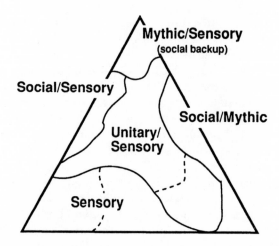

employees and relevant communities. Immediately beneath the CEO are people who have risen in the organization by their ability to support the leader, people who are often stereotyped as "yes-men," unitaries-sensories who are often effective maintainers of the organization's core functions. Beside them are the business technicians, accountants, planners, schedulers, industrial engineers, who share the same worldviews and are further clustered by their specialties. The managers who typically are of a social-sensory worldview may not be departmentally clustered but appear variously within the operational organization. Sales, marketing, human resource development people form separate clusters dominated by a social-mythic worldview. Clerical personnel, factory workers, and other entry-level positions will not be so clustered but are likely to be dominated by the unitary-sensory or even by a more earthy, sensory worldview.

This is a representation of a purely clustered organization, free of "project work" or residual story culture. But the clustering fragmentation occurs even in the evolution of transformative organizations based in stories and continues to stratify even the most open societies. It is a fundamental process in maintaining the dialectical balance necessary to a culture's maintenance.

This clustering process is an important factor in the history of organizational change and the failure to change or resolve conflicts over the past decades in the United States. In fact, most changes have been accomplished in situations in which clustering has not been allowed to "chop up" the space of realities into enclaves of narrowly defined worldviews. A particularly good example of the change efforts that initially seemed successful have been in the "green field" sites—new plants in which most of the employees were newly hired or systematically selected from the current staffs. These were designed to explicitly prevent clustering, keeping people in teams that supported *redundancy of function*. In a number of large companies where I worked in the early 1970s, we were able to recruit employees who we anticipated would work well in the participative, open systems, storied organization environment, selecting as few as 1 in 30 of those who applied.[17] Now, I recognize that we did not select them well. We should have been hiring people with strongly volitional worldviews. Not recognizing this, we often got employees we had attracted because they wished to work in a collective team environment. Many had strong humanistic views that I now recognize arose from holistic values and were of a dominantly unitary worldview. Our failure to distinguish between the holistic, unitary worldview and the social has lead to enduring difficulties, because, while these employees were easily molded into a strong team-based organization, the unitary dominance of the groups has made it difficult for any changes to be made once they were allowed to settle into their efficient work habits. The open-system organizations became "closed." The employee who asked why she could not have a supervisor is an indicator of our misunderstanding of the psychology of change and performance. In recent years, with the aid of psychological testing, the managers of "green field" start-ups have learned to pinpoint the desired characteristics more accurately.

To understand a "new paradigm" organization such as those developed at the green field sites, we need to consider not only the storied and clustered cultures but also those that evolve within the pluralistic worldviews. It is out of the very strength of the monistic views that the opposing pluralistic cultures emerge. The conventionalizing counterinvents differentiation. Thus two other culturing processes emerge from the dynamics of the four realities: the *materializing* that pluralizes the clustering and the *democratizing* that individuates the storying process. The relation among these four is organized graphically in Diagram 5.5. The four labeled processes are placed within the reality that dominates the particular process.

Materializing

The materializing culture is an unintended invention of the clustering process. An increasingly refined classification of a maturing clustered

Diagram 5.5 Four Culturing Processes

culture produces, de facto, a pluralistic worldview. When the break-down of the whole is supported by systems of *measurement*, the parts become "materialized." Measurement increases our ability to make comparisons, to monetize transactions, and thus to effectively *compete*. Whereas clustering depends on the ability to identify differences in *quality*, materializing extends the differentiation to measured inter-vals, increasing the plausibility that the things of our perception are real, that the sensory is *the fundamental reality*. Human life comes to mimic the natural world, denying any explanation except the scien-tific. The monetization of goods, a basic tool of conventionalization, turns out to provide an additional tool through which to treat each *thing* as though it has its own worth and thus its own existence. The monistic assumption gives way to the pluralistic, even while we still try to maintain a collective image of a truth.[18]

The emergence of materializing processes occurred at a cultural level in Europe around the thirteenth and fourteenth centuries, paralleling drastic changes in Western society. This development accompanied the awareness of space and time as measurable commodities, the rise of modern science and realistic painting, and the appearance of commercial enterprises. It also brought about changes in the way in which issues were argued and in the personal and social motivations that came to drive social efforts. The changes that took place on a grand scale over centuries of Western history also occurred at the level of the individual enterprise during a much briefer time scale. The enterprise that arises in a founding event follows a similar path through a clustering formalization. Typically, particularly in this culture, as the myths of its creation fade, the organization becomes highly materialized, with relations among employees turning on economic relations.

Materializing imposes the authority of truth through the use of tools of a sensory practice, thus establishing differences among people and phenomena as "scientific fact." Being able to "take measures" supports the switch in the authority structure that dominates a society. With the acceptance of deterministic theories, the authority of science usurps that of sacred authority, leading to a new, monolithic, linear decision structure we call "rational" that recognizes the authority neither of the individual nor of the whole. Whereas clustering processes develop a qualitative emphasis on classifying and comparing, materializing processes focus on identifying the basic units of our sensory world and on counting that which is "at hand." This focus on measuring contributes to an increased sense of limitations on both material and temporal resources. Time as well as goods are forever to be "scarce." Thus, in making changes in a materializing culture, we are faced with the rational allocation of scarce resources as a major constraint. It has become *inefficient* to "waste" resources.

The management of conflict has similarly shifted to an important degree to rational means, to bargaining and compromises, and simple retribution. A pure form of the materializing culture does not provide for affective influence or group effects beyond convincing members as to the quality of data and providing rational arguments based on empirical data and legal processes. It makes little difference whether the arguments are based on principle, so long as they satisfy the applicable rules of measurement. New social values accompany materialization. The "particularization" of the person as well as of physical things aided by the ease of measurement facilitated the emergence of new social motivators: *competition* and *achievement*. These create an entirely different context for change and conflict resolution than does the clustering culture.

Democratizing

Democratizing flows directly from the mythic founding of the culture at large or an organization. It occurs through the individuation of the myth of origin—as in the idea that "anyone may grow up to be president." The symbols that represent the founding story are transformed into metaphors that are owned by individuals and groups within the culture. The democratizing processes give each person the right to the whole story on which the whole culture is founded. Each person can ascribe to the visions and values given by the founding myth without exclusion due to classes or qualifications. Democratizing processes emerge directly from the storying culture, in parallel to the emergence of materializing process from the clustered culture. Democratization and materialization share the pluralistic worldview. In democratizing processes, however, the modes of managing conflict and change assume the personal agency of the person; that is, democratizing is a phenomenon of the social reality and will only emerge where there is a population dominated by the values of the social reality.

The democratic processes call for a continual adjustment with every change of situation and of membership. They do not provide objective reference by which to judge appropriateness; a group choice is a matter of attaining a value consensus. Choices are not limited by class or qualification. As a culture grows from the storied cultures, there is no fundamental role for "quality," thus no qualifications. No one has "rights" based on principles, thus there is no need to make provision for "equal opportunity" as there is in a clustering culture. Like the mythic culture from which it devolves, the lives of groups as well as individuals are "projects" uniquely participating in the whole of the culture's path. Those involved have little interest in comparisons of individual achievement. For example, while there were major elements of materializing competition in the culture of the American West, there were races and "shoots" and other demonstrations of skill that were more shows of participation in the "dream" than occasions of winning and losing. So, in democratic Greece, the fairness criteria of the social reality were strongly supported as suggested by a quotation from the times: "Whenever a celebrated champion with a reputation for invincibility is challenged by an obscure antagonist who is a markedly weaker competitor, the crowd at once bestows its sympathy upon the weaker party, cheers him, and cannot contain its partisanship on his behalf."[19]

The motivator of a democratizing culture is the opportunity to live out the stories, the myths, of founding. By the nature of the social reality, these will be stories of sharing and general welfare, of commitment to participation and affiliation. But, by the very act of individuating, each person or group is likely to develop its stories along different paths. Over time, the source of homogeneity in the founding myth leads to differentiation, to new mythic stories, and thus to new sources of internal conflict without providing overarching rules of resolution as there would be in a principled culture. A democratizing process depends on the founding story for coherence. That may not be so strong a restraining force as principled beliefs, but it is more adaptable to a changing environment.

There is a complex dialectic established between the clustering and democratizing cultures, emerging as they do from the same mythic base. The two cultures may appear to share the same values and traditions, even the same story, yet their members respond very differently to situations. For example, the gulf between the two is obvious in the response of Americans to national causes such as war, social rights, or environmental protection. Those coming from a unitary worldview derive *principles* from the nation's founders; those from the social worldview derive them from *values*. They can stand on opposite sides of a picket line championing the same hallowed words. Nowhere is there a deeper pathos in U.S. society than in the paradox of "hawks" and "doves" mourning together the loss of loved ones in a military action or street violence.[20]

A similar ongoing dialectic operates in organizations. The traditional leadership operates from a clustered view while employee ranks are more likely to make choices from a democratic process. Both groups can aspire to the dreams of the corporate founders yet envision totally different courses of operation. The words are the same but the logics are incomparable. I discuss the dialectic in the organizational setting further in the next section.

Consideration of the democratizing process in distinction to the clustering-materializing paths led me to recognize another configuration in which these processes could evolve. One interpretation[21] of Japanese society suggests it has achieved a paradoxical combination of democratizing and clustering processes, showing both a need for giving and receiving love and a deep respect for the traditions and history of the family and the society. I think Americans have mistaken this for an authoritarian society and, in so doing, have misunderstood Japanese management. When brought to the United States, its methods were transferred into a clustered authoritarian setting in which quality is a major criterion. In Japan, "quality," like a "turkey shoot," is evidence of attainment on the path of respect for the other person (and tradition). It is a milestone on a path within a social worldview rather than a standard in unitary thinking, as it is in the West. As such, its attainment is in the service of the vision of the society, not a principle to be maintained for itself. Whereas in the United States, as a materialized society, attainment of quality is a constraint on production efforts, in a democratizing society, it can be evidence of progress toward a meta-goal such as *integrity*.[22]

The Multiculturing Organization

Just as every person and society operates out of a variety of worldviews, so every community and organization will be constituted by a variety of culturing processes. Carrying the analogy of a map of alternative realities one step further, resolving issues in a community or organization is parallel to guiding a sailing vessel through a sea with strong currents and divergent winds. Diagram 5.4 earlier presented a "snapshot" of that sea in analogy with the traditional hierarchy. In Diagram 5.6, I name the "currents" in terms of the organizational cultures with which we are familiar. Charting a course through such a dynamic is obviously a more complex task than laying out the path through a placid territory of well-segregated alternative realities and immensely more complex than working within a homogeneous population that operates with only variations of a single worldview. Most of our strategies of change and conflict resolution assume the latter, homogeneous case to be typical. The conditions in a natural community may be less clustered and more fluid, but they are not likely to be homogeneous.

The complications arising from diverse realities suggest not only hypothetical conditions but ones immediately encountered in any attempt to make changes. Recently, a project undertaken to improve production introduced a sociotechnical work design into a high-tech computer company. The process involved several existing groups in the manufacturing operations. The diverse departments accepted the idea and cooperated in the formulation of the basic design. While there appeared to be cooperation at every step, implementation of the design produced such conflict that the attempt was eventually abandoned. A subsequent study (Osborn, 1990) indicated that the project spanned groups with diverse culturing processes closely akin to those described above. Some operated with a clustering culture—for example, the cost and quality control groups—and some by a rational-design worldview—the design and production engineers—and others by a social-mythic worldview that included both democratizing sentiments and generative ideation—the marketing group and the senior executive. In spite of the implication that the design involved no personal threat of economic loss, major changes in power relations, or career damage, conflicts continued to hamper the effort. The groups simply did not have the same meaning for the words they used or the intents they expressed. On review of the failed implementation, it was

Diagram 5.6 A Multiculturing Organization

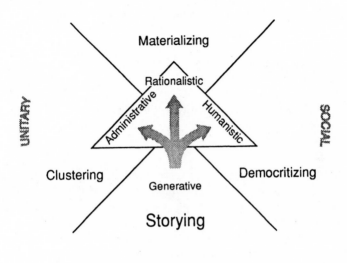

SENSORY

Materializing

Rationalistic

UNITARY

Administrative

Humanistic

SOCIAL

Clustering

Generative

Democritizing

Storying

MYTHIC

clear that no provision had been made to select tools and leadership to match the different cultures of those involved. The participants did not share a work culture; rather, they lived in organizations made up of a set of distinct subcultures whose members restrict their outside contacts to those who are of like mind or who are necessary for the conduct of day-to-day business. By so doing, they minimize both the effort and the conflicts involved in the ongoing daily work, but, conversely, the diversity of cultures makes it extremely difficult to introduce new work processes—or any other change.

The typical response to such blockage is to refound, to start a new story. An entrepreneur or technologist generates a new vision and heads for a "green field" site, abandoning the old site to let it settle into a clustered stability or selling it off to someone expecting to get a new start or a cheap resource. The cycle of death and rebirth is started anew. This is a long-standing habit of human beings, hinted at by the allusion to the green field. When we have drawn down the fertility from a field, we move on to "greener pastures." That strategy will no longer work with 4 billion "sources of conflict" roaming the fields of earth. We need more efffective modes of resolution and the courage to traverse the paths through the complex cultures that have evolved in modern societies.

With this discussion of resources—leaders and followers and the setting for the efforts of resolution—I have introduced the major elements of the meta-praxis. Before going on to the final question of implementation, I review what has been presented.

CONCLUSION

> The essential human quality is the ability to deal with (know) Absurdity.
>
> —Camus (*The Rebel*)

The development in the prior chapters is likely to have left the reader with misconceptions. The linearization of the ideas made necessary by the form of a book suggests that some ideas I have put forward should be treated as initiatory and others as summatory. I have not intended that to be the case; the relations among the major themes are at least circular and, in practice, better described as "contextual." Any explanation must be made from within one of the realities, and thus the exposition will be self-referential, a characteristic that often leads to paradox and irresolvable ambiguity. In addition, the narrative logic of the paths of change arises from a universe that is wholly unrelated to the logic of the multiple realities; there is no natural derivation from one to the other. Before I go ahead to consider the means of implementation, I review the elements in a different sequence to aid the reader to develop a gestalt of the whole presentation.

The sequence in which I presented elements, analytic first and expressive second, and the general bias toward rationalistic language were both used out of the habits of my work in the industrial environment. It would have been different if I had come from an anthropological or philosophical exploration. It is certainly not a necessary sequence or bias. I look forward to another occasion in which to frame the meta-praxis in an expressive language through which the theory of change will emerge in narrative form, but, for my own comfort and the presentation of theory, I found it easier to start along a somewhat more familiar route.

This meta-praxis is an approach to resolving issues through relating the infamous "two cultures" that appear chaotically laid upon one another in Western cultures. It is made up of *realities* that form the territory, *methods* that are the instruments of problem solving, and *archetypal stories* that set the direction, the paths, and courage that free us from disabling ambiguities. In this book, I have presented the following:

1. *A complex structuring that I propose describes the diversity of worldviews that are held in a typical Western population.* It displays the ontological differences that establish *the fundamental basis of conflict* due to the incompatibility of the positions on a variety of dimensions. These differences underlie the habits or styles by which we can characterize people and societies and identify methods of resolution that are natural to dominant realities. Thus the map of alternative realities provides a systematic linkage of

- problem-solving tools,
- styles of leaders and followers, and
- the culture in which the issue is embedded,

to an ontological mapping of alternative realities (Chapters 1, 3, and 5). This serves as a "bootstrapping" device to allow me to discuss third-order change and thus to transcend the limits of paradigmatic thinking. When (and if) we are able to work beyond classifying frameworks, the kind of structuring I have presented in these three chapters will be seen to be simply instrumental for resolving particular issues in particular cultural settings, that is, instruments of second-order change.

2. *An image of the processes of resolution that follows the paths of archetypal stories.* I use two interlinked myths as models for the typical paths of grand resolution efforts, showing how the plot line of these stories is pursued through the territory of alternative realities in the service of resolution (Chapter 4). These models are particularly relevant to the resolution of organizational and community issues in Western cultures. They are but two important instances of the archetypal myths and histories that do direct our paths toward resolution, more and less consciously.

3. *Elements of theory of change that relate the change processes inherent in the temporal story to the context of realities in which the resolution must be attained.* There were several elements of this emerging theory (Chapter 2). I (a) adopted two logically fundamental directions of change, differentiation and conventionalization; (b) noted how the direction determines what (reality) is assumed as given and in what reality the control (intention) will be expressed; (c) identified, by analogy with Bateson's work, three orders of change that provide increasing power to affect the habitual patterns of behavior of individuals and societies; (d) recognized the role of counterinvention, the normal force that

arises to offset changes; (e) related the dominant realities to the forms of play, indicating that we can see six levels of "games" that are analogous to the stages of resolving a conflict or constructing a program of action; and (f) presumed the essential ambiguity that denies the possibility of responding to conflicts from a position of certainty.

The theory weaves a fabric between the two languages—analytic and expressive. It is a fabric of paradoxes, inconsistences, and absurdities that is culture. I see no possibility of reducing the fabric to a consistent whole. Rather, I see the development of this meta-praxis and similar work leading us to greater facility in *working with the paradoxes and ambiguity* that envelop our attempts to settle conflicts. The theory does not lead to an overly optimistic view of our ability to resolve the issues that face humanity. It suggests that most of our problem-solving actions taken on little "trips" will grow messes in their footprints. It suggests, as our experience has told us, that we must follow through on the paths of change that we initiate.

V

—"For to Go to School"

During the Korean War, I was an Army Intelligence officer in the south of Korea. In the course of various investigations, I was often at the Pusan rail station when trains came in bearing wounded soldiers who were to be shipped home. I came to be interested in how they had been wounded and gradually my curiosity grew about *courage*. A number of them had been hit while recovering other wounded soldiers, acts of heroism that were often recognized with medals; others had led charges or repulsed attacks, against extreme odds.

They talked of their own acts of heroism and those of buddies as coming out of *friendship*. When they first got to Korea, especially as replacements, they didn't care about the other men. They were private about their feelings and focused on "covering my ass." With the first firefight, with deaths and terrible pain inflicted on these near strangers, their feelings changed. Then, they told me, sneaking out into no-man's land to bring back "a downed buddy" became almost automatic. "He" hurt, had a wife, wanted to go home to his Chevy just like the rest of the unit. And there was the pervasive, "he'd do it for me." There came a balance; it was as important to be a part of what was living as it was to be alive oneself.

I got another image of courage, riding the train to Seoul with a group of Turkish officers returning to the front after an R&R. They were magnificent—sensual in their brightly appointed uniforms, exuberant, often rising to confront one another and swearing and laughing and wildly gesticulating to describe how they had mowed down a Chinese soldier or would do it on their next encounter. Conversing in bits of our common French, they verified that they were wild about returning to action, to exercise their high skills with machine guns, pistols, and the short swords they preferred to the issue bayonets. They said they faced no risk, for they knew what they were doing—"chancing is for fools."

And still another image of courage: Many days when I came to the rail station I was accosted by the swarm of children who knew the Americans were soft touches. Most were orphans who had taken possession of every recess, coverlet, and empty packing crate in the rail yards. There were frequently things there to steal and many bored GIs to tease and beg from. Most visible among the waifs was a girl, perhaps 10 years old. She stood tall and handsome in her washed-out print dress. She had great "GI Joe" patois and could talk a few coins out of almost anyone. It helped her cause that she had an open bleeding gash running across her forehead and into her hair. Someone suggested it was such a good thing that she tore the scab off each morning. It also helped that she was radiantly joyful.

Shortly before I was ordered back to the "States," there was one of the periodic roundups of the waifs staged at the rail station. There was a well-run orphanage on nearby Cheju island. The children seldom went willingly as they fantasized it to be a form of prison. This girl was caught and, I was told, did everything she could to escape, swearing and screaming with the vilest GI oaths. She finally acceded to go on condition that she could return to her "home," a large drainage pipe under the tracks, to get her things—bits of clothes and a large, worn, and misshapen doll. Later, when they tried to separate her from the doll during the delousing, she again put up a wild protest. The Korean nurse, from whom I heard the story, finally settled her and found out why she was so attached to it. The doll was stuffed with over $6,000, a true fortune in the early 1950s. When the money was revealed, the girl turned to the officer and said, with calm determination and a perfect English accent, "It is for to go to school." They banked the money in her name. I know nothing further of her history.

Courage is about the choices one makes when everything is uncertain, amid personal danger, social distress, and lives and a world that have lost meaning. Courage is also about acting when there is no reality that we can assuredly accept. Rollo May said, "Courage is not the absence of despair; it is, rather, the capacity to move ahead *in spite of despair*."

6 Courage for the Journey

In the three circumstances described in the interlude, the soldiers and the orphan girl were actors making positive choices about their situations. Each created a context within which action was called for. The Turks had taken on the business of war as an honorable profession. The U.S. soldiers were there out of duty, and their courage arose out of their caring. The girl was creating an environment in which she would not be a victim. As an outsider to their circumstances, I judge that they all faced uncertainty; none had a course that would definitely lead to a happy or even predictable outcome. While they shared the overall circumstance of a nation at war, they created situations that called for different forms of risk and different orders of courage to enable them to confront ambiguity, paradox, and despair. They each had confronted the war resourcefully with adequate knowledge, skills, and tactics for their situations, but each had sacrificed a degree of consciousness—of aliveness—in taking on the courageous acts. The work of each brings about different orders of change indicating the manner in which courage is related to resolution of issues.

Courage is the last ingredient of this meta-praxis. The courage to follow a path is not a simple quality. The courage required varies with the order of change that is involved and with the role one takes in the processes of resolution. I begin this chapter with a look at courage in the context of alternative realities and the ways in which we use stories to lay out and traverse the paths of resolution. I then consider the impact of courage and the role of courage in *creating* resolutions. Ultimately, resolution is the

223

telling of a tale anew; that is, making the tale real for those involved in its implementation. I have argued that implementation calls for work in the three orders of change, beginning in the third order with the awareness of choice, continuing within the second order to set the context, and finally in the first order to solve problems within complex settings.

THE COURAGE TO CHOOSE
(OR COMMIT TO) ACTION

The first and most profound courage is that required to maintain awareness that the world we encounter is of our own choosing. This is the courage to affirm that there is *none among the alternative realities that will assure us of our being*. The theologian Paul Tillich (1952) called this the assumption of *nonbeing*. Any effort to make a change is an assertion of a belief in a specific worldview and accepting its "reality" while recognizing that our acceptance is simply a *matter of choice*. Rollo May (1975, p. 12), in writing about "the courage to create," notes the curious paradox that we must be fully committed to a reality while at the same time knowing that we can never be certain about a reality. So, as change calls for encounters with reality, we must incorporate this paradox into our understanding of designs of action. But an even more curious paradox is that, for the great majority of people, and during most of their lives, the first paradox must be ignored for it is too demanding a condition to sustain. We deny that our reality could be merely a choice. This normal avoidance is a critical *datum* for designing approaches to resolution.

The "amount" of courage required to act is reduced when we deny the possibility of being wrong, and it is increased with the consciousness of the consequences of our acts. The Turkish soldiers, it appeared, had successfully resolved all doubt about their profession—they had made a "profession," a declaration of their devotion to the rules of war. They had the least need for courage, for they affirmed their choice without maintaining consciousness of the alternatives or of the possibility of choice. (Soldiers, as well as business managers, police, nurses, and social workers, among others, are trained to be unconscious so that they will not need so much courage in their encounters with "harsh reality.") For a rationalistic context, Herbert Simon labeled such unseeing behavior "satisficing"—the mode of getting decisions made in the face of uncertainty. The U.S. soldiers who spoke of saving buddies lying wounded in the battlefield retained greater awareness of the alternatives. They need not have saved their dying companions, yet they held on to the consciousness of consequences and the awareness that they could not have tolerated being in their own community had they not tried. Only by so acting could they maintain the "fiction" that they were members of a community of caring human beings. The orphan girl called on still more courage to maintain a vision of something that was beyond her experience, an image of being she held while others around railed at their misfortune. She, like the biblical Job, refused to deny the possibilities of the self. Still more demanding is *moral courage*. Rollo May (1975, p. 9) also called it " 'perceptual courage' because it depends on one's capacity to perceive, to let one's self see the suffering of other people." His example is the Russian author Aleksandr Solzhenitsyn, who proclaimed "I would gladly give my life if it would advance the cause of truth." Each of these four forms of courage gives the holders the power to act within their worldviews. By retaining a belief in the truth, the self, the community, or the constancy of the material world, each has the ground (a reality of being) for action, a worldview on which to build expectations.

An ultimate level of courage is required for denial of the possibility of being right. Paul Tillich saw such courage as transcending the forms so far described. Its power comes from being "threatened neither by the loss of oneself (to become a thing within the whole of things) nor by the loss of one's world (in an empty self-relatedness.)"[1] It is within this space that third-order change arises. This is the courage it takes to make the first selection to *join as a part* or *assert one's individuality*—a choice between a conventionalizing and a differentiating path of change. The differentiating choice calls for the courage to commit to oneself. It is the belief that allows one to let go of the maintained worldview, that is, one's story, in search of a new one. It is the acceptance of the night journey into one's unconscious as an essential founding of a resolution. This is Dante's journey of renaissance. The conventionalizing choice calls for the courage to reject doubts of what is already espoused and to act out of one's belief. It is the belief that allows one to work from principle, as must a mathematician or judge. The Hindu hero Arjuna follows that path of revitalization with the courage to carry out the implications of his belief in a particular truth. The ritual of the Navajo sand painting, ritual dance, spiritual training—meditations, recitations—and military inductions are all instruments of instilling one or another form of courage to act consistently toward a resolution.

Courage responds to paradoxical conditions. I need the courage to be conscious of the alternatives and the courage to assert one (or some subset) of the alternatives. I need to deny the primacy of all paradigms to assert that *one* is the foundation from which to act. That is, I need courage to see and courage to act (or change). What made the Korean girl remarkable is that she exhibited both courages: holding the vision of what was possible and being "blind" to its improbability. Consciousness would create a cosmic hell for humanity had we not also been given courage to blind our consciousness in the service of action. To act, we must reduce our awareness of possibility—to go blind to those questions that would inhibit action, to the fear of losing opportunity. We can be disabled as easily by competing opportunities as by encircling threats. So we must act in transcendence of skills, community, self, and truth, taking on a reality and thus moral, intellectual, or authoritative preconditions. *Positing a specific reality is a precursor to a path of action.* The story must begin "somewhere" in some reality.

We have gained nothing by courageous activity unless we can stay conscious of the assumptions of conditions and honor the realities— usually different than our own—of those with whom we work. Relinquishing a particular worldview allows us to accept another's reality. In selecting the realities to which we will commit, we need to be guided by following the stories and myths that we all share through territories of differing realities and so committing ourselves to these stories holding the status of the "real" in the coengagement. Sharing a "plot" gets us through the mine field of conflicts. The failure to follow the plot opens us to the paradox that began this work, that new conflict *is induced by the attempts to eliminate existing conflicts, due to the differences in realities that we have asserted.*

But following in any form is a dangerous substitute for the expression of the two forms of courage. By *following,* I mean succumbing to a belief system without a consciousness of self and the consequences. The danger is differently experienced in each direction of change. In choosing a differentiating path, we often need to rely on another person to "vessel" us as we allow our boundaries to fall apart. It is tempting for both parties to maintain this relation: The voyager stays within the protective womb, and the "vesseler" (consultant) builds a following of dependent, unbounded souls. Overcoming these joint dangers is one of the major tasks that Ulysses faced in the *Odyssey*—escaping Circe and avoiding the Sirens. The danger for those on the conventionalizing path is that they will never achieve a commitment to principle—a faith—or gain a foundation (self-belief) from which to judge "truth"; thus they will wallow in indecision. This danger is visible in the current American culture in the acceptance of "gurus" who supply the business community with new solutions to its problems as "the program (or slogan) of the month," indicating how little courage of either type is displayed by the managers of our daily commerce. There is little display of consciousness of the consequences or persistence in follow-through. Admiral Hyman Rickover recognized both forms of courage in saying, "Good ideas are not adopted automatically. They must be driven into practice with courageous patience."[2] The replacement of legal proceedings by arbitration and mediation both in U.S. practice and in international issues (e.g., in the Irish national disputes) has required such courageous patience.

Keeping One's Eye on the (Moving) Target

Not only do good ideas not get adopted automatically but their very suggestion and attempted implementation lead to the creation of opposition. The most pervasive sources of *counterinventions* that block implementation are doubt of the supporting data, of the proposer's capability, of the advantage of the selected alternative over others, and, most of all, of the realities in which the idea is founded. In addition, there are sources in other human failings—for example, territoriality that is often expressed in the destructive not-invented-here syndrome and fear generated by a lack of understanding of the consequences. One way or another, almost every effort is faced with a counterinvention.

Regardless of the source, the more courageous (first sense) to open oneself one must be to initiate the effort, the more courage (second type) to close will be needed to block counterinventions. This joint need is recognized in the common assignment of responsibility for achievement to hands other than the source of an incentive. Great inventors and artists are not necessarily great entrepreneurs, and disciples are needed for even the most powerful ideas, from Christianity on. Thus one element of a design for implementation is the means that will be employed to maintain focus throughout the different stages of encounter. In the process of *resolving any issue*, not just problem solving, the path will require traversing domains of different realities, often calling for more adaptability than the initiator is capable of. The path will typically require shifts not only in reality but also in the direction of control. Thus one must let go of one reality and source of control and take on others in the course of implementation. The training for such courageous flexibility cannot come from within a traditional discipline or profession that, by definition, holds to a single worldview. Presidents seldom make good generals—Presidents Jimmy Carter and Saddam Hussein shared that lack of focused courage.

We learn from experience when to change tactics, to move from enforcer to persuader, from fantasy to engineering, from doubt to trust, but the deeper and more efficient guidance may come from *stories* given by example, read in biography and history, and extracted from myth and epic tales. The plots, such as those used by the Navajo in the tale of the Pollen Twins, exemplify the shifts that are needed and often the sequence in which to employ the tactics from the different worldviews.[3] In following such tales, the necessary courage is shifted from that required to act from a particular belief system to that required to accept the meta-reality of a path of resolution. Finding that courage is easier if one identifies with a real or mythic person who has followed the course in some real or mythic past. Having heroes helps.

Focus, and the courage to maintain it, *destabilizes* a system, setting it on a path of change and thus inducing conflict. One of the functions of counterinvention is to keep a system stable, to balance opposing forces and so to reduce conflict. In differentiating societies (as are many tribal cultures), the counterbalance is maintained via rituals of rebirth and social (power) inversions. In conventionalizing societies (such as the United States), the operating dialectic maintains an uncourageous polarization. Changes can come only by upsetting the balance, as Kurt Lewin noted in his force field model: A situation stays stuck as long as there is a balance of opposing forces. So, by imbalancing operations, changes may flow "naturally"—quietly or violently— on a course of coevolution.[4] The role of courage is to sustain change efforts; the role of consciousness is to know when to rebalance.

The question that is next in the flow of my argument is how we choose the particular stories that will encourage the desired changes. I confront that in a following section, but first I look at the question of how one finds validity for the worldviews that will be required in the course of a resolution effort that appears to require far more than simply accepting the first paradigm offered that will take us into a New Age.

Belief, Validity, and Courage[5]

Gregory Bateson wrote: "Man lives by those propositions whose validity is a function of his belief in them"[6] and "whose validity is really increased by the acceptance of them." (This is one of those self-referential statements that, if you disagree with, you are in concurrence with.) The logician Raymond Smullyan (1987) indicates that the proof of many assertions depends on the assumption that one accepts—believes in—the premise. Without belief in a premise, the proof does not "go through." You can't prove "it" if you have not adopted a ground on which to stand. Tillich (1952, p. 176) takes the argument one step further: "The paradox of every radical negativity, is that it must affirm itself in order to be able to negate itself." The denial of this proposition affirms it. So we must begin with belief in order to establish validity. In the above paragraphs, I indicated that, to follow the course of a resolution, we need to shift our beliefs from one worldview to another along the path, operating from a *meta-reality*. This process seemingly requires us to shift our beliefs from one to another reality systematically to maintain the validity of the actions we are taking along that path. Without belief in the requisite set of realities, we will not be able to resolve an issue—at best, we could deny its existence.[7] The validity of our choice of actions must be based either on our experience, thus on self-affirmation, or on belief in the lessons we learn from our adopted stories. And this observation takes us back to questions of courage.

Belief, validity, and courage all have to come together with both the courage to perceive and the courage to act. If we have little courage to perceive, then we have little need for belief and few challenges to the validity of what we do. With increasing courage to perceive the world around us, we have the courage to accept increasingly powerful worldviews, even to the point of transcending the local realities for a meta-reality. This, in turn, gives us the validity to act but, without the courage of the second type, we will not settle into the proper mind-set to act in ways that will take a resolution along its course. Courage facilitates our choice of action; it also underpins the sensed validity of the path we choose. Courage (of the second type) is the ability to say that something is right because one chooses it.

THE STORIES THAT GUIDE CHANGE

> We are *lived* by the stories of our race and place. . . . We are, each of us, locations where the stories of our place and time become tellable.[8]

Courage is often defined as "blind" and so I have characterized it here. It aids us in maintaining focus and the belief necessary for establishing the validity of our work. It does not, however, contribute to setting direction or to knowing the paths to resolution. To get such direction, we have to have a grand guide—for example, *the rational, scientific approach* has been, to quote Prigogine, "the greatest myth of the modern era."[9] We need a source of guidance, a plot to get us from one reality to another. What it comes down to is that guidance for change and the resolution of issues is to be found in *narrative forms*, in the various stories we call histories, biographies, epic tales, myths, and simply the stories that we tell about how we got to where we are.[10]

The Argument for Story

I lay out the fundamental argument for implementation in a bald form to ensure that I provide the reader a clear foundation for an unfamiliar proposition. The groundwork has been laid in the prior chapters and is supported by both by the students of mythology, such as Mircea Eliade and Joseph Campbell, and work in organizations as reported by Harrison Owens (1995) and Levy and Merry (1986), among others. Nevertheless, it is still surprising to me how central narrative logic is to the resolution of issues and conflicts. Succinctly put:

- The resolution of issues requires involvement of multiple worldviews.
- In typical populations, making changes that call on different realities will invoke new conflicts, deny resolution, and perhaps induce new messes.
- To achieve resolution without inducing messes, we need to work across the different realities in ways empathic with all the individuals and groups involved.
- Everyone is capable of working in any reality when there are conditions supporting movement beyond one's natural and habitual territories. As suggested in Chapter 4, the necessary freedom and support for operating in another reality come within a "storied space"—a space protected from secular threats, similar to what we experience in "retreats," on crusades, in fantasies, and on occasions of storytelling.
- We can operate beyond the familiarity of our worldviews only in the consciousness of narratives, the stories, myths, histories that we come to trust. That is, it is the courage that comes from knowing stories of success, mythic or real, that allows us to operate in unfamiliar realities. Like the adventurers of old, it helps to know someone has been there before and returned and that the land is not "godforsaken."
- Like the paths of resolution, there are an infinite variety of stories, but the vast majority follow a few great plots that serve as general guides and evocations. The great epics and histories provide guidance for deeper resolutions, both conventionalizing and differentiating. Biographies and the tales of our daily experience are like the reduced paths of resolution. They reflect on a limited range of human experiences and accordingly provided limited (even limiting) guidance.
- Tales that describe the past as histories aid in setting direction and values. Tales that describe a "life cycle"—the myths such as the Pollen Twins—guide us in forming strategies for future steps. The myths of origin serve as meta-guides, enabling new tales to be invented and thus novel resolutions to be achieved.
- The summary proposition is that *issues can only be resolved in storied contexts.*

This definitive proposition relies on the definitions of *issue, resolved,* and *storied.* It does not apply to situations that simply call for a problem to be solved. "Resolved" means the issue has been so thoroughly worked that new messes do not follow the course of the resolution. But the concept of "storied" is not so easily operationalized, for it arises in two realms that are not part of the scientific paradigm within which most of us were educated. These are *the unconscious* and *the sacred.* These are realms into which we go to separate ourselves from a problem-solving orientation and thus from counterinvention and priority setting. In entering these realms, Carl Jung (1968, p. 46) indicated, "Man is no longer a distinct individual, but his mind widens out and merges into the mind of mankind, here we are all the same." This is the state into which the "patient" is taken to gain courage through participation in the sand painting ritual or that executive groups go into during week-long retreats to explore their corporate futures—the state in which an individual or a group gains access to the story that will serve as guide through whatever ontological territories the path requires. The storied context enables an individual, even a whole culture, to transcend its worldview *so long as its symbols remain vital.* Conversely, the loss of the symbols, that is, of meaning, denies the culture guidance from values, beliefs, and facts and thus denies the possibility of resolution.

Campbell (1949) proposed, from his study of myth, that there was a pervasive "monomyth," one story that lay under all myths and epics of all cultures. Clearly his focus on the myth of transformation is justifiable but there are others such as that represented in the Hindu tale in which Arjuna plays a part. Campbell's form of the *myth of origin* is a potent archetype for evoking core purposes, extracting values, and, of course, enabling a rebirth. Jean Gebser (1985) further justifies the power of the myths of origin in asserting that purpose presumes an origin—only by being able to contact its origin can a person's self-sense, an organization, or a culture gain access to its purpose. Any other purpose it espouses is borrowed and thus inessential—and a poor motivator. Other myths, particularly those that follow conventionalizing directions, provide the plots, the strategies, that guide one's living a life, or doing business, by following a popular or morally desirable "model." The clearest criterion for choosing a guiding myth is probably that quality that suggests it is a story of "everyman." In terms of alternative realities and the concepts of courage that are developed here, a guiding story is one that requires the transit of all realities and the paradoxical encounters described in Chapter 2. The epitome of such tales is the *Odyssey.*

Typically, we do not go to the archetypes for our tales. We find them much closer to home. The primary source for individuals is the adults who were important to them while growing up, and next in importance are the heroes of the culture. Some suggest that we never mature without role models—without role stories. The power of the tales of historical figures is evident in the biographies of leaders and artists. Napoleon called on the romance of Charlemagne, Martin Luther King followed the life of Gandhi, and General Schwarzkopf followed General Patton, whose hero was Alexander the Great. Equally important are fictional characters, both in modern fiction and in fairy tale, myth, and epic. There are equally tales of organizations, of peoples, that serve the same purpose for later generations of members, such as the patriotic tales of a nation, the fabled heroism of a founding group, the drive and excitement of an entrepreneur or those who have worked on "the shop floor" in the "beginning." These tales carry the symbols of the organizational purpose. For example, in a recent effort for the *revitalization* of a missionary organization, the core purpose was *recovered* by finding the stories of organizational achievement to which the field-workers were most attuned. From this work came the insight that the heart of the organization was more focused on the personal act of conversion than it was on the avowed "propagation of the faith."[11] With that awareness, recruiting, training, and performance evaluations were shifted to bring back an integrity to the community. The choice of such stories is based in criteria such as integrity, familiarity, and the breadth of realities encountered in the telling.

With deeper probes for the relevant stories, material is likely to be brought from the unconscious of the participants—of the individual or the collective. Deeper, archetypal tales can be evoked with projective techniques as simple as having a group "make up" tales of their founding, history, and future or with elaborate explorations using archaic ritualistic processes.

While many consultants and organizations use stories to identify desired outcomes, we have less experience with calling upon stories to guide the paths of change and development.[12] The premise of this work is that, without such use, any efforts at issue resolution further imbalance the system and produce new dysfunctionalities. In more familiar terms, a focus on the ends without concern for the means is almost certain to be destructive. The discussion of implementation in the following sections calls for a systematic coordination of processes of change with the worldviews of those involved using the story for guidance.

FOLLOWING THE PATH (TO ACTION)

In any change effort, there is a founder or founding group, some person or body of people, formally constituted or not, who are the instigators of the change. The path of action begins with this person or group. Their effort is founded in their worldviews and in the conditions of the culture in which they are embedded. There is no choice on how to start. The path has been entered or it hasn't. The roles the instigators take depend on their leadership styles (following their dominant realities) and the culture that determines the direction of the effort. In a conventionalizing effort, the founder is by definition a part of the leadership. In a dialectic version of a conventionalizing change, the founder of the change is the contender for the leadership. In practice, if the founder of the effort is not the senior executive, territorial disputes are likely. Any effort started by an underling that looks like a second-order change is certain to produce a schism in the organization, thus is a threat regardless of whether or not the expected changes follow from the accepted "first principles." Even a benign intent leads to a dialectical revolution, following a path that has been repeated incessantly over the centuries in national as well as religious and organizational wars. In both instances, the founder is a *reformer*, leading the organization or community along its true course. The level of effort that is produced ultimately depends on the courage of those who join the reformer's path.

It is meaningless to discuss what would be an ideal starting point, for that concept itself is the product of a particular worldview and the time and place of instigation. The most definitive thing one can specify is that the instigators must have courage sufficient to transcend their own worldviews. It is clear from the general messiness of our world that the courage sufficient to sustain a thorough resolution of a full-blown issue is rare. We need all the understanding we can muster to ease the path.

The Setting

Starting a change process to resolve an issue without taking into account a person's worldview leads to a lot of pain. Setting a person or organization on a path of a large-scale change effort without preparation is analogous to introducing gross puns into serious dialogue. Puns are an odious form of humor that threaten conversation with systematic ambiguity.[13] The threat that there will be another pun puts an audience on the defensive, building dikes against a flood of new contexts entering the conversation, forcing us to be "of two or three minds" at any moment, listening for a tangential signal to take us off course. Puns "inflict" new meanings from an alien worldview, thus offend our realities with ambiguity, confuse our ability to make distinctions, and, under the most severe and ingenious attacks, are crazy making—as can be turbulent environments in which we attempt to guide changes. A pun introduces raw metaphors, meanings that are out of context and, in the extreme, threatening to the worldview of the listener. Puns, and change, if pursued relentlessly, deny boundaries between contexts. They eventually deny rationality, requiring an escape to a meta-reality that is rarely achieved. The maker of puns and the maker of changes are not popular in most settings.

To gain a reception for the juxtaposition of ideas such as occurs in deep change efforts or are brought out by a pun, one must bring the listener along by establishing a context. Here I have suggested that this be accomplished by embedding the paradoxes of change in stories in which the ideas are woven together along a familiar path. Just as we may set each interpretation of a pun in context to articulate the multiple meanings, we can present the course of change in ways that integrate the histories and visions of the involved people and the cultures with the new realities that must be encountered. Thus I create an environment for those involved wherein they may encounter new ideas and for the moment be "of two or three minds," safe from the demands of the particular realities of the secular world.

The first step in creating such an environment is to make articulate the founding and core stories. Ultimately, these tales of beginnings and heroes' journeys and of coming to terms with the death of institutions and persons provide guidance for the resolution. But, initially, the tales may be simple histories or tales of peak events in the life of the organization. In Billings, Montana, where I came to help with urban and regional renewal, I began the work by talking with Senia Hart, the grande dame whose father-in-law was a founder of the city. She arrived with boxes of newspaper clippings and photographs. Within three hours, we could see the seeds of the current conflicts in the decision made at the turn of the century to move the city center across the Yellowstone River. At a metaphorical level, the conflicts that arose by leaving some people on the other side of the river had never been resolved. The remembering of these events at the search conference set the context for everyone to tell tales of generation that focused the group onto long-term issues, eliminating much of the finger-pointing accusations and clearing the ground for dealing with the current situation.

Whether working with a group or a self-regenerating leader, starting within the storied world establishes a number of conditions critical to a resolution of an issue:

- suspension of various ego fears, motivations, territorialities;
- courage and some skills for entering any reality and using it empathetically—in short, for playing among the realities in the search for solutions (the processes by which the stories are generated or evoked provide scenarios through which each person's concerns can be respected);
- recovery of core values and "core energy" (resurfacing the values and energy produces a founding event that initiates—sanctifies—the resolution effort);
- sanctions to evoke and support the core stories and to accept that storytelling does not require special intellectual training or background;
- uncovering the source of irrational organizational behaviors that have been an enigma for the current membership;
- courage to "stay the course" and to block counterinventions; and
- rituals that support the courage and focus by reaffirming accords and shared expectations (which are often performed in returns to "the sanctuary" and in memorializing the process with symbols, slogans, and celebrations).

The intended outcome of greatest importance is the *adoption and the shared awareness of a path of resolution* that is necessary for revitalization or rebirth or for following the lesser, reduced paths.

So, in practice, we begin by considering the setting in which to evoke the stories. In Billings, we had a clear historical antecedent to uncover. The search conference for the college site described in Chapter 4 was designed to allow the typical political process to be forgotten while the participants uncovered their archetypal bases through play. The now widely employed organizational retreats, in which groups of executives or employees work for several days in isolation, can provide the necessary separation from secular demands. In these efforts, it is not expected that all the participants will move beyond their familiar territories, but, with sufficient "vesseling," the group can identify what a core story is and what the sources of core energy are and so attain a collective courage to proceed. The collective can be wiser and more courageous than the individual moving alone toward the freedom of third-order changes.

The first step of a third-order sequence is *getting out of one's own way* to make room for choosing, for "coming clear." That is, we have to be clear of the *presumed realities* with their definitions, rules, and judgments as well as of *attachment to particular stories* that we have experienced as leading to favorable outcomes or that simply are supportive of our worldviews. By so doing, we get space in which to "see" freshly and to engage with stories that we individually or collectively "know" to be relevant to the resolution. Equally important, we thereby shed the armor that fends off the insights that others present to us. This space, which I label "the storied world," does not operate within the realities of the secular, mundane world. The meta-reality of third-order work is not a comfortable place to work in, being without the intellectual protection afforded by classification systems and expectations, but experience of it is necessary for the facilitators of change and, in the cases of deep renaissance, for all those who would be a party to the founding of a new mission or organization.

Issues of the Third Order: Moses or Merlin

The most difficult question that arises in the use of this meta-praxis is that of guidance. In simplest form, the question is this: Does guidance come from one person who sets the course and maintains it, or may it come from a dual leadership in which one person provides guidance and another provides the active leadership for the resolution? Throughout history and in all cultures, there are examples of both alternatives. It is a question not only for the theory and practice of change but for leadership in general. Over most of history, the question has been confronted in terms of the joining or separating the *secular* and the *sacred processes*—the secular having to do with the material and political processes, and the sacred with the generative and culture maintaining processes. So long as the respective leaders work from specific worldviews, it is inevitable that conflict will arise between the two authorities. This is implied by the concept of alternative realities and attested to by many of the great dramas of history. But there have been occasions of emergent leadership in which the secular and sacred were merged *and* of great synchrony when they were separately expressed.

An archetype of the first type is the image of Moses as the political and military leader of the Israelites who also took into his hands the spiritual direction of his followers. Prophet and political leader were combined in one person. Muhammad also followed this path. By collapsing the two into one, the leader defines a single worldview, politically correct or theologically true. This dual role appears to have been most successful when the leadership was generative, displaying a mythic creativeness in founding new organizations, states, or cultures; that is, in establishing second-order changes. The combined role is also successful when the leadership is authoritarian, holding on to power by denying either the sacred or the secular worldview, whether it produces a Mayan theocracy or a monarchy such as those of Peter the Great or Henry VIII that denied the authority of the Holy Father. Often the leader gains the unified "authority" from some heroic figure of an earlier time. Great revigorations such as was initiated by John Kennedy arise out of old traditions that, having decayed, need to be reconnected to their founding stories to regain their vitality. While such leadership focuses an organization's energy, it usually inhibits the further innovation characteristic of second-order change. The tale typically ends in an authoritarian regime in the hands of a unitary personality such as Joseph Stalin or a "yes-man" on whom a leadership vacancy fell.

The model of dual leadership splits the secular and sacred functions, leaving the political leadership to one and the source of ideas and support for change to another. This is the more common form in Western democratic cultures. Most leadership and most change efforts follow from the joint effort of one who commands resources—a political leader—and one who is the "sanctified" source of ideas and advice. Such a person comes with different labels: *adviser, counsel, guide, mentor,* and, most commonly if least elegantly, *consultant.* The category *sacred* and the attribute *sanctified* indicate that the latter role is denied *substantial* engagement in the enterprise. That is, the sanctified cannot attain significant power or wealth through this work. Sometimes they play a visible but low-key role, occupying an office next to the executive's; sometimes they are completely invisible to the members, limiting their encounters with the executives to retreats and apparently casual meetings.

One form of adviser contributes to changes of the *first order* wherein advice is limited by the dominance of a unifying theology, administrative regime, or pervasive science. Here advisers would speak from a single truth system as experts or technical advisers helping to train others in the use of a skill or to incorporate second-order concepts that have been established elsewhere in the culture. U.S. managements appear to grasp unendingly for such technical advice, acting as though each new idea is a message derived from a source from which arises their evaluations and feelings of self-worth. The adoption of each new fad indicates both their need for the guidance from the wise adviser and their lack of courage to operate from their own skills.

The second type of adviser creates *second-order* change. They bring innovative ideas and practices to a community, sometimes as scholars, sometimes as activists. In recent decades, Kurt Lewin, Douglas McGregor, Saul Alinski, Carl Rogers, Eric Trist and Fred Emery, and Roger Fisher at the Harvard Program for Negotiation, among others, have brought out ideas for second-order changes with increasing frequency and effectiveness. Their collective impact has contributed importantly to opening Western cultures to new approaches to issue and conflict resolution, to bringing about the paradigm change that is so widely heralded.

The adviser working with *third-order change* provides secular leaders contact with the "sacred," which is essentially a *process* for engaging outside of the logics of the secular society and worldviews. This is achieved in two ways: first, by *vesseling*, that is, providing the psychological setting for the leaders (and member) to explore their concepts of reality and by being a companion to the seekers—playing Virgil to guide Dante through one's personal hell. In part, this is done by stepping away from the assumed realities to make room for their choosing worldviews anew, and in part, by locating the essential stories/paths/ myths for traversing the space of realities as has been discussed here. Advisers identify the paths in stories evoked from the participants or call them up from the collective conscious (and the unconscious) of the community or of humanity at large. That path becomes the essential core of the resolutionary work. Whereas problem solving is defined by the realities of the situation, the path of resolution is a narrative, a core theme that guides without the limitations and territoriality of the realities. The desired outcomes of third-order work are an organization of resources over time such as to minimize resistance as the secular leaders follow the "sacredly" determined paths *and* the courage (and conviction) to complete the journey. These are outcomes provided for leaders by guides over all of history—as exemplified here in the tale of Arjuna and the Navajo sand paintings ceremonies—but, for the most part, those guides have not been sufficiently free of bias to allow resolution of the issues to be accomplished.

Freedom from bias is difficult to sustain. The better the adviser's reputation, the greater is the temptation for the client to take every word and gesture as advice. Seldom can advice, bad or good, be taken without creating counterforces. Too often, the solved problem produces new "messes." When members know their organization is in trouble, when pain is surfacing or indicators are pointing to future losses, it would seem an adviser is justified in offering help by displaying opportunities and designing projects to work on the issues. But such offerings can be destructive even when they have been requested. By offering solutions to their troubles, advisers discount the realities within which many people in the client populations define themselves. By accepting the proffered solution, most of those involved are disconnected from their natural bases of belief and, in so disowning their own positions, become followers and the adviser becomes the leader. This is a common, if unfortunate, outcome of "successful consulting." I believe that I (or anyone else) can be effective in *resolving issues* only if I accept that I know neither the solution nor the criteria for a solution in the terms of the presenting difficulties. If I presume answers to either of these questions, I assume dominance over the choice of realities. This occurs because the resolution must be defined and its qualities measured in terms of the realities in which my answers were established and in which control is vested. I cannot both make choices for the organization and expect the issue to be resolved, regardless of how well the presenting problem is handled. It is *relatively easy* for consultants to resist giving answers—that's done mostly by training ourselves to ask questions; it is far more difficult to avoid imposing our realities. The choices of reality and of story must be made by the leaders and members of the community if the changes are not to end up inducing further conflicts, violent or subtle.

The archetypal meta-practitioner is Merlin—not the magician of a child's fantasies but the sage that we encounter when we turn away from the everyday culture for guidance. Like Merlin, most such practitioners are by their role *liminal figures*, residing at the edge of the organization or society lest they be "captured" as leaders, teachers, or experts. In such a role, their names are not widely known. They may be as insubstantial as was Merlin, or they may perform more visible roles in the society or organization that provide a "cover" for the supportive and narrative roles through which they support resolution. Strangely, those who acquire a reputation for expertise and power as consultants disable themselves from this work for their reputations demand that the client accept the consultants' realities and apparent directions. The confrontation of a powerful secular leader with a celebrated consultant is not likely to produce third-order learning. The tale of the English King Henry II's encounter with his archbishop, Thomas à Becket, illustrates the tension produced by the secularization of the consultant. The lesson from such a tale, and from history, is that leadership must eventually be taken on by the leader who is being guided. Resolutions follow from persistent commitment to second-order processes identified in the explorations and commitment made in the sacred domains of third-order work.

Managing a resolutionary process calls for communication and for selecting and providing resources for the *modes of change* called for along the path of resolution. This meta-praxis requires the manager to assume a particular reality and exercise control through another reality *for each stage of the path*. That is, managers need to match methods, people, and situations to the dominant relevant realities and to sustain the direction—or, more accurately, sustain the directed balance between the directions—as is called for in each stage of the storied path.

In the conventionalizing change, the managers sequentially develop strategies, set budgets and short-terms plans, assign resources, and evaluate performances. In differentiating paths, their emphasis is on communication and enabling others to make resource allocations.

It is naturally difficult for managers to move with a story. Their competencies and past successes have been typically built working within a given worldview. To the degree that work has been success-ful, those involved believe their worldview and paradigm to be valid. Local success induces habitual behaviors and dulls one's consciousness. Habitualizing behavior and the development of *professions* have been useful tactics in the relatively slow-moving cultures of past millennia. They become less useful as the change rate of the environment rises. Even more in the face of complexity, one needs to confront the para-dox of displaying the courage to be skeptical *and* the courage to take on a belief—the paradox that *the truth is our choice*. It is not enough to select operating principles based on "what worked last time," "what worked in Japan," or, sadly, "what I am best at doing." The most de-structive form of management, worse even than "management by pun" (i.e., systematically induced ambiguity), is using processes that use logics that are out of tune with the path of resolution—for exam-ple, using processes that call for personal openness in a highly judg-mental environment. Such violations of the story eliminate the possibility of resolving the issue and lead to efforts that, no matter how locally useful, disrupt the system, the person, the organization, and the community. So, even if managers are not involved in the third-level work, they need to stay in tune with the storied culture if the change processes are to continue through to resolutions.

The management of meta-praxis itself parallels the evolution of cour-age, beginning with skill development, followed by increasing depth of encounter with new alternatives, transcendence of choice, and the return to focused efforts along the path of resolution (Diagram 6.1). Regardless of the path that is called for, the great majority of this work is done "in the streets" and "on the shop floor," more first level than second or third. It is unlikely to be successful, however, if it is not done with a continuing observation of the self and the process in the light of third-order concerns.

The Paths of Change Coevolve

A critique of the myth-story base for developing paths of resolution might raise the objection that this approach literally depends on "ar-chaic" processes to deal with issues more complex than encountered in

Diagram 6.1 Evolution of One's Meta-Praxis

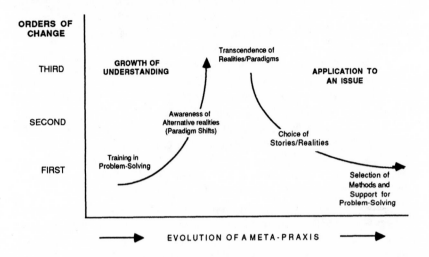

any time before the current era. This critique is a concern for me. It would be damning if the knowledge of how to use the narrative logics in this context were not subject to inquiry, development, and comparison with other modes of directing the resolution of issues. In the synthesis I have formed with the typology of alternative realities, the "Wagnerian" theories of change, and the use of story, the meta-praxis has the properties of a science of human behavior. As a praxis, it is continually tested by its applications. And, as appropriate for a change strategy based in part in the human narrative, it intrinsically *coevolves* with use as do the situations in which its methods are used. The praxis and the applications are related as a macrocosm and microcosm.

Issues do not get resolved if "everything else" remains the same. Major changes in a system that accompany a resolution (though not a problem solving) change the embedding society or organization. Issues such as the national debt, a homeland for the Palestinians, or domestic violence are not resolved without having an impact on the environment of these issues. The resolution of an issue coevolves the system and the environment, if it is successful, with direction coming from the shared story.

A simple example of this coevolution is a project undertaken in the mid-1980s in Saudi Arabia. A Saudi government commission under the direction of Hisham Naser, at that time minister for planning, had built two new cities on opposite sides of the Arab peninsula to support the newly laid trans-Arabic pipeline. As the cities neared completion, it became obvious that provisions for their governance had been neglected.

The contract to train the city managers, and in so doing create the governing processes themselves, was given to UCLA. I joined the project explicitly to experience working with a dominantly unitary population, one that would not be open to new "transformational" thinking.[14]

The contract called for educating groups of young engineers and managers, many of them already with master's degrees from Western universities, in new organizational and public administration concepts. As we worked with the student groups and their elders in the commission, two "stories" emerged as to how the cities would be governed. One "plot" followed the development of government in "new towns" in the United States and England. This was the one Hisham Naser advocated. The other was a "shadow plot" that the in-place traditional managers were confident would be the tale by which the actual government was formed. It was literally a shadow plot, for it was developed in the late hours of the night within Arabic homes, isolated from Western "intruders." The "elders" formulated these plans, for they knew they could "wait us out." The only way to resolve the issue—here between the needs of a new high-technology urbanization and the old guard—was to merge the plots. So, in planning for the second city, Jubail, we adopted the metaphor of a "pilgrimage," using a plot structurally similar to the *hajj*, the religious pilgrimage. The language was sufficiently different to ensure that the usage would not infringe on dogma, yet its images were close enough to be familiar and trustworthy.

We began a systematic tuning of the two images by finding parallels in the two processes. I was assured there would be fundamental parallels as both were models of "founding," of spiritual rebirth and social construction. For example, the UCLA plan called for considerable personal development of the managers preliminary to the explicit planning, as we did in the site selection described in Chapter 4. I expected objections from the traditionalists, because the notion of personal change unacceptably called for them to become more consciously choiceful, thus skeptical of dogma. We found an appropriate convergence. In the Koran, there is a well-known maxim of the Prophet Muhammad, "God loves for each of you to excel in his work." As God's work, personal development is highly desired. Because our formulation was shifted from a social reality to the unitary principled development our plans and efforts brought into convergence the two paths. So it was all along the path. In developing the rationale for authority, and to tie in the more participative aspects of the UCLA model, we called on pastoral traditions used by the Saudi family rather than the more sophisticated concepts that had been adopted in the coastal cities. In some cases, forming the parallels appeared cosmetic; for example, organization charts had to be designed so they would display visual symmetry. But more important than any structural parallels was the need to tune together the pacing, the modes of decision making, the commitments, and the respect for "channels" ultimately describing the work as a journey or pilgrimage. To some degree, we created a path that, if violated, would be a rejection of spiritual principles. That is, we cocreated a path that required the Saudis to make "no changes," allowing them to celebrate their own ways.[15] Nevertheless, even with these concessions, the governmental structure now supports more open communication of information, development and advancement of employees, and incorporation of modern logistics; thus five years later (1990), the conflict between traditional and new approaches is not an important issue.

Such a coevolution transfers energy back and forth between the parties to the disagreement and in so doing brings them into *accord*. In the Moslem unitary culture, the coevolution was not viewed as a *change*, because change would be viewed as a pluralistic interference, but as a conventionalizing clarification, achieved by reaffirmation. The design process directed an interpretation of traditional practices. If the work had been done in a world dominated by a social reality, "change" would have been openly espoused. If the sensory, contemporary Western logics had dominated, the design would have employed analytic modes throughout the process, producing a PERT chart instead of a Koranic maxim. The commonality is in the logic of the story itself; the differences are in the path that guides the choice of realities, rules of operation, and criteria variously along the route. This coevolution example is a microcosm of the kind of changes that can follow from the deep application of meta-praxis.

CONCLUSION: THE BEGINNINGS OF AN EXPLORATION

My drive to write is the pain I feel from seeing the difference between what is possible and what is being done in society and organizations. Over the years, I have felt impatient that the implementation of new ideas for resolution of conflicts and issues has shown such slow progress. I recognized that developing the praxis had to be self-reflexive—creating a process that would itself use the praxis to achieve implementation. Clearly, presentation of the ideas by publishing a book is a critical step in gaining acceptance of the ideas. Further steps must, in turn, be responsive to the dominant realities of the communities into which the ideas are to find their use.

So, for example, work on strengthening the *Realities Inquiry* instrument will both improve the efficiency of change efforts and gain acceptance for the theory from other theorists and academics. A study of creative behavior (Junge, 1991) has already deepened our understanding of the use of realities in practice and explored problems in third-order learning that will lead to better education. A handbook is being prepared for more conscious use of the various modes of problem solving. It will be particularly supportive of people coming from design (unitary-sensory) and participative orientations. Several studies are developing uses of story and myth in organizational settings, supportive of facilitative leaders. Case studies of implementation—that is, stories—are being collected to encourage organizational and community leaders to set their organizations on paths of change via meta-praxis. Each of these efforts supports a portion of the population of developers of ideas and potential users. We have a long journey before I might be able to claim a theory of change that will work in Western cultures, much less one that is appropriate for all of the human cultures.

There are paradoxes inherent in a propagating a meta-praxis, for its bald adoption would be counterproductive, interfering with the basic intent of creating a conscious involvement rather than a new paradigmatic dogma. The implementation strategies must have elements that will lead to a transcendence of the ideas and forms that are being implemented. The difficulties identified in gaining acceptance for resolutions will be re-created in the implementation of a practice. The strategy of propagation itself becomes a deep issue in the design of *games for the second board*. So, in essence, the implementation must be a self-practice in the acceptance of diversity and, at the same time, a support to the commitment experienced by the participants to a change. It must support the courage to see and the courage to be focused.

If our societies were to implement this meta-praxis in the resolution of the major issues that they encountered, what would be the outcomes and would they be attractive? To answer these "futures" questions is impossible for there are too many other involved structures and processes to know what forces would become dominant. I can, however, list some changes that I think would occur in a society that are directly related to a broad implementation of meta-praxis in a community or at large. I associate these changes with three aspects of the meta-praxis: the alternative realities themselves, the paths of change with the related development of narrative logics, and the appropriate use of the modes of changes, that is, of the relevant tools.

Alternative Realities

- A high degree of awareness of the way others construct reality and, in general, their worldviews.
- A high degree of understanding and acceptance of the worldviews of others. (I would add "of the right to hold other worldviews" except that itself comes from the unitary view so I leave it simple as "acceptance.")
- A movement away from the dominance of unitary thinking in large portions of the world's populations (that is, from what Ken Wilber calls the "pre-egotic" level of development).
- Recognition of the illogical structures that are left over from earlier paradigms, leading to the restructuring of many activities that are focused on what we now call social issues (for example, criminal justice, in which we place scientific assertion of fact, religious principles, and reeducation all within the purview of a system designed to preserve sociopolitical expectations—the anomalies of our educational and economic systems would become similarly unacceptable).
- Opening up of conflict resolution efforts beyond the current disciplines to reduce the hold on society exercised by professionals such as lawyers, MDs, and "high-science" academicians.
- Reconstruction of Western thinking on a variety of logics, arising from the awareness of the need to use *alogical* devices to produce changes (in particular, the review of alternative logics leads to an expansion of the theory of games to include games of the second and third boards—maybe even of the sixth board).
- Intensive and extensive regionalization to come from the combined effect of immensely increased flow of information and wide acceptance of alternative worldviews (which will reduce the influence of the large, dominantly unitary authorities, placing many of their functions within a great variety of interwoven subcultures).

Paths of Change

- Reemergence of narrative as a critical element in our practical lives, ranging from history and biography to stories and myth. (This reawakening will be supported by the development of narrative logics that is currently under way; I anticipate that these developments will free us from dependence on the part/whole logics that date from Aristotle.)

- The use of the grand paths in systemically "destabilizing" cultures and organizations in ways that allow change to take place without the severe backlash such as is beginning to occur in civil rights in the United States and other Western countries.
- New understandings of the roles of leadership and the skills necessary to set and hold the course along any path of change.
- Strengthening democratic culturing processes, thus enabling more effective participation of a population in its enterprises and governance.

Modes of Change

- Improvement in the strategic design and use of problem-solving tools, allowing better match between the users, the situations, and the desired outcomes—in part, this gain will be based on better understanding of the relation between effectiveness of the tools and the maintained realities and, in part, from using the strategically appropriate direction of change and the proper placement of the problem in overall issue management.
- Within the context of meta-praxis, the problem-solving methods may be used more directly on the anomalies and contradictions that underlie problems rather than staying above with the cultural shields that block penetration to the level of the issue (that is, problems will be placed on the board wherein they are most likely to find immediate solutions; in others terms, there will be less waste on inappropriate analyses, "playing politics," and anguishing over mission).

These effects in combination with changes due to other factors in society could lead to additional changes that are clearly of central concern, such as international strife, maldistribution of resources, domestic violence, and the impact of bigotry, to new concepts of work and remuneration and of education that will encourage creative and evolutionary thinking. These will remain but dreams until we have a far greater understanding of the self-destructive drives of the human species.

Epilogue   The Querencia and the Arabesque

In a bullfight I saw some years ago in Spain, a young and not yet skillful matador get into trouble. As the fight progressed, the bull increasingly could not be teased into charging the cape. The bull had established himself in a spot near the *barrera* and, when it came time for the kill, no matter how prodded, he remained there. As the matador would come in over the bull's horns to sink the sword between the shoulder blades, the bull countered, twisting his head to drive his horns toward the belly of the matador. The matador had to shy off and thus lost his thrust. The bull knew his ground; he had learned quickly to counter the attacks. Within the rules of that deadly game, the bull had become unkillable. He was simply slaughtered to make way for the next event. The next day, I located in Ernest Hemingway's *Death in the Afternoon* an explanation of what had happened. The bull had been allowed to establish a *querencia*, a preferred spot in the ring in which he could hold his own. The querencia is "where the bull makes his home—a place where he has had some success."

A *querencia* is the Spanish word for a nest or haunt of a wild beast. It is not only for beasts but for humans as well. All of us adopt querencias as that bull did; some are as simple as a certain chair I would take in a meeting room or as pervasive as religious faith and worldviews. We are often unconscious of our choices until we are denied them. A newcomer may innocently occupy "my" chair; a personal failure may threaten someone's religious beliefs; or a scientist may be threatened by a "fact" completely unexplainable by his or her intellectual stronghold. The physical and psychic places are ones from which we display the maximum degree of confidence. They are places from which there is no retreat and, in that, they become places of power. The root of *querencia* is the verb *querer*, which means to desire, to love, and to will, so it is not only a place of security but a place wherein we can learn, love, and sense success. With such a feeling attainable in the comfortable, though limiting, querencia, it is natural that we, like the bull, would develop strong tendencies to stay within its boundaries.

Those of us who wish other people to make changes in their worlds are often like the bullfighter, calling out those others to operate in an unfamiliar world in which they usually feel discomfort and at a disadvantage. Yet, change in the open arena clearly can be to our mutual advantage. Even in the bullring, there is achieved, on rare occasions, a common good. Later that season, there was a fight in which a bull defended himself with such bravery and endurance that the matador stopped the fight and, ceremonially touching the forehead of the exhausted bull with his sword, honored him with a rare reprieve. Perhaps for that moment, the two combatants shared a querencia forged from the oneness of an encounter with death.

Increasingly, our world is becoming like the bullring, a place without natural querencia, without safe homes unchallenged by demands to which we must respond. The broad cultures of the last centuries are giving way before an onslaught of change brought about by a growing consciousness in the human species that is manifested in technologies that have swelled the living population beyond its capacity to manage the changes or to sustain querencias for very many of us. The multiplicity of realities has become "the real fact" of our daily lives. That which is alien to our querencias now penetrates the physical and psychical boundaries as easily as the matador penetrates the bull's defenses. The time of *closed door policies* and *iron curtains* is past. Trade barriers and old wealth have lost their exclusive power. Not the family, nor the tribe, nor the church can shelter growing children any more.

With an increasing level of consciousness, free flow of information, and our mutual dependence on the physical resources of the earth, there will be great difficulty in finding querencia in which each of us may flourish. Less often will we find large social querencias shared by populations of one mind. Less often will we find the silence in which to organize our perceptions and rebalance our psyches. All of us will live in a great media arena of communications crammed with messages that tease and infuriate as well as inform and guide. If we are not more conscious than we have been, the earth may come to feel to the participants like a great bullring in which the courage of neither the bull nor the matador will be sufficient. We must change our way of engaging if we are to survive.

I see another possibility emerging, one that is better characterized by the metaphor of an *arabesque* than of a bullring. It would be a world created by the rhythmic succession of motifs, giving form to but not filling total spaces. They are generated by the repeated application of a rule of composition, metaphorically following "paths" produced over and over in greater and lesser representations. The rules were derived out of natural patterns—rosettes, lotus leaves, cloud forms—and sacred calligraphy, echoing natural and spiritual sources and defining forms balanced between the positive and negative spaces. The patterns trace along the paths of change, images of the impressions made by our efforts to change the courses of our personal and social lives.

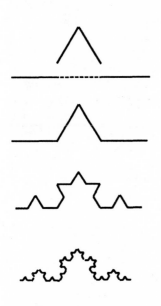

Arabesques are analogous to *fractals*, which are mathematical structures that are similarly created by the recursive application of a rule. The rule may take an extremely simple form, such as this: "Insert an inverted 'V' into the middle of a line and repeat the insertion into every line segment, indefinitely." The process generates an arabesque-like figure by the repeated application at every level of one or more rules, producing a figure of increasing complexity but one that never totally occupies a space or defines a boundary. Two aspects of the fractal process that make such arabesques provide a metaphor for my image of a viable society. One aspect is that the form is created by the application of a rule, which by analogy is a "path" that appears at every level, just as the great mythic patterns guide the lives of "everyman," communities, organizations, and whole cultures. Once we have generally accepted multiple worldviews, our society may be characterized by such an elaboration of rules forming patterns of behavior interwoven at macro and micro levels. Jorge Lois Borges, in *Pascal's Sphere*, envisioned such a society as following from "the diverse intonation of a few metaphors." The second aspect is that a fractal never occupies more than some *fraction* of the dimension of the space on which it is laid out, so that, in the immediate neighborhood of every pattern, there are spaces that have not been included, spaces that have not been "encountered" in the recursion of the generating process. In the fractal arabesque, there will always be unexplored spaces, always dark next to the light, always unknowns within the figure as well as beyond the outer edges. We can look inward to find novelty and mystery as we have, by habit, looked outward. In pursuing the repetitions of the patterns, we can span all the realities and experience the range of opportunities at scales that are appropriate to our persons and our purposes.

This is not what we are used to. In our current society, we export uncertainty and inquiry to those on "the outer limits," allowing the vast majority of us to expect to stay within the comforting boundaries of our thinking, our disciplines, and the dogmas of religions and sciences, family traditions, and civil codes. We export evil into the dark. We have little experience choosing our realities or working out the consequences of our choosing the assumptions of a particular reality. We are accustomed to working with established sets of definitions that form our reigning paradigm. We stay close to our home bases in which we are assured of caring and consistency. So, even as we find that opening to alternative realities along paths set by ancient guides is successful in settling issues, we will follow these paths hesitantly.

Individuals and groups will not easily give up well-formed boundaries or become comfortable with third-order change. A fractal society will leave everyone on an edge. Acceptance of alternative worldviews and the courageous use of varied logics and narrative processes will come slowly, and movement toward processes of third-order change will be interrupted by *sporadic, frequently violent, periods of paradigmatic closure.* We will still encounter religious wars, acts of bigotry, denial of opportunities to others, and "true beliefs" as we learn the paths of meta-praxes. We will all have to learn to *manage* the evils that can no longer be banished from our neighborhoods and our persons. What we have gained by moving from the limiting territorial and material definitions of human culture to those of a generative arabesque is that which human beings, looking skyward on a starry night, have always strived for —to reach out to the Infinite. With the arabesques of consciousness, we may search for the infinite that is within.

Notes

Introduction

1. We are not alone in this conclusion. Support comes, for example, from Nils Brunsson's *The Irrational Organization* (1985) in which he documents the irrationality of large-scale programs conducted in industry and government.

2. There is good evidence for the stability of the response to the *Realities Inquiry* (see Junge, 1991), but better evidence is provided by long-term studies of particular realities; for example, what I call the unitary reality is a form of authoritarianism and social reality is the INS category in the Myers-Briggs typologies, both of which are considered to be inborn personality characteristics.

3. Adapted from Smith (1982, p. 292).

4. Between most chapters, there are *interludes*, occasions for me to speak in a different voice than that used in essays as our standard for communicating analytic material. They provide analogies, comments, and stories that forward the discussions. The epilogue is a prologue to a new language for a new society.

Chapter 1. Alternative Realities

1. I have no evidence to say that these views are held in non-Western cultures. I expect to find that they extend to the Middle Eastern cultures but my scanty evidence suggests that the Oriental mentalities may differ substantially.

2. Similar systems based on two dimensions have been proposed by Jackson and Keys (1984) and Schneider (1986). Each of the many societal and personal typologies strongly overlap if for no other reason than the geometry calls for at least two of the types in any set to match those of any other set—based on the fact that two planes meet along a line. The closest to the current design is that of Bolman and Deal

(1991). Their explanation and experiences with the classification can help the reader apply the alternative realities.

3. Such compromises underlie the many paradoxes of "classes" that Russell and Whitehead (1913) introduced with their mathematical investigations of classification.

4. Søren Kierkegaard (1954) labeled this axis the *absolute paradox*, specifying its extremes as *finitude* (objective determinism) and *infinitude* (subjective free will). The psychologist Rotter labeled these extremes *outer control* and *inner control* and developed an instrument to measure a person's preference for acting out of one or the other worldview. This measure correlates closely with the scores on the *Realities Inquiry*, which I developed to conduct the research reported herein.

5. See Grazzaniga's *The Social Brain* (1985).

6. I don't have enough research yet to know the rules by which a person selects one reality versus another. It is an important consideration and one that must be understood to extend the usefulness of this model of choice making.

7. All the literature and the more formal testing that I have done concerns people from Western cultures. From reading, anecdotal information, and a small sampling, I sense that the beliefs of people brought up in Chinese and Japanese cultures may not be well captured by this categorization. Thus, both to limit my story to that for which I have solid evidence and to continually keep ourselves aware of the ethnocentric quality of this work, I call attention to the fact that it is Western images of the world I am discussing.

8. The realities map produces a personality typology quite similar to descriptive schema such as the well-known Myers-Briggs Personality Types, the lesser known but well-based Driver Decision Style Indicator (Driver & Rowe, 1979), and such pop psychology pieces as Kathy Kolby's (1989) Conative Index. While they all have adequate means for describing the pure types, they do not do as well with mixtures; they don't explain which personality function would be dominant in a particular situation. Even more problematic is that they are not equipped to deal with the paradoxes that are inherent in the concept of change or action. Some ideas for resolving this paradox are provided in Chapter 2 and in the discussion of problem-solving methods in Chapter 3.

9. P. Robinson in *Psychology Today* (February, 1980, p. 112).

10. In quantum physics, it is hypothesized that space and time and many other qualities are determinable only up to a probability distribution. But relation itself is deterministic. So, in this worldview, events may not be strictly predictable even though they precisely follow physical laws.

11. I use *sentient* as a more general term than *conscious*, thus allowing other degrees of awareness such as *a-*, *sub-*, and *unconscious*.

12. Remember that this is not an argument about reality but about belief systems. There is no issue here concerning the existence of an unperceivable understratum of reality.

13. The most problematic unitary phenomenon for me is mathematics, particularly the number system, which is formal in its cause but also appears to be universal, more fundamental than any sensory truth.

14. A more extreme form of this attribution to the power of myth is Lèvi-Strauss's statement: "We are not, therefore claiming to show how men think the myths, but rather how the myths think themselves out in men and without men's knowledge" (as quoted by Leach, 1970, p. 50).

15. An alternative interpretation of the mythic position is that there are a multiplicity of people (and things), but they are all at one with God so anything they do is what God wanted. Each is a perfect reflection of God. I see this view as much closer to the unitary reality, and it will be discussed under that label.

16. Western culture has not allowed for the emergence of many such charismatic women: What has blocked their appearance?

17. See Bohm and Peat (1987).

18. A person dominated by any of these views of reality will appear pathological to those holding other worldviews. So, for example, the psychoanalyst Manfred Kets de Vries (1980) views Nixon and other leaders as suffering from various Freudian diseases. Psychoanalysis may be a useful diagnostic device, but it blocks us from seeing the role that such charismatics and others play in social change.

Chapter 2. The Dialectics of Change

1. In preliminary studies for this work, I explored carefully the question of ambiguity and concluded that the resolution of issues is subject to uncertainties that are akin to the limitations on the completeness of logic proved by Gödel and on measurement of conditions that appear in any formally complex system. Thus it appears to me that the ambiguity, uncertainties, and many of the paradoxes of intentional change are *essential*—absolutely beyond removal. I have chosen to leave these arguments out of the current discussion simply because, with all the obvious ambiguities, I need not burden the reader with worrying about whether every last self-referential ambiguity can be removed.

2. See Maxine Junge's (1991) journal of creating artwork in the manner of each of the four realities. It gives support to the schizmogenic nature of Learning III.

3. Bartunek and Moch (1987) introduce the idea of third-order change in a very similar context, indicating that the third-order work aids the user to select among the schemata of the second order. They allude to the problems of establishing criteria for selecting among schemata but do not recognize the illogic of developing logics for working at the third level. Morris Berman (1981) views Learning III more radically, considering it to be "identical to religious conversions of the archaic tradition." I take this to be a plausible but not a necessary definition. A closer parallel is Gurdjieff's *fourth way*, which calls for an experience grounded in everyday experience that includes experience of categories, that is, of boundaries (see P. D. Ouspensky's, 1971, *The Fourth Way*).

4. Such points always lead to wondering about the consciousness of higher animals. Do animals sense conflict, or is the fight for survival simply a "fact of life"? The social customs among mammals certainly point to an awareness of the need to accommodate differences.

5. The source for many of the ideas in this subsection is the anthropologist Roy Wagner (1975).

6. The form of the cause differs with the realities involved. For a differentiated base, the cause might be *efficient*; for example, the "cause" of a problem I am trying to solve is the antecedent context, just as the hand of cards I hold in a bridge game is the cause of my play. For a conventionalized base, the cause might be *formal*. For example, the classification of a natural phenomenon is *explained by a general rule*—an apple falls *because* of gravity.

Chapter 3. Modes of Change

1. Even within mathematics, there are difficulties as exemplified by the various limitative theories, of which the most famous is Gödel's. And as mentioned below,

the proof methods are often not drawn from existing principles of argument—a major point in Roger Penrose's (1989) *The Emperor's New Mind*.

2. I do not claim a general proof of disjunction between action and a consistent logic but assert that we will not find such consistency between action and the logics we currently employ in rhetoric or in the physical and social sciences.

3. My argument for this comes from the ontological model presented in Chapter 1. Quite different arguments coming up with the same conclusion are presented by Popper (1963) and, more directly, Paul Feyerabend (1975) in his infamous work *Against Method*. An informative attack on the common conclusion is made by Arvid Aulin (1987); his position is taken without recognition of the logical inconsistency that is argued here.

4. Allison (1971, p. 277).

5. Reframing is discussed as a general strategy in Chapter 4, following the work of Paul Watzlawick.

6. This statement derives from Kenneth Arrow's proof of the impossibility of interpersonal comparisons of utilities.

7. This form of participation has been deeply explored in the work of Habermas (e.g., 1972). Also see Friedman (1989) on the dialogic processes.

8. This feature of evaluative problem solving was wrestled with under the label of "the effect of irrelevant alternatives" by Luce and Raiffa (1957), among other decision theorists.

9. In the language I have adopted here, *conflict resolution* is usually viewed as a form of problem solving. That is, most of the issues that are handled are separable problems about allocating conflicting claims. They are territorial or membership disputes.

10. There is no clearer argument of this position than that in the tale of "The Grand Inquisitor" in Dostoevski's *Brothers Karamazov*.

11. Gertrude J. Spilka (personal communication, 1991, Philadelphia).

12. See particularly James Gleick's *Chaos* (1987).

Chapter 4. Paths of Resolution

1. For example, see Chirot (1986).

2. See particularly Bennis, Benne, Chin, and Covey (1976) and Beckhard and Harris (1977) for a summary of these methods and approaches.

3. Other important work in the use of myth in working with organizations includes Adams (1984), Boje, Fedor, and Rowland (1982), and Owens (1983). With the exception of Owens, little of this work saw myth as an instrument of change or conflict resolution.

4. One argument against their uniqueness is that these tales are identified as male. They are certainly dominant in contemporary society. There must be tales that are more appropriate to women, for example, the Athena legends, and certainly there are archtales of *human beings*. Storm (1972) notes that many of the tales of the Dakota Indians could be read in either gender.

5. For example, Evelyn Underhill (1961) presents similar descriptions of the two paths of development in ancient Greek society in her work on mysticism.

6. A provocative view of Russia's renaissance is Susan Welsh's (1990) *Alchemy of Revolution*.

7. This view has been greatly popularized by the work of Joseph Campbell (1949), particularly in his *The Hero with a Thousand Faces*. See also McWhinney and

Batista (1988) for examples of the use of myth in modern contexts. A fuller description of psychological and political dynamics of the second path is provided in McWhinney (1980).

8. A quotation from a corporate president from Ramanantsoa and Thiery Basle (1987).

9. The description of the revitalization process presented here arose from looking at organizational and political situations. Anthropologist Anthony Wallace (1966, pp. 158-163) indicates that religious revitalizations typically follow a remarkably similar pattern to those of organizations.

10. The Navajo painting is constructed from the view of the objects (persons) in the painting, not that of the painter, so the right and left sides are reversed.

11. Paraphrased from Levy and Merry (1986, p. 59).

12. Anthony Wallace (1966) similarly describes this process in the formation of new religions when the culture of the old has become contaminated. His description, particularly of the Iroquois spiritual leader Handsome Lake, is the archetypal story of a new CEO revitalizing a failing company.

13. A recent article by Beer, Einsenstat, and Sector (1991) presents a perfect example of the "revitalization," as they label it. The most interesting point of fit is the switch from the stage of embodiment—with a very masculine "velvet glove"—to the more feminine effort "spreading, without push from the top" in the accepting stage.

14. Dante Alighieri, *The Inferno* (1954, p. 28).

15. A study by Welsh (1990) suggests that the Russian Revolution was the beginning of a grand regressive reconstruction that is just now coming out of the hellish downward trip into a period of integration perhaps to become a postindustrial, supranational entity.

16. Note that the core process is related to what Maturana and Varela (1980) label an *autopoietic machine*. It is the abstract, self-maintaining operations that define the essential living entity. The idea of community that I wish to convey here is like that defined by anthropologist Victor Turner as *communitas*. Turner (1969, p. 126) quotes Martin Buber in saying that *communitas* is "the being no longer side by side (and, one might add, above and below) but *with* one another in a multitude of person. And this multitude, though it moves towards one goal, yet experiences everywhere a turning to, a dynamic facing of, the others, a flowing from I to Thou."

17. See Clark and Krone (1971) and Jayaram (1976).

18. Early examples include the Procter & Gamble "green field" plants beginning about 1970; the reconstruction of housing following the 1965 riots in Watts (Los Angeles) through an artist cooperative; and the redevelopment of industry in Jamestown in upstate New York in the late 1970s (Trist, 1981).

19. This is but one of the many uses of the term *dialectic*. It is related to but not the same as that used in the next section to describe a particular form of the interweaving.

20. This example came from Terry Golbeck through his designing an employment process for a new operation in ESSO Resources in Canada.

21. I don't have the data to know the occasions on which the analytic is used as a problem-solving mode and when it is been viewed as a path of resolution. Evidence that the strategic approach is being (ill-)used is visible in how quickly we jump to hypotheses as to what the solution is, often before we have collected any data whatsoever. Dr. Albert Shanker (in *Medical Encounter*, volume 7, number 1, 1990) comments that physicians far too frequently begin their diagnosis with a hypothesis before any questions have been posed as to the patient's condition. I doubt such practice is limited to physicians.

22. The work in artificial intelligence has increasingly made the split between a pure designer view in the unitary-sensory domain and the need for nonalgorithmic

approaches increasingly sharp. Many writers believe that, in theory, we will be able to create all mental processes with computer-based algorithms; others believe that meaning can only come from a values-based reality. For discussion, see Searle (1981).

23. See Romeo, Mauch, and Morrison (1990); the following quotes are from pages 1254-1255.

24. While I have used the male pronoun with the charismatic in prior instances, here there are so many examples of charismatic women taking hold of a belief system that it is appropriate to be specific in recognizing that the genders have equally exhibited this power.

25. My choice is "indefensible" on "logical" grounds. I have to enter the "playing field" somewhere, but I cannot use the rules of the games to decide what game to play. The problems of such choices are discussed in the final chapter as a central issue in achieving resolutions.

Chapter 5. Leaders, Followers, and Culture

1. I recognize an inconsistency in the labeling of these styles, because, as I have indicated in Chapter 2, a change occurs only with an act of control in a reality different than one's given reality. In the following text, I have accounted for this inconsistency in the case of the four single worldviews. The six styles based on pairs of realities formally represent only half of the possible styles for, within each pair, there are two different styles depending on the reality taken as given and that taken as controlling. From my experience and reading of the literature, I have not found appropriately distinct names, so I have ignored that inconsistency in the text.

2. I recognized this concept of "given" and "controlling" years after I designed the *Realities Inquiry* research instrument, so I don't have the body of data to validate these conjectures. I am in the process now of designing an instrument to test them.

3. See Conger and Kanungo (1987) for an extensive listing of the studies.

4. The quotes in this paragraph are from Wagner (1975, p. 122).

5. It is extremely awkward to avoid the singular pronoun in discussing those of a mythic worldview. From a mythic person's worldview, there is but one, so the use of the plural is an implied put-down from the pluralistic worldviews. I use the male pronoun both out of convention and because to date most recognized charismatics have been male. I am not endorsing a position that men are more likely to be charismatic than women.

6. See Conger and Kanungo (1987) for a summary of the behavioral factors.

7. A method and approach to using archetypal material, generally under the label of remythologizing, is presented in McWhinney and Batista (1988).

8. A sad result of this worldview is that task-oriented administrations assume training is done by presenting facts. Its adherents assume that, once knowledge is delivered to the students, their behavior will certainly change. The practical result is that the vast majority of training efforts are wasted. Training officers and other personnel specialists are highly likely to be dominated by a unitary worldview, so this result is pervasive in Western industrial settings.

9. That this article was the most requested reprint from the *HBR* for many years is testimony both to the authors' insights and to the need in U.S. society to deal with the schism between the deterministic and the person-centered worldviews. Management is devoted to sewing together the edges of the chasm to hide this deep conflict that never seems to stay safely covered.

10. The style arising from the reversal of this style is oddly similar. Its story is of the leader who is so devoted to the participatory mode that he ensures open involvement and fairness by establishing rules and laws of interaction, thereby destroying the freedoms. This is the classic double bind of a democratic society protecting itself against the freedom to deny others freedom. This oddity again points to the paradox that there is a deep compatibility between behaviors at the extreme opposite worldviews: mythic and sensory, social and unitary.

11. My reference search for ideas and information on followers turned up very few items, so few that I sense we lack a *theory of followership* that approaches the richness of the studies of leadership. It's not surprising that our focus would be on the dramatics of leadership but disconcerting that in a democratic society we have not given more attention to the masses. The most important studies have had an economic base such as those done by Herbert Simon, referred to below, and the anecdotal ones, such as the widely read *Working* by Studs Terkel.

12. Following Herbert Simon's clear modeling of the employment relation in his seminal works from *Administrative Behavior* (1947) on, most organizational theorists have taken the exchange theory as adequate to explain all membership relations. It has become a tautological proposition—if people stay, they must be getting sufficient rewards.

13. Turner (1969) uses the term *communitas* for this grouping, noting that the outsiders are typically viewed as marginal groups in a society that has an "open" versus a "closed morality" of structured hierarchical organizations. His writing suggests that, in the past, teams, as they are being promoted in the current high-performing organizations, are out-groups, supporting humanistic views that the established society protects itself against. With the averred change in paradigms, this form of out-group may be the avenue for the emergence of new organizational forms.

14. Quinn and McGrath (1985) present a deceptively similar set of cultures based on the information processing model. The set led to quite similar classifications. For some purposes, I find it more useful than what I present here, as the ontological base is not as familiar to practitioners as is the language of decision making. I continually emphasize that it is meaningless to judge these models on their "accuracy" or "truth"—criteria that are themselves embedded in the models and thus cannot be used to evaluate them.

15. The members in a storied organization show the *redundancy of function* of which Fred Emery wrote (1977), as they each are supposed to carry the total image of the ultimate goal. Those members of a clustering organization are more likely to be redundant as *parts*, as they would be in a machine.

16. Actual distributions of psychological types across an organization have been studied and reported, which substantiates this sort of mapping. For example, see Osborn (1990).

17. This was the ratio at a number of Procter & Gamble's green site plants opened in the 1970s. Currently, the well-reputed Worthington Steel claims that, even today, it takes months to locate and acclimate a new employee to work in their high-performing plants and offices.

18. Wagner (1975, p. 126): "Americans differentiate *in the interests of collectivizing.* This is what we mean by 'competition.' Differentiation and contradiction are rationalized and 'worked into the system' as 'means' to a single monolithic 'end'—a better life, a more democratic administration, a sounder species, and so forth."

19. A quote from Polybius in Arnold J. Toynbee's (1953) *Greek Civilization and Character.*

20. Writer John Kroll, while reading this material in draft, noted the paradox that, at the peak of the battle in the Gulf in February 1991, the most popular film in the United States was *Dances with Wolves*, a compassionate rejection of the American traditional belief in the righteousness of its causes.

21. Kumon (1990).

22. See Clark and Fujimoto (1990).

Chapter 6. Courage for the Journey

1. Tillich (1952), intermixing quotes from pages 163 and 155.

2. Quoted in Warren Bennis and Bert Nanus (1985).

3. Larry Greiner's "Evolution and Revolution as Organizations Grow" (1972) is a theoretical formulation of such a path. Many other authors have subsequently described this path in various languages following the same basic plot.

4. I have used a "romantic" approach to the subject of coevolution, using the insight-generating and accessible metaphor of "courage." An analytic approach to the problem of balance between the forms of courage can be found in the work on coevolution being done by S. A. Kauffman (1990) and his associates at the Santa Fe Institute, using a formal mathematical language and models from game theory and biological evolution. Here the argument is phrased in questions of persistence, depth of search, and other concepts that come from strategic thinking. In work suggested by Jeff Newman, we are looking at coevolution as a new level of game theory played on the second board. It will form a theory of "intergame" transition strategies.

5. The writing of this material presents me with the same problems that anyone has trying to resolve an issue. Here I presume the unitary mind-set to gain the reader's permission to use the narrative to establish the logical truth or validity of the mind-set through which I will resolve issues. I bootstrap my way up through a series of spirals to free myself from preconditions so that I can set conditions to act in ways that do not reevoke the reader's doubt in the process of establishing the processes of resolution. These conditions are the stories that are themselves outside of the logics they employ to solve the issues. The logic of my argument, in turn, arises from within such a story; see, for example, Howard (1991). I shall not try to disentangle the Gordian knot but ask you to join in re-creating the tales by which it all comes to have meaning.

6. Quoted by Berman (1981, p. 218).

7. Note that this is not as strong a proposition as its baldness suggests for it is subject to the paradoxical proposition at the beginning of the paragraph—that we live by propositions whose validity is a function of our belief.

8. Quote from M. Mair by Howard (1991, p. 195).

9. Quoted from a lecture delivered at the Claremont Colleges in spring 1985.

10. George Howard (1991) points out that most of our logics are themselves but stories stripped of context.

11. See Mary E. Boyce (1990).

12. Two interesting exceptions: In one particularly creative division of the Walt Disney Company, *management by story* was employed to redevelop the creative leadership as the division was built up to design the new parks in Europe and the United States. In a Norwegian aluminum company, a visualizing of the entire industrial community as creating a flower garden provided a complete guidance system for ecological and economic revitalization. See *Creating Shared Vision* by Marjorie Parker (1990).

13. The *Oxford English Dictionary* lists among the early uses of *pun*: "Debauch'd from sense, let doubtful meanings run, The Vague conundrum and the prurient pun."

14. The in-country team was composed of J. Chuck Reis, Robert Andrews, Jimmie M. Knight, and me.

15. The project had an ironic twist. It was eventually successful both in developing a group of young managers and in gaining acceptance for the new designs with the in-place administrators. I say "eventually" because they needed to delay acceptance long enough to obscure the sources of ideas and to avoid any sense that they were *introducing something new*. Naser, however, was not pleased. The plan did not appear to be novel as it failed to *appear* to have modernized the governing processes and it did not increase his personal power vis-à-vis the old guard's. We are seldom if ever successful at *making* large-scale changes—everyone must come along the path if the change is not to be blocked by counterinvention.

References

Ackoff, Russell L. (1974). *Redesigning the future*. New York: John Wiley.

Ackoff, Russell L., & Emery, F. E. (1972). *On purposeful systems*. London: Tavistock.

Adams, John D. (Ed.). (1984). *Transforming work: A collection of organizational transformation readings*. Alexandria, VA: Miles River.

Adizes, Ichak. (1978). *A manual for the dialectic convergence method for management of conflict*. Los Angeles: MDOR.

Alighieri, Dante. (1954). *The inferno* (J. Ciardi, Trans.). New York: New American Library.

Alinsky, Saul. (1969). *Reville for radicals*. New York: Vintage.

Allison, Graham. (1971). *Essence of decision: Explaining the Cuban missile crisis*. Boston: Little, Brown. (Original work published 1969)

Argyris, Chris, & Schön, D. (1978). *Organizational learning: A theory of action perspective*. Reading, MA: Addison-Wesley.

Aulin, Arvid. (1987). Methodological criticism. *Systems Research, 4*(2), 71-82.

Bartunek, Jean M., & Moch, M. K. (1987). First-order, second-order, and third-order change and organizational development interventions: A cognitive approach. *Journal of Applied Behavioral Science, 23*(4), 483-500.

Bateson, Gregory. (1972). *Steps to an ecology of the mind*. New York: Ballantine.

Becker, Ernst. (1973). *The denial of death*. New York: Free Press.

Beckhard, Robert, & Harris, H. T. (1977). *Organizational transitions: Managing complex change*. Reading, MA: Addison-Wesley.

Beer, Michael, Eisenstat, R. A., & Sector, Bert. (1990, November-December). Why change programs don't produce change. *Harvard Business Review*, pp. 158-166.

Beer, Stafford. (1985). *Diagnosing the system for organizations*. New York: John Wiley.

Bennis, Warren G., Benne, K. D., Chin, R., & Covey, K. E. (Eds.). (1964). *The planning of change: Readings in the applied behavioral sciences*. New York: Holt, Rinehart & Winston.

Bennis, Warren G., Benne, K. D., Chin, R., & Covey, K. E. (Eds.). (1976). *The planning of change* (3rd ed.). New York: Holt, Rinehart & Winston.

Bennis, Warren, & Nanus, B. (1985). *Leaders: Strategies for taking charge.* New York: Harper & Row.

Berg, Per-Olof. (1985). Organizational change as a symbolic transformation process. In P. J. Frost, L. F. Moore, M. R. Louis, C. C. Lundberg, & J. Martin (Eds.), *Organizational culture.* Beverly Hills, CA: Sage.

Berger, Peter L., & Luckmann, T. (1967). *The social construction of reality.* New York: Anchor.

Berlin, I. (1980). *Personal impression.* New York: Viking.

Berman, Morris. (1981). *The reenchantment of the world.* Ithaca, NY: Cornell University Press.

Bliss, Tamara J. (1996). *Leveling the playing field: How citizen advocacy groups influence corporate behavior.* Unpublished doctoral dissertation, Fielding Institute, Santa Barbara, CA.

Bohm, David, & Peat, F. D. (1987). *Science, order, and creativity.* New York: Bantam.

Boje, M. David, Fedor, D. B., & Rowland, K. M. (1982). Myth making: A qualitative step in O.D. intervention. *Journal of Applied Behavioral Science, 1,* 17-28.

Bolman, Lee G., & Deal, T. E. (1991). *Reframing organizations: Artistry, choice and leadership.* San Francisco: Jossey-Bass.

de Bono, Edward. (1996). *The master thinker's handbook.* Largemont, NY: Institute for Creative Thinking.

Boyce, Mary E. (1990). *Stories and storytelling in organizational life.* Unpublished doctoral dissertation, Fielding Institute, Santa Barbara, CA.

Bradley, F. H. (1966). *Appearance and reality.* London: Oxford University Press.

Brinton, Crane. (1952). *The anatomy of revolution.* New York: Vintage.

Brunsson, Nils. (1985). *The irrational organization.* New York: John Wiley.

Burns, James M. (1978). *Leadership.* New York: Harper & Row.

Burrell, Gibson, & Morgan, G. (1979). *Sociological paradigms and organisational analysis.* London: Heinemann.

Campbell, Joseph. (1949). *The hero with a thousand faces.* New York: Bollingen Foundation.

Campbell, Kathleen. (1989). *A Jungian view of the search conference process.* Unpublished doctoral dissertation, Fielding Institute, Santa Barbara, CA.

Camus, Albert. (1956). *The rebel.* New York: Vintage.

Carse, James P. (1986). *Finite and infinite games.* New York: Ballantine.

Chirot, Daniel. (1986). *Social change in the modern era.* Boston: Harcourt Brace Jovanovich.

Clark, James V., & Krone, Charles G. (1971). Towards an overall view of organizational development in the early 1970s. In John M. Thomas & Warren G. Bennis (Eds.), *Management of change and conflict.* Harmondsworth, England: Penguin.

Clark, Kim B., & Fujimoto, Takahiro. (1990, November-December). The power of product integrity. *Harvard Business Review,* pp. 107-118

Conger, Jay A., & Kanungo, R. N. (1987). Toward a behavioral theory of charismatic leadership in organizational settings. *Academy of Management Review, 12,* 637-647.

Cooperrider, David L., & Srivastva, Suresh. (1987). Appreciative inquiry in organizational life. *Research in Organizational Life and Development, 1,* 129-169.

Culbert, Samuel A., & McDonough, John J. (1980). *The invisible war: Pursuing self-interests at work.* New York: John Wiley.

Deal, Terrence E., & Kennedy, Allen A. (1982). *Corporate cultures: The rites and rituals of corporate life.* Reading, MA: Addison-Wesley.

Driver, Michael, & Rowe, Allen J. (1979). Decision-making styles: A new approach to management decision-making. In Cary L. Cooper (Ed.), *Behavioral problems in organizations* (pp. 141-182). Englewood Cliffs, NJ: Prentice-Hall.

Einstein, Albert. (1934). *Essays in science.* New York: Philosophical Library.

Eisenstadt, S. N. (1985). Cultural tradition, power relations and modes of change. In Orlando Fals Borda (Ed.), *Challenges of social change.* Beverly Hills, CA: Sage.

Elgin, David. (1977). Limits to the management of large, complex systems. In *Assessment of future national and international problem areas.* Palo Alto, CA: Stanford Research International.

Emery, Fred E. (1977). *Futures we are in.* Leiden, the Netherlands: Martinus Nijhoff.

Emery, Merrelyn & Perser, Ron. (1996). *The search conference.* San Francisco: Jossey-Bass.

Emery, Fred E., & Trist, Eric. (1965). The causal texture of organizational environments. *Human Relations, 18,* 21-32.

Feyerabend, Paul K. (1975). *Against method.* London: New Left Books.

Feynman, Richard P. (1988). *What do you care what other people think?* New York: Norton.

Fisher, Roger, & Ury, William L. (1981). *Getting to yes.* New York: Penguin.

Freire, Paulo. (1972). *Pedagogy of the oppressed.* New York: Seabury.

Friedman, M. (1989). Philosophical anthropology, the image of the human, and dialogue as keys to the integration of the human sciences. *Humanistic Psychologist, 14*(1), 4-21

Friedmann, John. (1973). *Planning in the public domain: From knowledge to action.* Princeton, NJ: Princeton University Press.

Frost, Peter J., Moore, L. F., Louis, M. R., Lundberg, C. C., & Martin, J. (Eds.). (1985). *Organizational culture.* Beverly Hills, CA: Sage.

Gebser, Jean. (1985). *The ever-present origin* (Noel Barstad with Algis Mickunas, Trans.). Athens: Ohio University Press. (Original work published in German in 1949 and 1953)

Gersick, Connie J. G. (1991). Revolutionary change theories: A multilevel exploration of the punctuated equilibrium paradigm. *Academy of Management Review, 16*(1), 10-36.

Gleick, James. (1987). *Chaos.* New York: Viking.

Gordon, William J. J. (1961). *Synetics: The creative capacity.* New York: Harper & Row.

Grazzaniga, Michael S. (1985). *The social brain: Discovery of the networks of the mind.* New York: Basic Books.

Greiner, Larry E. (1972, July-August). Evolution and revolution as organizations grow. *Harvard Business Review,* pp. 37-46.

Habermas, Jürgen. (1972). *Knowledge and human interest.* London: Heinemann.

Harris, Peter R. (1983). *New world, new ways, new management.* New York: AMACOM.

Hirschman, A. O., & Lindblom, C. E. (1962). Economic development, research and development, policy making: Some convergent views. *Behavioral Science, 7,* 221-222.

Hoffer, Eric. (1951). *The true believer.* New York: Harper.

Howard, George S. (1991). Culture tales: A narrative approach to thinking, cross-cultural psychology and psychotherapy. *American Psychologist, 46*(3), 187-197.

Hurst, David K. (1986, Autumn). Why strategic management is bankrupt. *Organizational Dynamic,* pp. 5-27.

Jackson, Michael C., & Keys, P. (1984). Toward a system of systems methodologies. *Journal of the Operational Research Society, 35,* 473-486.

James, William. (1963). *Pragmatism and other essays.* New York: Washington Square.

Janis, Irwin L. (1989). *Crucial decisions: Leadership in policymaking and crisis management.* New York: Free Press.

Jayaram, G. K. (1976). Open system planning. In W. G. Bennis, K. D. Benne, R. Chin, & K. E. Covey (Eds.), *The planning of change* (3rd ed.). New York: Holt, Rinehart & Winston.

Johnson, Chalmers. (1968). *Revolutionary change.* London: University of London Press.

Jung, Carl. (1968). *Analytic psychology: Its theory and practice.* New York: Pantheon.

Junge, Maxine. (1991). *Creativity and realities: The search for meanings.* Unpublished doctoral dissertation, Fielding Institute, Santa Barbara, CA.

Kauffman, S. A. (1990). *The origins of order: Self-organization and selection in evolution.* London: Oxford University Press.

Kets de Vries, Manfred. (1980). *Organizational paradoxes: Clinical approaches to management.* London: Tavistock.

Kierkegaard, Søren. (1954). *Fear and trembling and sickness unto death* (W. Lowrie, Trans.). Princeton, NJ: Princeton University Press.

Kolby, Kathy. (1989). *The conative connection: Uncovering the link between who you are and how you perform.* Reading, MA: Addison-Wesley.

Kuhn, Thomas. (1972). *The structure of scientific revolution* (2nd ed.). Chicago: University of Chicago Press.

Kumon, Shumpei. (1990). Toward co-emulation: Japan and the United States in the Information Age. *Whole Earth, 69,* 54-64.

Leach, Edmund. (1970). *Claude Lévi-Strauss.* New York: Viking.

LeShan, Lawrence. (1976). *Alternative realities.* New York: Ballantine.

Levy, Amir, & Merry, Uri. (1986). *Organizational transformation: Approaches, strategies, theories.* New York: Praeger.

Lilienfeld, Robert. (1978). *The rise of systems theory.* New York: John Wiley.

Lindblom, C. E., & Braybrooke, D. (1970). *A strategy of decision.* New York: Free Press.

Locke, Karen. (1996). Rewriting *The Discovery of Grounded Theory* after 25 years. *Journal of Management Inquiry, 5,* 239-245.

Luce, Robert D., & Raiffa, Howard. (1957). *Games and decisions.* New York: John Wiley.

Maccoby, Michael. (1988). *Why work: Leading the new generation.* New York: Simon & Schuster.

Mao Tse-tung. (1960). *On contradiction.* New York: International Publications.

Mason, Richard O., & Mitroff, Ian I. (1981). *Challenging strategic planning assumptions.* New York: John Wiley.

Maturana, Humberto, & Varela, Francisco. (1980). *Autopoesis and cognition.* Boston: Reidel.

May, Rollo. (1975). *The courage to create.* New York: Bantam.

McWhinney, Will. (1980). Paedogenesis and other modes of design. In T. G. Cummings (Ed.), *Systems theory for organizational development.* New York: John Wiley.

McWhinney, Will. (1985). The realities of leadership. In Robert Tannenbaum et al. (Eds.), *Human systems development.* San Francisco: Jossey-Bass.

McWhinney, Will. (1991). *Metaphors & models.* Venice, CA: Enthusion.

McWhinney, Will, & Batista, José. (1988, Autumn). How remythologizing can revitalize organizations. *Organizational Dynamics,* pp. 46-58.

Miller, Eric J. (1975). Socio-technical systems in weaving, 1953-1970: A follow-up study. *Human Relations, 28,* 349-386.

Ouspensky, P. D. (1971). *The fourth way.* New York: Vintage.

Osborn, Susan. (1990). *Performance management: Paradigm shift as a factor in diffusion of the socio-technical systems approach.* Unpublished doctoral dissertation, Fielding Institute, Santa Barbara, CA.

Owens, Harrison. (1995). *Tales from open space.* Potomac, MD: Abbott.

Parker, Marjorie. (1990). *Creating shared vision*. Oslo: Norwegian Center for Leadership Development.

Pava, Calvin. (1986). New strategies of systems change: Reclaiming nonsynoptic methods. *Human Relations, 39*(7), 615-633.

Penrose, Roger. (1989). *The emperor's new mind*. New York: Oxford University Press.

Pepper, Stephen C. (1942). *World hypothesis: A study of evidence*. Berkeley: University of California Press.

Peters, Thomas J., & Waterman, R. H. (1982). *In search of excellence*. New York: Harper & Row.

Piven, F. F., & Cloward, R. A. (1979). *Poor people's movements: Why they succeed, how they fail*. New York: Pantheon.

Polkinghorne, Donald E. (1988). *Narrative knowing and the human sciences*. Albany: State University of New York Press.

Popper, Karl P. (1963). *Conjunctures and refutations*. London: Routledge.

Prigogine, Ilya. (1980). *From being to becoming: Time and complexity in the physical sciences*. San Francisco: Freeman.

Quinn, Robert E., & McGrath, M. R. (1985). The transformation of organizational cultures. In P. J. Frost, L. F. Moore, M. R. Louis, C. C. Lundberg, & J. Martin (Eds.), *Organizational culture*. Beverly Hills, CA: Sage.

Ramanantsoa, B., & Thiery Basle, C. (1987). *The metaphor in top manager's speech: Symbolic creation or instrument of power*. Paper presented at the Third International Conference on Organizational Symbolism and Corporate Culture, Milan.

Rapoport, Anatol. (1970). *N-Person Game Theory: Concepts and applications*. Ann Arbor: University of Michigan Press.

Reigal, K. F. (1976, October). The dialectics of human development. *American Psychologist*, pp. 689-699.

Romeo, Thomas D., Mauch, Danna, & Morrison, Elizabeth. (1990). The art of strategic mental health planning in Rhode Island. *American Psychologist, 45*(11), 1253-1256.

Sandner, Donald. (1979). *Navajo symbols of healing*. New York: Harcourt Brace Jovanovich.

Schneider, Kirk J. (1986). Encountering and integrating Kierkegaard's absolute paradox. *Journal of Humanistic Psychology, 26*(3), 62-80.

Schön, Donald A. (1971). *Beyond the stable state*. New York: Norton.

Schutz, Alfred. (1967). *Collected papers: Vol. 2. Studies in social reality*. The Hague, the Netherlands: Martinus Nijhoff. (Original work published 1945)

Searle, John R. (1981). Minds, brains, programs. In Douglas R. Hofstadter (Ed.), *The mind's I*. New York: Basic Books.

Shils, Edward. (1965). Charisma, order and status. *American Sociological Review, 30*, 199-213.

Simon, Herbert. (1947). *Administrative behavior*. New York: Macmillan.

Slater, Philip. (1974). *Earthwalk*. Garden City, NY: Doubleday.

Smith, K. K. (1982). Rabbits, lynxes, and organizational transitions. In J. Kimberly & R. Quinn (Eds.), *New futures: The challenge of managing corporate transitions*. Homewood, IL: Dow Jones-Irwin.

Smullyan, Raymond M. (1987). *Forever undecided: A puzzle guide to Gödel*. New York: Knopf.

Storm, Hyemeyohsts. (1972). *Seven arrows*. New York: Harper & Row.

Stravinsky, Igor. (1960). *Poetic of music* (Arthur Knodel & Ingof Dahl, Trans.). New York: Random House.

Tannenbaum, Robert, & Schmidt, W. H. (1973). How to choose a leadership pattern. *Harvard Business Review, 51*, 95-102

Teilhard de Chardin, Pierre. (1960). *The phenomenon of man* (Bernard Wall, Trans.). New York: Harper Torchbook.

Tichy, Noel M. (1983). *Managing strategic change.* New York: John Wiley.

Tillich, Paul. (1952). *The courage to be.* New Haven, CT: Yale University Press.

Toulmin, Stephen. (1972). *Human understanding.* Princeton, NJ: Princeton University Press.

Toynbee, Arnold J. (1953). *Greek civilization and character.* New York: Mentor.

Trist, Eric. (1981). *The evolution of socio-technical systems.* Toronto: Ontario Quality of Working Life Centre.

Trist, Eric. (1985). Intervention strategies for interorganizational domains. In R. Tannenbaum et al. (Eds.), *Human systems development.* San Francisco: Jossey-Bass.

Trist, Eric, & Bamforth, Kenneth W. (1951). Some social and psychological consequences of the longwall method of coal getting. *Human Relations, 4*, 3-38.

Turner, Victor. (1969). *The ritual process: Structure and anti-structure.* Ithaca, NY: Cornell University Press.

Turner, Victor. (1974). *Dramas, fields, and metaphors: Symbolic action in human society.* Ithaca, NY: Cornell University Press.

de Unamuno, Miguel. (1967). *Our Lord Don Quixote* (Anthony Kerrigan, Trans.). Princeton, NJ: Princeton University Press.

Van Eijnatten, F. (1993). *The paradigm that changed the workplace.* Winona Lake, IN: Van Gorcum/Eisenbrauns.

Von Glasersfeld, Edward. (1984). *The construction of knowledge.* Seaside, CA: Intersystems.

Wagner, Roy. (1975). *The invention of culture.* Chicago: University of Chicago.

Wallace, Anthony F. C. (1966). *Religion: An anthropological view.* New York: Random House.

Watzlawick, Paul. (1974). *How real is real?* New York: Random House.

Watzlawick, Paul. (1984). *The invented reality: How do we know what we believe we know?* New York: Norton.

Watzlawick, Paul, Weakland, John H., & Fisch, Richard. (1974). *Change: Principles of problem formation and problem resolution.* New York: Norton.

Weber, Max. (1968). *Economy and society* (Guenther Roth & Claus Wittich, Eds.). New York: Bedminster. (Original work published 1947)

Welsh, Susan. (1990). *Alchemy of revolution.* Unpublished doctoral dissertation, Fielding Institute, Santa Barbara, CA.

Wilber, Ken. (1981). *Up from Eden: A transpersonal view of human evolution.* Garden City, NY: Doubleday.

Zaltman, Gerald, & Duncan, Robert. (1976). *Strategies for planned change.* New York: John Wiley.

Index

About the Author

Will McWhinney is a designer, consultant, and educator. He first worked with the Bell System in the early 1950s designing computer and operations research applications. In the early 1960s, he helped organize the business school at Leeds University (England) and was there introduced to the design of Socio-Technical Systems. He then joined in creating the first American STS program at the UCLA Graduate School of Management. By the 1970s, he was working with the earliest of the high-performing open-system organizations in manufacturing plants and in community development. In 1980, he helped found at the Fielding Institute in Santa Barbara the innovative doctoral program in human and organizational systems for midcareer professionals.

He works with organizations to establish new directions, typically beginning with retreat sessions in which the myths of origins and core missions are uncovered and tested for their current relevance, either to guide future directions or to display the ways in which they block progress. The methods used in this work, in concurrence with the ideas expressed in *Paths of Change*, provide understanding of the leadership and enculturing processes, and guide the selection of problem-solving tools that are particularly appropriate to the situation and the talents that are involved. While the focus is the organization, the work has profound impact on the individual participants and communities.

His doctorate is in industrial administration from Carnegie-Mellon University. He is past president of the Association for Humanistic Psychology and currently vice-president of International Synergy, and heads his own consulting organization (Enthusion, Inc.).

NOTES